JOHN POWELL, S.J.

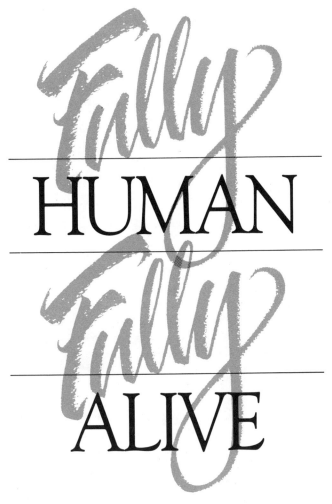

Fully HUMAN Fully ALIVE

A New Life through a New Vision

TABOR®
PUBLISHING

Allen, Texas

Acknowledgments

Grateful acknowledgment is made to the authors and publishers for permission to reprint the following:

From *Escape from Freedom* by Erich Fromm. Copyright 1941, © 1969 by Erich Fromm. Reprinted by permission of Holt, Rinehart and Winston, Publishers.

From *Yes, World: A Mosaic of Meditation* by Mary Jean Irion. Copyright © 1970 by Mary Jean Irion. Published by Cambria Press, a division of Richard W. Baron Publishing Company.

Continued on page 147

Photo Credits

Dennis Full   148
Algimantas Kezys, S.J.   20, 46
Jean-Claude Lejeune   iv, 8, 34, 60, 78, 104, 130

Cover Design: Karen Malzeke-McDonald

Calligraphy: Bob Niles

Tabor Publishing
One DLM Park
Allen, Texas 75002

Library of Congress Catalog Card Number 76-41586

Printed in the United States of America

ISBN 1-55924-281-7

2 3 4 5   93 92 91 90

Contents

A matter of insight

"The Glory of God is a human being who is fully alive!"
Saint Irenaeus, second century

My brothers and sisters: I am sure that the most persistent and restless desire of my life is to be fully human and fully alive. On the other side of the coin, my deepest and most haunting fear is the possibility of wasting the glorious opportunity of life. My personal prayers vary according to the experience and needs of each day, but one prayer is never omitted: "Oh God, my Father, don't let me die without having really lived and really loved!" This is my hope and prayer for you, too. As much as I can be aware of my own motivation, the desire to see you live fully is the reason for this book. I have found something good, energizing, and life-giving, and I want to share it with you.

Over the course of my own life and in my quest for the full experience of human life, the most fulfilling and transforming moments have been moments of "insight." Sometimes these precious insights, which have widened the dimensions of my world and intensified my participation in life, have exploded like the Fourth of July. Sometimes they have come like the dawn, slowly and gradually bestowing a gift of light and life. I felt the joy of recognition and the warmth of kinship for Carl Jung, the great psychiatrist, when he added insight to the three traditional theological virtues; he said that the most meaningful moments of his own life were the moments of faith, hope, love, and *insight* (*Man in Search of a Soul*).

It is necessary, of course, to test insights in the laboratory of life. Any knowledge that does not change the quality of life is sterile and of questionable value. On the other hand, if the quality and emotional patterns of life are changed, the change is usually traceable to some new insight or perception. This has been the story of my own life, and I am sure that it is the story of all human lives.

May I digress with a few personal examples? In my own adult life, among the insights that have profoundly changed me and my life, I would have to list the following:

1. Obnoxious qualities (lying, bragging, gossiping, temper tantrums, and so forth) in myself and in others are really cries of pain and appeals for help.

2. A good self-image is the most valuable psychological possession of a human being.

3. The success or failure of human relationships is determined primarily by success or failure at communication.

4. The full and free experience and expression of all our feelings is necessary for personal peace and meaningful relationships.

5. I am not personally responsible for solving the problems of others. Attempts to do this can only keep the other persons immature and train them to be dependent on me.

6. Love must be unconditional or it is a form of manipulation. Unconditional love is the only kind of love that affirms a human being and enables that person to grow.

These insights, along with many others, have been the subject matter of my previous books. I felt it was worthwhile to list some of these intuitions and realizations that have so deeply affected me, my life-style, and the dimensions of my world because the relationship between perceptions and life is the insight I want to share with you in this book. In one sentence: Our participation in the happiness of a full and human life is determined by our personal perception of reality. In the course of these pages I will often be calling this personalized perception of reality a "vision." As the saying goes, "What you see is what you get!"

Through the eyes of our minds you and I look out at reality (ourselves, other people, life, the world, and God). However, we see these things differently. Your vision of reality is not mine and, conversely, mine is not yours. Both of our visions are limited and inadequate, but not to the same extent. We have both misinterpreted and distorted reality, but in different ways. We have each seen something of the available truth and beauty to which the other has been blind. The main point is that it is the dimensions and clarity of this vision that determine the dimensions of our worlds and the quality of our lives. To the extent that we are blind or have distorted reality, our lives and our happiness have been diminished. Consequently, if we are to change — to grow — there must first be a change in this basic vision, or perception of reality.

It has been generally agreed that true and full human living is based on three components, like the legs of a tripod: intrapersonal dynamics, interpersonal relationships, and a frame of reference. In my previous attempts to write, I have been mostly concerned with the first two. My present concern is with the third: a frame of reference, a basic perception of reality through which we integrate, evaluate, and interpret new persons, events, and ideas. As a flexible person continues to integrate the "new," his or her basic perception or vision is itself changed. But it is always this vision, however modified, that controls the quality of and participation in human life.

This insight has made a great contribution not only to my life but also to my reflections on the human condition. I had come, in my own way, to the realization that love is the essential ingredient in a program of full human living and that love works if people are willing to work at it. I had come to see that communication is the lifeblood of love and that the experience and expression of emotions is the essential "stuff" of communication. I had also come to realize that no one can cause emotions in another but can only stimulate emotions that are already there waiting to be aroused.

After moving through these insights like milestones of understanding into ever new and exciting territory, I was left with a lingering question. Supposing a person were to act on all these insights, feeling perfectly free to experience and in a mature way to express his or her loneliness, fear, anger, and so forth. Where does the person go from here? Will the simple and open expression of these negative and burdensome emotions be sufficiently healing to change the patterns of his or her reactions? Fritz Perls and Gestalt therapists suggest that it will. Eric Berne and transactional analysts do not share this optimism. My own experience, with myself and with others, leads me to believe that a change in undesirable emotional patterns can come only with a change in thinking—with a change in one's perception of reality, or vision. This is also the contention of Albert Ellis and the practitioners of Rational Emotive Therapy.

It now seems obvious to me that our emotional reactions are not permanent parts of our makeup, the way we were in the beginning, are now, and ever shall be. Rather they grow out of the way we see ourselves, other people, life, the world, and God. Our perceptions become the habitual frame of reference within which we act and react. Our ideas and attitudes generate our emotional responses. Persistently negative emotions are an indication that there is a distortion or delusion in our thinking, an astigmatism in our vision.

For example, if I see myself as a worthless person, I can certainly anticipate many painful and persistent emotions—discouragement, depression, sadness, and maybe even suicidal feelings. But if I can be brought to realize, by the affirming and unconditional love of another, that I am really a decent and lovable person of considerable worth, this whole pattern of emotional reaction will be radically changed. As the distortion in my perception of myself is eliminated, I will be gradually transformed into a self-confident, assured, and happy person.

If I think of you as a friend and collaborator, my emotions on meeting you will be warm and positive. If I see you as an enemy and competitor, my emotions will be just the opposite. You will remember the little verse:

> Two men looked out from prison bars.
> One saw mud, one saw stars.

In the pursuit of the fullness of human life, everything depends on this frame of reference, this habitual outlook, this basic vision which I have of myself, others, life, the world, and God. What we see is what we get.

Consequently, if you or I are to change, to grow into persons who are more fully human and more fully alive, we shall certainly have to become aware of our vision and patiently work at redressing its imbalances and eliminating its distortions. All real and permanent growth must begin here. A shy person can be coaxed into assuming an air of confidence, but it will only be a mask—one mask replacing another. There can be no real change, no real growth in any of us until and unless our basic perception of reality, our vision, is changed.

A portrait of the fully alive human being

It would seem that the amount of destructiveness to be found in individuals is proportionate to the amount to which expansiveness of life is curtailed. By this we do not refer to individual frustrations of this or that instinctive desire but to the thwarting of the whole of life, the blockage of spontaneity of the growth and expression of man's sensuous, emotional, and intellectual capacities. Life has an inner dynamism of its own; it tends to grow, to be expressed, to be lived. It seems that if this tendency is thwarted the energy directed towards life undergoes a process of decomposition and changes into energies directed towards destruction. In other words: the drive for life and the drive for destruction are not mutually independent factors but are in a reversed interdepend-ence. The more the drive towards life is thwarted, the stronger is the drive towards destruction; the more life is realized, the less is the strength of destructiveness. Destructiveness is the outcome of unlived life.

Erich Fromm, *Escape from Freedom*

Some time ago a friend told me of an occasion when, vacationing in the Bahamas, he saw a large and restless crowd gathered on a pier. Upon investigation he discovered that the object of all the attention was a young man making the last-minute preparations for a solo journey around the world in a homemade boat. Without exception everyone on the pier was vocally pessimistic. All were actively volunteering to tell the ambitious sailor all the things that could possibly go wrong. "The sun will broil you! . . . You won't have enough food! . . . That boat of yours won't withstand the waves in a storm! . . . You'll never make it!"

When my friend heard all these discouraging warnings to the adventurous young man, he felt an irresistible desire to offer some optimism and encouragement. As the little craft began drifting away from the pier toward the horizon, my friend went to the end of the pier, waving both arms wildly like semaphores spelling confidence. He kept shouting: "*Bon voyage!* You're really something! We're with you! We're proud of you! Good luck, brother!"

Sometimes it seems to me that there are two kinds of people. There are those who feel obligated to tell us all the things that can go wrong as we set out over the uncharted waters of our unique lives. "Wait till you get out into the

cold, cruel world, my friend. Take it from me." Then there
are those who stand at the end of the pier, cheering us on,
exuding a contagious confidence: *"Bon Voyage!"*

The history of psychology has been very heavily popu-
lated by learned people who have worked mainly with the
sick, trying to discover what made them sick and warning
the rest of us about the things that can go wrong. They
have been well intentioned, and their good efforts have
no doubt benefited all of us. However, an honored place
in this history of psychology must certainly be awarded to
the "father of humanistic psychology," the late Abraham
Maslow. He did not concern himself primarily with the sick
and the causes of sickness. He devoted most of his life and
energies to a study of the healthy ("self-actualizing" people) and asked about the causes of health. Abe Maslow was
definitely a *Bon Voyage* type. He was more concerned with
what can go right than with what can go wrong, more
anxious to lead us to the wellsprings of a full human life
than to warn us about crippling injuries which we might
sustain while trying to move along.

In the tradition of Maslow's humanistic psychology, I
would like to begin now with a verbal portrait of people
who are fully alive and offer some observations about what
makes them healthy.

By way of a general description, fully alive people are
those who are using all of their human faculties, powers,
and talents. They are using them to the full. These individuals are fully functioning in their external and internal
senses. They are comfortable with and open to the full
experience and expression of all human emotions. Such
people are vibrantly alive in mind, heart, and will. There is
an instinctive fear in most of us, I think, to travel with our

engines at full throttle. We prefer, for the sake of safety, to take life in small and dainty doses. The fully alive person travels with the confidence that if one is alive and fully functioning in all parts and powers, the result will be harmony, not chaos.

Fully alive human beings are alive in their external and internal *senses.* They see a beautiful world. They hear its music and poetry. They smell the fragrance of each new day and taste the deliciousness of every moment. Of course their senses are also insulted by ugliness and offended by odors. To be fully alive means to be open to the whole human experience. It is a struggle to climb a mountain, but the view from the top is magnificent. Fully alive individuals have activated imaginations and cultivated senses of humor. They are alive, too, in their *emotions.* They are able to experience the full gamut and galaxy of human feelings—wonder, awe, tenderness, compassion, both agony and ecstasy.

Fully alive people are also alive in their *minds.* They are very much aware of the wisdom in the statement of Socrates that "the unreflected life isn't worth living." Fully alive people are always thoughtful and reflective. They are capable of asking the right questions of life and flexible enough to let life question them. They will not live an unreflected life in an unexamined world. Most of all, perhaps, these people are alive in *will* and *heart.* They love much. They truly love and sincerely respect themselves. All love begins here and builds on this. Fully alive people are glad to be alive and to be who they are. In a delicate and sensitive way they also love others. Their general disposition toward all is one of concern and love. And there are individuals in their lives who are so dear to them that the happiness, success, and security of these loved ones are as real to them as their own. They are committed and faithful to those they love in this special way.

For such people life has the color of joy and the sound of celebration. Their lives are not a perennial funeral procession. Each tomorrow is a new opportunity which is eagerly anticipated. There is a reason to live and a reason to die. And when such people come to die, their hearts will be filled with gratitude for all that has been, for "the way we were," for a beautiful and full experience. A smile will spread throughout their whole being as their lives pass in review. And the world will always be a better place, a happier place, and a more human place because they lived and laughed and loved here.

The fullness of life must not be misrepresented as the proverbial "bowl of cherries." Fully alive people, precisely because they are fully alive, obviously experience failure as well as success. They are open to both pain and pleasure. They have many questions and some answers. They cry and they laugh. They dream and they hope. The only things that remain alien to their experience of life are passivity and apathy. They say a strong "yes" to life and a resounding "amen" to love. They feel the strong stings of growing—of going from the old into the new—but their sleeves are always rolled up, their minds are whirring, and their hearts are ablaze. They are always moving, growing, beings-in-process, creatures of continual evolution.

How does one get this way? How do we learn to join the dance and sing the songs of life in all of its fullness? It seems to me that the contemporary wisdom on this subject can be distilled and formulated into five essential steps to fuller living. These are normally taken in the order suggested, and each one builds upon the previous accomplishments. As will be obvious from a description of the steps, while each one builds on and grows out of the previous steps, none is ever fully and finally completed. Each will always remain an ideal to keep us reaching. In terms of a vision, or basic frame of reference, each of the five steps is essentially a new awareness or perception. The more deeply these perceptions are realized, the more one is enabled to find the fullness of life.

Briefly, and before discussing each, the five essential steps into the fullness of life are these: (1) to *accept* oneself, (2) to *be* oneself, (3) to *forget* oneself in loving, (4) to *believe,* (5) to *belong.* Obviously all growth begins with a joyful self-acceptance. Otherwise one is perpetually locked into an interior, painful, and endless civil war. However, the more we approve and accept ourselves, the more we are liberated from doubt about whether others will approve of and accept us. We are freed to be ourselves with confidence. But whether we are authentic or not, loving and living for oneself alone becomes a small and imprisoning world. We must learn to go out of ourselves into genuine love relationships. Of course the genuineness of these relationships will be directly dependent on one's ability to be authentic, to be himself or herself. Having been led out of self by love, one must then find a faith. Everyone must learn to believe in someone or something so deeply that life is charged with meaning and a sense of mission. And the more one dedicates oneself to this meaning and mission, the more such a person will develop a sense of profound and personal belonging and discover the reality of community. Let us now look at each of these steps more closely.

1. *To Accept Oneself.*   Fully alive people accept and love themselves as they are. They do not live for the promise of some tomorrow or the potential that may someday be revealed in them. They usually feel about themselves as they are the same warm and glad emotions that you and I feel when we meet someone whom we really like and admire. Fully alive people are sensitively aware of all that is good in themselves, from the little things, like the way they smile or walk, through the natural talents they have been given, to the virtues they have worked to cultivate. When these people find imperfections and limitations in themselves, they are compassionate. They try to understand, not to condemn themselves. "Beyond a wholesome discipline," *Desiderata* says, "be gentle with yourself." The wellsprings for the fullness of life rise from within a person. And, psychologically speaking, a joyful self-acceptance, a good self-image, and a sense of self-celebration are the bedrock beginning of the fountain that rises up into the fullness of life.

2. *To Be Oneself.* Fully alive people are liberated by their self-acceptance to be authentic and real. Only people who have joyfully accepted themselves can take all the risks and responsibilities of being themselves. "I gotta be me!" the song lyrics insist, but most of us get seduced into wearing masks and playing games. The old ego defense mechanisms are built up to protect us from further vulnerability. But they buffer us from reality and reduce our visibility. They diminish our capacity for living. Being ourselves has many implications. It means that we are free to have and to report our emotions, ideas, and preferences. Authentic individuals can think their own thoughts, make their own choices. They have risen above the nagging need for the approval of others. They do not sell out to anyone. Their feelings, thoughts, and choices are simply not for hire.

"To thine own self be true . . ." is their life principle and life-style.

3. *To Forget Oneself in Loving.* Having learned to accept and to be themselves, fully alive people proceed to master the art of forgetting themselves—the art of loving. They learn to go out of themselves in genuine caring and concern for others. The size of a person's world is the size of his or her heart. We can be at home in the world of reality only to the extent that we have learned to love it. Fully alive men and women escape from the dark and diminished world of egocentricity, which always has a population of one. They are filled with an empathy that enables them to feel deeply and spontaneously with others. Because they can enter into the feeling world of others—almost as if they were inside others or others were inside them—their world is greatly enlarged and their potential for human experience greatly enhanced. There are others so dear to them that they have personally experienced the "greater love than this" sense of commitment. They would protect their loved ones with their own lives.

Being a loving person is far different from being a so-called "do-gooder." Do-gooders merely use other people as opportunities for practicing their acts of virtue, of which they keep careful count. People who love learn to move the focus of their attention and concern from themselves out to others. They care deeply about others. The difference between do-gooders and people who love is the difference between a life which is an on-stage performance and a life which is an act of love. Real love cannot be successfully imitated. Our care and concern for others must be genuine, or our love means nothing. This much is certain: There is no learning to live without learning to love.

4. *To Believe.* Having learned to transcend purely self-directed concern, fully alive people discover "meaning" in their lives. This meaning is found in what Viktor Frankl calls "a specific vocation or mission in life." It is a matter of commitment to a person or a cause in which one can believe and to which one can be dedicated. This faith commitment shapes the lives of fully alive individuals, making all of their efforts seem significant and worthwhile. Devotion to this life task raises them above the pettiness and paltriness that necessarily devour meaningless lives. When there is no such meaning in a human life, one is left almost entirely to the pursuit of sensations. One can only experiment, looking for new "kicks," new ways to break the monotony and boredom of a stagnant life. A person without meaning usually gets lost in the forest of chemically induced delusions, the alcoholic fog, the prolonged orgy, the restless eagerness to scratch without even having an itch. Human nature abhors a vacuum. We must find a cause to believe in or spend the rest of our lives compensating ourselves for failure.

5. *To Belong.* The fifth and final component of the full life would no doubt be a "place called home," a sense of community. A community is a union of persons who "have in common," who share in mutuality their most precious possessions—themselves. They know and are open to one another. They are "for" one another. They share in love their persons and their lives. Fully alive people have such a sense of belonging—to their families, to their church, to the human family. There are others with whom such people feel completely comfortable and at home, with whom they experience a sense of mutual belonging. There is a place where their absence would be felt and their deaths mourned. When they are with these others, fully alive people find equal satisfaction in giving and receiving. A contrary sense of isolation is always diminishing and destructive. It drives us into the pits of loneliness and alienation, where we can only perish. The inescapable law built into human nature is this: We are never less than individuals but we are never merely individuals. No man is an island. Butterflies are free, but we need the heart of another as a home for our hearts. Fully alive people have the deep peace and contentment that can be experienced only in such a home.

So this is the profile, the portrait of fully alive men and women. Having succeeded in taking the five steps just discussed, their basic question as they address themselves to life is: How can I most fully experience, enjoy, and profit from this day, this person, this challenge? People like this stand eagerly on the growing edge of life. In general they will be constructive rather than destructive in their words and actions. They will be flexible rather than rigid in their attitudes. They will be capable of constant and satisfying relationships. They will be relatively free from the physical and psychological symptoms produced by stress. They will perform well, in reasonable proportion to their talents. They will prove adaptable and confident when change is thrust upon them or when they have to make a decision that will change the course of their lives. We would all want to be like these people, and all of us can be more like them. In the last analysis, it is a question of vision. It is our perceptions that make us fragmented or whole. Health is basically an inner attitude, a life-giving vision.

Bon Voyage!

The statistics, the status quo, the speculation

Normal Day,
let me be aware of the treasure you are.
Let me learn from you,
love you, savor you, bless you,
before you depart.

Let me not pass you by
in quest of some rare
and perfect tomorrow.
Let me hold you while I may,
for it will not always be so.

One day I shall dig my fingers
into the earth,
or bury my face in the pillow,
or stretch myself taut,
or raise my hands to the sky,
and want more than all the world:
your return.

Mary Jean Irion,
Yes, World: A Mosaic of Meditation

The proposal being made in these pages is that one's vision, the way one interprets and evaluates reality, is the key to one's emotional and mental health. The theory is that our perceptions cause our emotions and affect our behavior. Consequently, we must begin with our thinking, with the way we are seeing things, with our vision. If we believe this, we will direct our personal growth efforts to becoming more aware of our vision and eliminating the faulty or distorted perceptions that have become a part of that vision.

Not everyone would agree with this theory or build an approach to mental and emotional health on this premise. In fact there are at least several other different theories about what makes people sick and what makes them well. And there are hundreds of different approaches to personal health and growth built on these basic theories. In this chapter I would like to locate my "new life through a new vision" approach in the context of contemporary problems and the current theorizing about those problems.

Unfortunately the vast majority of our human brothers and sisters do not look very much like the fully alive human being described in the last chapter. Abraham Maslow estimated that only one person in a hundred could be called self-actualizing or fully functioning. He felt that most of the others exist without really living. By common estimation most people realize only about 10 percent of their life potential. They see only 10 percent of the world's beauty and hear only 10 percent of the music and poetry of the universe. They are alive to only 10 percent of the deep and rich feelings possible to human beings. They stumble along the path of an unreflective life in an unexamined world. They survive with only a shriveled capacity for giving and receiving love.

Internal aches and pains tend to capture and hold hostage the attention of most people. They live "lives of quiet desperation," as Thoreau once said. The greater part of their energies is siphoned off by fears, angers, guilt feelings, hatreds, loneliness, and frustrations. They have little zest and even less strength to join the dance of life or sing its songs. "Getting high on life" is a meaningless cliché, a cruel hoax dangled before the hungry hearts of the naive.

Most people feel like tightrope walkers trying to keep their balance, afraid of the stress that can tip them into emotional or mental imbalance. Under any increase of social stress, the quiet desperation has for many flared up into acute and painful symptoms. A man loses his job and develops bleeding ulcers. A mother whose child dies goes into severe and prolonged depression. Actors, politicians, and others who live and perform in the fishbowl of public scrutiny often break down physically or psychologically. The protracted stress of the Vietnam War has left the American psyche strained and sour. The shadow of violence on the streets or in the home has darkened the minds and souls of most American city dwellers. There are so many sources of stress that make contemporary life a precarious adventure. Most people would be willing to settle for survival and safety.

You may know the statistics. There is something in us that rebels at and is reluctant to face them, so please be patient. One out of every ten Americans, according to the United States Institute of Mental Health, suffers from some kind of emotional or mental imbalance. One-half million Americans are in mental hospitals. Ten million Americans are classified "mentally ill," and more than 250,000 are admitted each day into mental hospitals for treatment. Two out of every three American hospital beds are occupied by mental patients. The most modest estimate of American suicides is 25,000 each year. However, it is commonly acknowledged that there are at least ten times that number of suicide attempts. Five percent of the adult American population is classified "alcoholic." There are people whose life-style is "characterized by intense and painful emotional isolation from family and friends accompanied by fear, distrust, guilt and shame," according to the Menninger Alcoholism Recovery Program. The second highest cause of infant mortality in this country is child abuse.

The fullness of life, the glorious opportunity of living and loving, means very little to most people. They have "had it" with life. Their hopes are dashed and their dreams are broken.

It is necessary to acknowledge that the emotional and mental problems of which we are speaking are classified as either "organic" or "functional." Organic disturbances are those that result from some deficiency in the physical organism, such as mongolism, retardation, and senility. Functional problems cover a wide spectrum, from the very serious to the very slight. The most serious form of the functional disturbance is "psychosis," a split or cleavage between the person and the real world. The most common mild form of functional problem or imbalance is called a "neurosis." The neurotic person is in touch with reality, but his or her ability to adjust to reality and function peacefully is diminished by emotional problems. The neurotic person usually has exaggerated reactions to certain persons, places, or things which may relate to job, family, or health.

If neurotic people cannot distinguish their emotional needs from physical hungers, they may turn into compulsive eaters. If they do not feel free to have and to express their emotions, they may well work them out destructively on their own bodies in consistently poor health, or they may displace these emotions on innocent bystanders. They may be perpetually edgy or have uncontrollable outbursts of temper or tears. All these, of course, are symptoms, not causes. Neurotic people are usually aware of their condition and the effects it has on others. Still, they feel quite powerless to do much about it.

The United Nations World Health Organization has singled out one type of imbalance as the world's greatest health problem: depression. The more severe form of this disturbance is called "deep depression" or "depressive psychosis." If this alternates with periods of exaltation, excitement, and intense activity, this up-and-down condition is usually called a "manic-depressive" state. Most people who suffer from depression experience feelings of loneliness and especially of helplessness and uselessness. Often they feel unworthy and guilt-ridden. When a person gets worn down by these emotions of depression and shows little interest in life and other people, he or she experiences what is commonly called a "nervous breakdown." More women suffer from depression than men, and the suicide rate among depressives is thirty-six times greater than among the general population.

The most serious and widespread form of mental illness is "schizophrenia." In the United States it is the main cause for hospitalization, and it is estimated that three out of every hundred Americans will be afflicted by some form of schizophrenia at some time in life, with the highest incidence coming between the ages of sixteen and thirty. The usual symptoms include withdrawal from all meaningful social life and retreat into an inner fantasy world. Schizophrenes are always deluded about reality and may hallucinate. There are marked and serious changes in sense perceptions, emotional reactions, and general behavior. People and objects assume strange appearances. Food and drink often taste very strange. Sounds come through as unbearably loud or scarcely audible. Internally the schizophrene often experiences depression, tension, and fatigue.

A paranoid schizophrenic person experiences delusions of grandeur, alternated with a sense of hostility and a feeling of being persecuted. But in general schizophrenes are more dangerous to themselves than to other people. The suicide rate among those so afflicted is twenty times greater than the normal rate. The general opinion is that one-third of all schizophrenes recover spontaneously, one-third remain as they are, and the other third experience progressive deterioration.

Because it is usually some form of social stress that precipitates these disturbances in those who seem predisposed, there have been many mass movements to places where there are no traffic problems, no demanding bosses, no pressures to produce, no regimenting clocks and calendars, few decisions, and no deadlines. Communal and country living have become very popular. Those who cannot physically get away attempt to escape by daydreaming a lot, getting drunk, or using other drugs. Some charter a perpetual flight into the future, living in the haven of a rosy tomorrow. Others find escape from stress in intellectualism—a world of books. Still others take on a perpetual frivolity, allowing any sin except "getting serious."

Of course, each individual's susceptibility to stress is different. Some individuals have a high tolerance for frustration and can take stress in large doses. There are even some who seem to thrive on tension and live on nerves. Others are more fragile and break apart quite easily. This lesser or greater susceptibility to stress obviously must be related to one's environment and biological heredity. The kind of home we live in, the chemistry of our bodies and brains, our diet and metabolism—all are factors that influence our ability to find the fullness of life. It would be a sizeable omission if this were not acknowledged. If a person is seriously troubled, there is immediate need for a competent diagnosis by a professional.

This has been a quick overview of the types of problems that cripple human beings and force them to forfeit the experience of life to the full. Now let us briefly turn to the methods of treatment that have been and are being used to help the troubled.

Even into our own day, treatment has been largely a matter of experimentation. Probably there is no one best way to help all people. Prior to the nineteenth century, physical cruelty and abuse were commonly accepted as the treatment of choice. Even the mentally ill King George III of England was subjected to beatings. Since the late nineteenth century, many theories have been proposed. Some of the theoreticians, like Freud and Adler, approached the emotional and mental disturbances of men and women through the minds of the sufferers. Others have been convinced that these disturbances originate in some bodily imbalance. Psychosurgery was once very popular, then fell into disrepute, and is now slowly regaining some of its lost popularity.

Another commonly used technique—based on the somatic, or bodily, approach—is "shock therapy." After induced convulsions, which scramble the brainwaves, many patients seemed to recover at least temporarily from painful emotional and mental disturbances. At first (in the 1930s) these convulsions were induced by injections of insulin. After ten years, other forms of shock therapy replaced insulin shock. The drug Metrazol was used for a while and was eventually replaced by electroshock (ECT), the application of electric currents to the brain. Today it is the practice to use ECT only after psychotherapy and chemotherapy (drugs) have been proven ineffective. Shock treatments usually effect some remission of symptoms. They obviously cannot reach the basic psychological disturbance. Consequently, there is a high rate of relapse among patients who undergo ECT without further psychotherapy.

Many recently discovered drugs, such as the antidepressants, have given welcome relief to many patients. But drugs, like ECT, can only be a crutch. Conceivably they could delay rather than hasten recovery since they alleviate the symptoms without touching the cause.

Another avenue of approach and experimentation is the so-called "orthomolecular psychiatry" of Dr. Linus Pauling. Pauling bases his theory on the fact that the proper functioning of the brain requires the presence in the brain of certain diverse molecules. These substances reach the brain through the bloodstream. If the body fails to utilize properly the vitamins and minerals found in food because of some genetic defect, this can be compensated by massive doses of vitamins or diet adjustment. Many psychiatrists have reported dramatic improvement in their patients through this means, while others remain critical and unconvinced.

We have been reviewing some of the somatic approaches to mental health. They are based on the belief that we must work through the body to help the mind. Basically, however, suffering persons know that they need help with their *thinking.* Many have sought help through psychotherapy from a psychiatrist or clinical psychologist. The results, when studied statistically, are not very impressive. The number of sick people who improve or recover without this professional help is almost as great as the number of those who improve or recover with professional help. This is not intended to downgrade the psychotherapeutic professions. It is undeniable that many people have been helped, and the professionals are only to be praised for their intentions and efforts.

As we have said, there are many systems of psychotherapy, as opposed to the somatic approaches, and they are rapidly multiplying. However, there are four distinct and basic hypotheses from which most of these systems have been derived.

1. *The Misconception Hypothesis.* This is the basic assumption on which the reasoning of our "vision therapy" is based. It is called a "cognitive" approach to emotional and mental health because it supposes that cognition (the way we perceive reality) is at the basis of emotional reactions and behavior. It further supposes that when faulty or distorted perceptions are eliminated, a person will be enabled to function and live more fully. It presumes that fears, complexes, and generally negative emotions are all traceable to faulty ideas, distorted perceptions, and destructive attitudes. These misconceptions are distortions in our vision of reality. Chronologically, this is the oldest of the four major hypotheses, and is associated today with Albert Ellis and Rational Emotive Therapy.

2. *The Expression of Emotion Hypothesis.* The theory of this hypothesis is that the way to a fuller life is through the release of pent-up emotions. Sometimes there are marked changes in people after they are encouraged to act out their fears, rages, and so forth, in experimental situations. This ventilation seems to be only part of the picture. Probably more critical than the simple emotional catharsis is the new awareness of the person regarding his or her emotional repression and the severing of the tie between stimulus and emotional response. The person ventilating has probably been repressing emotions, reacting to the emotional stimuli in life with outward calm in deference to the expectations of others. In the act of ventilation he or she asserts the right to open expression of feelings and discovers that he or she is constitutionally capable of such expression. Today we associate this hypothesis with Fritz Perls's Gestalt Therapy, Casriel's Scream Therapy, and Janov's Primal Therapy.

3. *The Redistribution-of-Energy Hypothesis.* This is the theory of Freud and the classical psychoanalysts. The so-called psychic energies of a person can be concentrated in or controlled by the *id* (basic, blind desires) and the *superego* (censor or conscience). When this happens, the personality becomes unbalanced and there are symptoms of maladjustment. When the balance of energy is restored by the *ego* (the mediator between the id and reality), the way is then open to the fullness of life. The person is freed from his or her intellectual conflicts and consequently liberated from the need to hold unconscious drives in tight control. When this happens, the person can then use the released energy in dealing constructively with his or her environment.

4. *The Behavior-Change Hypothesis.* This hypothesis bypasses as relatively unimportant the historical sources and origins of crippling emotions and behavior, and moves directly to changing the behavior itself through conditioning. Observable behavior is definitely changed through systematic desensitization, modeling (doing something in front of the person to show how easy it is), and self-demonstration (asking and helping the person to do what he or she feels incapable of doing). Observable behavior is the only concern of the behaviorists. We associate this hypothesis with the names of Wolpe, Eysenck, Skinner, and Ullmann. We are also familiar with the behavioral techniques of Stampfl's Implosive Therapy (a procedure of desensitization by repeatedly imagining the situation in which there is an anxiety response) and Assertiveness Training.

Psychologist Victor Raimy in his book *Misunderstandings of the Self* gives an adequate and reasonably objective description of each of these hypotheses. More importantly, he illustrates that in each of the last three there is some inclusion and incorporation of the misconception hypothesis. For example, the open expression of emotions (number 2) effects a very real change in the person's concept of himself or herself. After acting out their anger, fears, or frustrations, people see that they can express these feelings without falling apart or being utterly rejected. This new awareness will obviously change people's visions of themselves, of their ability to express emotions, and of the readiness of others to accept their emotions. In the redistribution hypothesis (number 3), there is an evident effort on the part of the analyst to help patients "work through their illusions" and arrive at new insights. (See Karl Menninger, *Theory of Psychoanalytic Technique,* p. 38.)

In the behavior-change hypothesis (number 4), the very conditioning and desensitizing procedures are geared to and always result in the elimination of some misconception. This misconception may be about an object ("All dogs are dangerous") or an action ("I can't give a speech in public"). In either case the person must be brought to the insight that his or her previous fears were without foundation. In Assertiveness Training people are taught through role-playing or performing tasks of graded difficulty how to assert their own rights. The coaches in this type of training help underconfident people to see themselves as individuals with rights. They help their participants to see that these rights must be asserted if they are to have any meaning, and that seeing oneself as subordinate and deferential represents a distorted outlook. It is obvious that such a technique presumes and builds upon the misconception hypothesis.

This brings us back to the basic supposition of our vision therapy: All change in the quality of a person's life must grow out of a change in his or her vision of reality. There can be no real and permanent change unless this vision is changed. We are now ready to investigate this truth in greater detail.

The vision that shapes our lives

Unfortunately,
children are excellent observers
but bad interpreters.
They observe keenly what goes on
but do not always
draw the correct conclusions.

Most children who feel rejected
are not rejected,
but assume that they are
because their impressions
and interpretations of what they observe
are faulty.

We are trying to change goals,
concepts, and notions.
Only such changes
can bring about permanent improvement.

Psychiatrist Rudolf Dreikurs,
Contemporary Psychotherapies
(M. I. Stein, editor)

Every baby born into this world is a living question mark. The first question asked is about self: Who am I? The baby proceeds to discover physical reality: hands, feet, and so forth. There is the experience of wetness and hunger. Then comes the discovery of personal emotional reality: security, insecurity, the need for gratification and attention. Somewhere in the course of this ongoing awareness of self, the infant gradually discovers that he or she is not the whole of reality, that all other beings are not merely extensions of self. This initiates the startling discovery of *otherness*. Who are they? Some are warm; some are cold. Some can be manipulated by crying; others cannot.

The thing that all other people have in common for the baby is that they are there. They are a part of the world. He or she must learn to relate to them. Thus, from the first days of life, the infant must begin the work of interpreting and adjusting to reality. As the eyes of the small body start to draw physical reality into focus, the small mind begins its own work of understanding, interpreting, and evaluating. It is the beginning of a vision that will shape a human life.

The human body is instinctively adaptive. The pores close in cold weather. The pupils of the eyes contract in bright light. Certain interior organs can take over the function of others if those others are defective. So, as the baby grows up, he or she will develop a whole repertoire of psychologically adaptive reactions comparable to those of the body. As each new being in this world is perceived, some adjustment to it must be made. This process will eventually constitute the personalized interpretation of and adjustment to reality of a unique human being. Most parents claim to see the first emergence of a distinct personality in each of their children even during infancy. The perceptual patterns and adaptive reactions of each child within a family also have very different emotional colorations. It is very important to realize that the individual adjustment and emotional reactions are the result of a very personal perception and interpretation of inner and outer reality.

At all times in every life there is at least a tentative vision. It is a necessary result of the dynamism of the human mind. The senses pick up phenomenological data—sights, smells, tastes, sounds, and sensations of touch. These are transmitted to the mind, which immediately begins to process and evaluate this material. Like a computer, the mind interprets all the different impulses, first grasped by the senses, and organizes reality into intelligible perceptual patterns.

It is something like receiving one by one the pieces of a mosaic or a jigsaw puzzle. The mosaic is "reality." It does not come all at once in a neat box. It comes piece by piece in packages marked "days." Each day brings new pieces. Every new piece adds its own contribution of deeper understanding to the total picture of reality. We put the pieces together differently because each of us perceives reality in his or her own way. The qualities most needed for the construction of an adequate and accurate vision are *openness* and *flexibility*. The trap to be avoided is *rigidity*.

Rigid people cannot live comfortably with doubt. They need to complete their pictures in a hurry. So they put together only a few of the pieces in a small and tight pattern. These few pieces are all they need. More pieces would only confuse them. And that is the way it was in the beginning, is now, and ever shall be. To hear such people talk, they would appear to have more certainties than anyone else. On the other hand, flexible and open people keep accepting new pieces, rearranging them to modify their tentative patterns. They are always ready to review and revise. They appear to have fewer certainties than the rigid people, and their conclusions are always tentative.

To use another analogy, rigid people are like detectives who take the first scraps of evidence discovered and immediately come to a definite and unshakeable conclusion about the mystery they are trying to solve. If any new evidence is uncovered, they insist on bending it to fit their original, premature conclusions. Flexible and open people are contented with tentative judgments, which they keep revising as new evidence comes in. Instead of bending the facts to fit their conclusions, they keep revising their conclusions to accommodate all the known facts.

Rigid people live fixed and static lives in a small world. They keep their world small so they can handle it. Though they won't admit it, they are terribly afraid to attempt any more. If they should open to reality, it would certainly overwhelm them. Their computers would be jammed. This tunnel vision preserves them from doubt and confusion. On the other hand, flexible people are growing people who live in an ever-expanding world. They sanely acknowledge that change involves both danger and opportunity. They know they can get hurt by possible miscalculations, but they also know that nothing is ever final or irrevocable. If one continues to review and revise, there can be no final failure.

The fact is this: We all need a vision, whether it is prematurely fixed or in the process of constant revision. A vision is necessary because of the restless insistence of the mind to find answers to its questions and to organize reality into understandable patterns. A vision also gives us direction for behavior. It gives life predictability. My vision serves me as a frame of reference, a source of adjustment to reality. Because of my vision, whether it be large or small, tentative or fixed, I know how to act.

If my vision or perception of myself is that I am no good and that people will not like me, then at least I know what my options are. For example, I can play at being a loner or I can become so repulsive that people will leave me alone. Or I can take the offensive, which is proverbially the best defense. By causing some kind of trouble I can get at least "negative strokes."

If in my vision of reality I perceive others as evil or dishonest, I will know how to adjust to them. I will lock my doors at night, put zippers on my pockets, and confide in no one. Similarly, if I perceive life to be an ugly struggle in a valley of tears, I know how to act: Cop out! Get high on drugs, liquor, or daydreams. Come into contact with reality only when necessary or unavoidable.

In other words, we all have a vision because of the very nature of the mind and its instinct to interpret reality. There is also a special need for this vision because it gives life consistency and predictability. A vision enables us to know how to act. Without some kind of vision we would be psychologically blind, stumbling and groping through completely uncharted territory. We would soon be confused and fragmented.

This vision serves as an inner resource by which we can gauge appropriate responses to persons, places, and things. It also becomes the source of our emotional responses. As we have said, all our emotional patterns and reactions are based on our perceptions. It doesn't matter whether the perception is accurate or not, the emotional response will inevitably be proportionate to our perception. For example, let us imagine that a child leaves a toy rubber snake on the lawn. If I perceive it as a real snake, it doesn't matter whether it is real or not. My emotional reaction will follow my perception.

Emotions are always the result of a given perception and interpretation. However, emotional reactions to a given perception can have a profound effect on further perceptions and interpretations. Have you ever been alone in a large, remotely situated house? You hear a noise in the night which you cannot locate or explain. It may have been a shutter blown closed by the wind. From that point on, every creak and shadow becomes suspicious. It is a kind of vicious circle. A perception causes emotional reactions, and the emotional reactions color and distort further perceptions.

We can laugh when remembering the night in the lonely house. However, such vicious circles can be crippling when they involve us in prejudices against other human beings. One bad experience can distort our perceptions of whole classes of people. Also, one experience perceived as disastrous can prove very crippling. It can distort the perception of ourselves and the interpretation of our abilities. For example: "I could never become a teacher. I tried to teach a class once and made a fool of myself." Or, "Some years ago I took a flight in an airplane, and we had to make a crash landing. I could never go up again."

Thus far we have seen that this vision, which is a highly individualized interpretation of reality, results from the nature of the mind. As soon as we discover otherness in the form of other creatures to which we must somehow relate, we begin to make this interpretation and to construct a personal adjustment to reality. This vision gives life predictability and guides our behavior by indicating appropriate responses. Finally, this vision is the basis of emotional patterns that define us as happy or sad, courageous or afraid, affectionate or angry.

There is one other result of this vision, which has a great and pervasive influence on the quality of a human life. I would like to call this result a "basic question," or mindset. It consists of a disposition in advance, or anticipation. Some people are sure of eventual failure whenever they attempt anything. "Old arsenic lips! Everything I kiss falls over dead." Each of us eventually develops a habitual, individual attitude as we approach life: persons, events, specific situations, work, study, and play. The question each of us habitually asks is always an outgrowth of his or her vision, or frame of reference. Sample basic questions: (Is yours listed here?)

What do I have to fear?

How could I get hurt?

What do I have to do to meet the expectations of others?

How could things go wrong?

How could I be tricked or taken advantage of?

Will I have to make any decisions, meet any deadlines, or take any responsibility?

Will I look good or bad in the eyes of others?

How can this bring me attention?

What "strokes" (rewards) are in it for me?

Will I have to reveal myself?

There won't be any trouble, will there?

Of course, the basic question with which each of us approaches the various persons and situations of life is not applied in all situations with absolute universality. Most of us are capable of some variation. But the vision that shapes our personalities is a habitual outlook, and we are creatures of habit. Habit makes us repetitive. The natural, human tendency to unity and a unified approach leads us into habitual rhythms, cycles, and reactions. At any rate, the point is that the basic question, or mind-set, is a consequence of one's fundamental vision of reality.

The basic question of the fully alive person, I would suggest, is this: How can I *enjoy* this person, place, situation, or challenge? No suggestion of hedonism or self-centeredness is intended. Nor is there any intention of limiting the *joy* in *enjoy* to sensual pleasure or emotional satisfaction, though these would be included. The essential condition for true human satisfaction requires that we remain fully active in all of our parts and powers—senses, emotions, mind, will, and heart. I cannot indulge my senses or emotions at the expense of shutting down my mind or turning off my heart.

In the question, How can I enjoy this? there is implied a strong positive mental attitude, a spirit of creativity. This basic question is also multidimensional: How can I get and give the most? How can I grow through this and help someone else to grow? How can I most deeply "live" this experience? What are the opportunities for loving and being loved in this day, this encounter, this situation?

Fully alive people find enjoyment in what others regard as drudgery or duty. They don't *have* to; they *want* to. They are aware of the thorns but concentrate on the roses. Each day has a newness about it; it is never a carbon copy of yesterday. No person is today who he or she was yesterday. Since their vision is always tentative and open to modification, fully alive people eagerly await new insights. These insights will renew them and their vision of reality.

Caution! In describing fully alive people, their vision and basic questions, I feel a certain uneasiness. I don't want to seem to be describing an ideal that is essentially unrealistic. It is quite possible for some people to get drunk on the raw liquor of Pollyannish hopes. Everything is always "ginger peachy!" Life is always beautiful! Obviously such people have lost touch with reality. I know of a wealthy businessman who demands the answer "Great!" whenever he inquires, "How are you?" There are many pop-psychologists who tell us authoritatively that all we have to do is think positively and optimistically. We should ignore our failures and just streak along the primrose path. This will change everything! This is obvious and dangerous nonsense.

It is obvious nonsense because changing one's thoughts about reality can change one's attitudes toward the facts but it cannot change the facts themselves. There is still grief over the death of a dear one. Failure still stings, and being overlooked still saddens. Of course, fully alive people will feel "the slings and arrows of outrageous fortune." They will grow into deeper, more sensitive, and more compassionate individuals precisely because they have suffered; but they will suffer.

The danger in the "Keep smiling!" quackery is that such romanticism and glamorization always end in sad disillusion when reality intrudes. "You can do anything you want to. Where there's a will there's a way!" is true only in soap operas and pulp-magazine stories. Usually the person who gets hooked on dreams is eventually buried in bitter disappointment.

Also, I have the feeling that the enthusiasts can force the positive mental attitude kind of happiness on people whose basic vision is, in fact, negative and pessimistic. This is really quite cruel. It amounts to urging the person to put a smiling mask over his or her essential sadness.

What we have to do is work with our vision. We must become more and more aware of its contents, discover its distortions, and replace faulty perceptions with those that are true. The truth alone can make us free. This is not a simple matter. If a person has spent twenty years building up a specific interpretation of and adjustment to reality, he or she cannot be expected to change that vision in twenty minutes. It is not as simple as wearing a smile or an "I think positively!" button. There is no real growth until the basic vision is changed, and growing is a gradual procedure, often accompanied by growing pains.

C H A P T E R   F O U R

The sources of our vision

From its earliest days,
the child had to learn
degrees of approach and withdrawal
toward everyone around him.
He had to learn whom he could touch,
in whose arms
comfort and warmth could be sought,
where distance was the safer course.

Margaret Mead,
"Sex and Society," in *The Catechist*

If we could compare a human being to a tree, we would find under ground level at least five major roots. These roots nourish and tend to shape the total development of the person. They include a person's biological inheritance (brain, nervous system, and so forth), physical diet, metabolism, social environment, and a unique structure of personality. All of these affect to a great extent the way people will perceive themselves and the world around them.

There is an undeniable, even if somewhat mysterious, interaction of body and mind. It is undeniable that mental and emotional states affect the health of the body. Anxiety can precipitate an attack of asthma. I am personally convinced that health is basically an inner attitude. However, there is no doubt that bodily conditions, conversely, can affect psychological states. Anemia or an imbalance in the chemistry of the brain can bring on depression. This depression of physical origin can consequently distort the way one perceives reality. In other words, our vision of ourselves and the world around us can be profoundly influenced by physical factors.

After making this acknowledgment, I must leave all discussion and diagnosis of these possibilities to the biochemists and the medical doctors who are qualified and competent. I am not. I must limit this present discussion of human visions and their origins to the psychological, environmental influences.

As infants—and later children—begin to discover and interpret reality, they are acquiring a vision that is largely shaped by parents and other family members. Children may distort some family messages, and their most impressionable stages may unfortunately coincide with darker days in the life of their families. They may not hear what others intended to say, or they may be most open to parents and others during periods when they are least apt to transmit a healthy outlook. However, for better or for worse, a child's first tentative vision will by and large be that of his or her parents and family.

Children will see themselves very much as their parents and other relatives have seen them. They will learn to fear the things that their parents fear, to love that which they love, to value whatever they value. This process of osmosis by which children absorb into themselves the parental vision of reality actually begins with intrauterine or prenatal experiences. The peace or turbulence of a mother while she is carrying her child is transmitted to the child through blood-chemistry changes and muscular contractions. The child records these messages in his or her developing brain cells and nervous system. The mother's tranquillity and her traumas become the child's. The mother is saying to her child through these bodily messages that the world is safe and peaceful or that it is dangerous and insecure. To some extent, at least, these messages will affect the child's evaluation of reality and the basic vision with which he or she will begin life.

We have already described the newborn as living question marks. From the very moment children receive the gift of life, they also begin to receive answers and evaluations. Along with these answers and evaluations an emotional coloration is supplied: "Living in this world is difficult; the appropriate response to life is depression." Or, "Life is an exciting adventure; the appropriate response is a sense of eagerness and exhilaration." Children are generally docile and ready to accept the evaluations and suggested emotional responses that their parents communicate to them.

Of course these perceptions, interpretations, and suggested emotional responses are not swallowed whole or all at once. Repetition is the mother of learning. The dynamics in the development of a vision are these: A child, in a definite human situation and in response to definite stimuli, thinks a certain thought, for example: "I have no worth of myself. My only worth is to please others." In successive, repeated situations of a similar nature, the child thinks this same thought, repeatedly perceiving the supposed fact of personal worthlessness and the need to please. The original perception is reinforced by each incident. After sufficient repetition, what was at first a thought and only a questionable fact becomes an attitude and a conviction.

When this happens, the original perception has become a part of the child's vision. His or her emotional responses and behavior will correspond to this habitual perception. The child will be sad and constantly seeking the approval of others. It is another example of the fact that we humans are creatures of habit. Our habits define us. Our thoughts crystallize into attitudes, and our attitudes coalesce into a habitual frame of reference, a way of looking at things, a vision.

Both in the transmission of messages and in the ways they are received, the combinations and variables are infinite. Consequently, people develop unique visions and act very differently. For example: Through coded or explicit parental messages children, rightly or wrongly, may perceive their worth to reside in causing no trouble, or in getting good grades, or in being quiet, or in looking nice, or in being brave, and so forth, *ad infinitum*. Whether children have heard the messages correctly or not, whatever they have heard will have a profound effect on their lives.

In terms of the fullness of life, these early perceptions are extremely important. If children perceive themselves to be affirmed by their parents for what they look like, succeed at, or avoid doing, they will be trapped into frustrating visions and lives. To the extent that they are loved unconditionally they will perceive in themselves real worth identified with their persons and not with appearances or accomplishments. If they perceive only conditional love, which will be withdrawn as soon as they stop fulfilling the imposed conditions, they will perceive themselves as worthless. They will feel "used." The emotional response to this conditional love will probably be a blend of anger, insecurity, and a strong need for approval.

We have said that a baby's first question concerns self: Who am I? The perceived answers to this question, and consequent perception of self, will be the most important of all the parts of the vision that is being formulated. If children are loved or perceive themselves to be loved for themselves, they will develop a good self-image and be on their way to fulfilling lives. If they are loved for what they look like or can do for others, they are on their way to diminished lives.

The second question of children is about others: Who are they? Parents will answer this question more by example than precept. Children watch and listen for answers. They watch the expressions on the faces of their parents and listen to the inflections of their voices as they talk to and about other people. Parental reactions are repeated; messages are reinforced; child thoughts become adult attitudes. Eventually they know: Other people are essentially good or bad, friendly or angry, trustworthy or suspicious, safe or dangerous. They feel secure in this knowledge. If you can't believe your parents, whom can you trust?

Again it should be noted that the combinations and variables are infinite. For example: "Our family and relatives are good; everyone else is suspect." Or, "All people are basically good and decent if they are treated well." Or, "Some people are all right, but it is a safe rule to test thoroughly before trusting." Or, "People will be good to you if you are good to them." Or, "Be sure to bring pan scales when you deal with other people; that way you can carefully measure what you are giving and what you are getting. You won't be a sucker."

The third category in the total vision that opens or closes a person to the fullness of life is life itself. The child asks: What is life for? Who is a success and who is a failure at life? What is the most important thing to do in and with life? What is a full and satisfying life? The answers received will become an integral part of the child's first vision and evaluation of reality. The child's first goals and ambitions will be drawn from this frame of reference.

The general attitudes and value systems of one's parents are deciphered from their actions as well as their lecturing, from their reactions of satisfaction and disappointment as well as their stated principles. Their example more than their words will carry an indelible message to the growing child about the nature and purposes of life. The life situation of the parents during these early formative years of a child is very important. It may be that the parents are generally well adjusted and possessed of reasonable goals and value systems. But it may also happen that financial reverses, health problems, or one of many possible traumas can tip them off balance for prolonged periods. The life messages transmitted to their children during these periods will probably be filled with distortions.

Possible messages about the nature and purposes of life (check one or more):

Life is exciting; it is a real adventure.

Life isn't easy; it is everyone for himself.

Life is to have things: your own home, enough money for an emergency, security for old age.

Life is to get ahead, to prove yourself, to make people respect you.

Success in life is judged by how popular you are—by how many people love you.

You are worth only what you are worth in God's eyes.

Success in life is spelled M-O-N-E-Y.

Be sure you own your own business. Don't ever work for anyone else.

You only go around once, so grab all you can while you can.

Life is for having good times.

It isn't whether you win or lose; it's how you play the game.

Get your own plot of land and build high fences around it.

If you've got your health, you'll be all right.

Education is what is important. They can take everything away from you except your mind.

Eventually the child will be graduated from the home and family situation, but the old parental messages will continue to play softly on the tape recorder of the brain: "Life is . . ." "Success is . . ." "The most important thing is . . ."

This first inherited vision has parts called *self, other people,* and *life.* There will also be transmitted an attitude toward the physical world in which we live. Blessed are the children who receive a life-giving, energizing vision of the universe. They will be taught to wonder, to be filled with curiosity, to admire. Their leisure will be filled with nature walks, stargazing, planting gardens, bird-watching, and collecting rocks or seashells. They will learn to care for their own pets, to distinguish species of flowers and trees as well as cloud formations.

Sad are the children of parents who have no time for such "nonsense." (Unfortunately, many parents know that summer has arrived only because someone has turned on an air conditioner.) Such people are preoccupied with grubbing out a living, with making ends meet, and with watching sports spectaculars on television. "Mabel, did you hear what the kid said? He wants a new pair of binoculars for bird-watching! That's really a good one! No kid of mine will ever be a bird-watcher." Children of such parents will begin life with a "deprived" outlook. They will be able to see only a dingy little world. They will hear only the sound of the air conditioner and the voice of the announcer, endlessly describing a game that some athletes are playing on a field somewhere . . . somewhere they aren't. They will smell only the odors of stale beer and pungent cigars.

Finally, in the last category of reality, the child will receive an inherited vision of *God*. Many people have differing thoughts about God, who he or she is, what he or she does, and so forth. I do not have any last or even late work on the subject. I would deal here only with one truth about God, which is an unquestionable part of all Jewish and Christian teaching: the love of God for us.

There are two ways that God can be presented. One is very healthy; it will affirm a child and invite him or her to live more fully. The other is unhealthy; it can only threaten a child and diminish his or her prospects for life. In this second, distorted (as it appears to me) version, God loves us only *conditionally*. He loves us if, and only if, we make ourselves pleasing to him by obeying all his laws. However, if we fail—in thought, word, or deed—he will immediately withdraw his love. We will feel at once the shadows of divine displeasure falling across our lives. If we fulfill the condition of perfect faithfulness, he will then love us. If not, he will certainly vomit us out of his heart. It is a pretty heavy load to lay on a young mind and heart. If children later reject belief in this God, they are certainly one step closer to the truth.

The truth of God, as I find it in Jewish-Christian teaching and personally believe it, is that God loves us *unconditionally*. He says through his prophet Isaiah, "I have loved you with an everlasting love! . . . If a mother should forget the child of her womb, I would never forget you. . . . I have carved your name on the palms of my hands so I would never forget you." Of course we can refuse God and reject his love. If you ever offered your love to someone who did not want it, you will know what this means. Such a rejection of God's love constitutes the reality of sin. However, God changelessly continues to offer us his changeless love. He is not diminished in any way by our rejection. His arms are always open to receive us.

The ideal of unconditional love was dramatized for me in a story recently related by a well-known psychologist. It seems that a troubled married couple consulted a counselor. The wife complained that her husband was loving only when she kept their house in perfect order. The man agreed that this was true, but maintained that he had the right to expect a house in perfect order when he returned from a hard day's work. The wife countered: "But I need to know that he loves me whether the house is clean or not, just to have the strength to clean the house." The counselor agreed with her.

Children should not be taught that they have to win, earn, or be worthy of love—either the love of God or the love of parents. Real love is a gift. Real love is unconditional. There is no fine print in the contract. There is no price of admission. Simply: "I love you!" (I have described this ideal of love at greater length in my book *The Secret of Staying in Love.*) The God I know would say to the person striving to earn or be worthy of his love: "You have it backwards. You are trying to change so that you can win my love. It just doesn't and cannot work that way. I have given you my love so that you can change. If you accept my love as a gift, it will enable you to grow. You need to know I love you whether you do your best or not so that you will have the strength to do your best."

At any rate, Margaret Mead is right: The child has to learn from his first teachers "degrees of approach and withdrawal . . . whom he can touch, in whose arms comfort and warmth can be sought, and where distance is the safer course." Children learn who they are and what they are worth, who other people are and what they are worth. Children learn to cherish life as a beautiful opportunity or to despise it as a drudgery. They discover that the world is wide and warm and beautiful, or they walk along with eyes cast down through an unexamined world. It is all a matter of the vision they inherit. This vision is certainly the most important legacy of a child's parents and first teachers.

Inevitably children will revise this inherited vision. Their own observations and experiences will to some extent contradict, enlarge, and modify the pictures that were drawn for them. We have said earlier that the key to revising and modifying one's first vision—the key to growth as a person—is openness and flexibility. We called rigidity the trap to be avoided. Obviously, the more open and flexible a person is or becomes, the more he or she will be able to change the inherited vision and eliminate the distortions that diminish capacity for the fullness of life.

The rub is that some message of flexibility or rigidity is also a part of one's inherited vision. Parents transmit a disposition to rigidity or flexibility depending on their own willingness to risk and revise. If they are open to the new evidence that daily living constantly presents to us, their children will perceive this as an appropriate response. However, if parents are unwilling to live with doubt and are consequently rigid, their children will probably see this as the safer course. They will, in the beginning at least, imitate their parents in these inflexible postures.

For example: If a little girl comes home in tears after a disagreement with a playmate, her father may bellow some rigid, categorical sentiment such as: "I told you that kid's no good! Her whole family is no good!" Or, "You can't get along with anyone. From now on just stay home!" Or, "Stay away from those Catholics (or Protestants or Jews or blacks or whites)!"

For the kind of person who says these things, "all the evidence is in" on all questions. He is the personification of rigidity, and rigidity is the formula for nongrowth. It is also contagious. Rigid parents tend to beget rigid children.

Fortunately, as we grow up, new influences and other messages come to us from significant other persons. There is a constant turnover of new evidence in our lives. Through these sources we can modify inherited tendencies to rigidity and inflexibility as well as the other distortions in our inherited visions. But it isn't easy. Just to be aware of one's vision is very difficult. We are so easily deluded by our own ego defense mechanisms. Each of us has to contend with the deceits of an illusory self, the person we would like others to see and accept. It is hard for most of us to distinguish this illusory self from a real but repressed self.

The most profound problem of change probably lies at an even deeper level. The vision I work with gives me certainty. It makes sense of life. It gives life predictability and gives me a basis for adjustment to reality. With my vision, for better or for worse, I can cope. Without it, where would I be? What would happen to me if I gave it up in search of a new vision? It is now time to discuss these important questions.

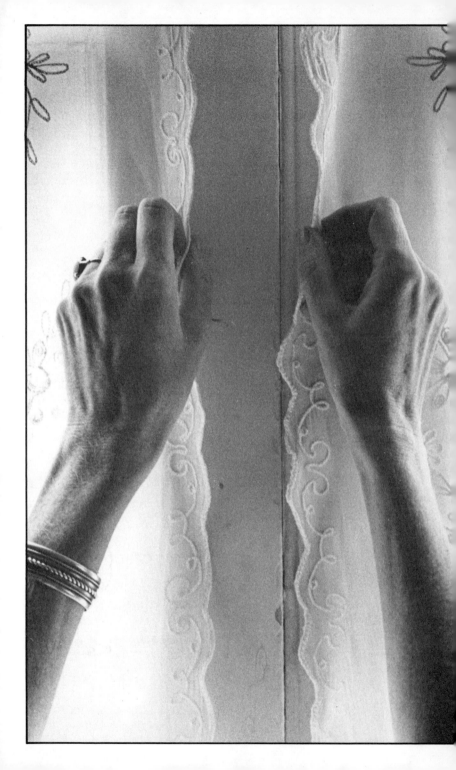

Persistence and awareness (of a vision)

Take stock of those around you and you will . . . hear them talk in precise terms about themselves and their surroundings, which would seem to point to them having ideas on the matter. But start to analyse those ideas and you will find that they hardly reflect in any way the reality to which they appear to refer, and if you go deeper you will discover that there is not even an attempt to adjust the ideas to this reality. Quite the contrary: through these notions the individual is trying to cut off any personal vision of reality, of his own very life. For life is at the start a chaos in which one is lost. The individual suspects this, but he is frightened at finding himself face to face with this terrible reality, and tries to cover it over with a curtain of fan-

tasy, where everything is clear. It does not worry him that his "ideas" are not true, he uses them as trenches for the defense of his existence, as scarecrows to frighten away reality.

José Ortega y Gasset,
The Revolt of the Masses

I would like at this point to investigate a very interesting question. It concerns the persistence of our first, inherited vision. Why does one's early vision tend to have such a lasting influence throughout life? Are first impressions really that lasting? It would seem that we would be eager to give up the distortions that limit our happiness and diminish our possession of life. Of course some change is inevitable in everyone. It is the lack of profound changes that is puzzling.

Let us imagine a man with a totally distorted vision. He sees himself as a one-man slum. He regards other people as mean and menacing. Life for him is an endurance contest, the world is a snake pit, and God is little more than a cruel illusion. Obviously such a man would want to stop the world and get off. His perceptions punish him brutally. Why doesn't such a person rethink and revise his vision? He must notice that there are other people who are relatively happy. Some of the people who pass him on the street are smiling or whistling. Did they swallow some secret of joy? Are they high on something he hasn't found? What do they know that he doesn't? If he were only willing to rethink and revise his basic vision, he could turn self-contempt into self-celebration. He could move from pessimism into optimism, from cynicism into trust. He could replace a negative mental attitude with one that is positive. Why doesn't he? To a lesser or greater degree we all somehow resemble this poor man. Are we all masochists?

On the principle that if a thing is worth saying once it is probably worth saying twice, we have been repeating that the only possible way to grow and live more fully requires a change in our perceptions. A limiting, punishing vision is like a set of chains that keeps us bound. We are held fast in the same place, each day a carbon copy of the previous, and each year a repetition of last year's sadness. To understand why many of us remain voluntary prisoners of distorted visions, we must review briefly what a vision does for us. It may shed some light on why we are so reluctant to rethink and revise the vision with which we began the journey of life.

When we human beings first look inward at our own reality and outward at the rest of reality, we immediately begin looking for order, patterns, cycles. We learn to relate causes with their effects. We are looking for, in one word, *predictability.* Knowing what to expect gives us a sense of security. It enables us to make decisions about how to act. Soon our own actions and reactions fall into patterns which are based on our perceptions and adjustments to reality. Life becomes predictable, and our reactions take on *consistency.* We are usually willing to act well or badly to maintain this consistency. The opposite of predictability and consistency is *chaos.* Chaos implies unpredictability and inconsistency. Chaos boggles the mind and fragments the spirit. People who go through a period of chaos are often referred to as "disoriented." In their confusion, disoriented people have lost all sense of direction. Chaos is a very frightening experience.

And this is perhaps the main reason why we are so reluctant to change our vision, even when it is a cruelly imprisoning vision. There is a lingering fear that in giving up the old vision, which has provided predictability and consistency, I might fall into the chaos. I will be lost without a guide. For example, if I were to give up a poor self-image and learn to like myself, how would I act? What would happen? How would I relate to other people? If I were to give up my prejudice that others are basically dishonest and out to get me, how would I treat them? Would I have to start trusting others? Would I have to go so far as to reveal myself to others?

The trouble is that there are no guarantees that the new will be better than the old. Isn't it a question of one bird in the hand being better than two in the bush? Who wants to trade in a known for an unknown without some kind of reassurance? I know what I have; I am not sure what I will get or even what I stand to lose. In every change there is a death and a rebirth. Dying to the old and being born into the new is a frightening prospect. And there is always that terrible moment between death and rebirth when I will have nothing. If I give up the old vision, which made some sense of life and provided a source of direction for my behavior, will a new vision keep my life intact in the same way?

What we have been saying may sound like pure abstraction. I remember a personal experience that may help to illustrate more concretely the reality of this fear. A college girl came to me repeatedly in a counseling situation. For each visit she had a different problem. Finally, after working through very many problems, I asked her: "Do you think you will ever run out of problems? We must have hit the hundred mark by now." She looked down a bit sheepishly and said softly: "If I do, I won't be able to come and see you any more." The poor girl saw herself as completely inadequate in an adult social relationship. Because of her own self-perception she could not relate as one equal to another. The only way she could adjust to the reality of dealing with others was by playing a role of the "perpetually troubled little child."

Now let us suppose that someone were to say to this girl: "You see yourself as inadequate, and you have adjusted to this supposed inferiority by remaining a little girl. Now the fact of the matter is that you are not at all inadequate. You have fine gifts and you are a fine person. You must learn how to relate to others on a basis of equality, as one adult to another." What would be her reaction to this? Theoretically, she should want to believe in her adequacy and equality. However, she has based all her perceptions and adjustments on the supposition that she is inadequate and inferior. She has become comfortable and practiced in this role. A suggestion that she should change this faulty vision and begin acting in a radically different way would strike terror into her heart. She feels safe behind her fences and the face of helplessness. Consequently, she will tend to cling to her original orientation. Unfortunately, in doing so she has walled out a fuller and more human life.

A new example could be given for almost every person. All of us make definite evaluations of our human situation and develop definite ways of coping, of living within that situation. From that point on it is practice till functionally perfect. To revise the original evaluation would be like starting all over again and there would be no certainty of success. Consider the young man who has perceived himself as unlovable and has adapted to that supposed situation by becoming a professional introvert and loner. What if he were invited to revise his original judgments and leave his human hiding places, to come and join in the celebration of life? He would most probably cling to his vision and adaptation with white knuckles rather than risk the chaos of a conversion.

The famous psychiatrist of interpersonal relationships, Dr. Harry Stack Sullivan, in his book *The Psychiatric Interview,* calls these adjustments which result from a false or inadequate vision a "security operation." Once people have taken flight into such an operation, they have to fend off any new evidence that would threaten their original perceptions and subsequent adjustments. Dr. Sullivan calls this deliberate blindness "selective inattention." He attributes the security operation and consequent selective inattention to a desire to protect oneself, to stay safely within what we have called predictability and consistency. He says that this stubborn defense of a barricaded position "seriously reduces one's capacity to profit from experience." We have called this "rigidity."

Do you remember trying to pry something dangerous or undesirable from an infant's hand? Usually the little fist will tighten around its possession. The indicated psychological ploy is to dangle some attractive distraction before the child: a replacement. It works not only with the very young; we are all susceptible to a reasonable exchange. However, in this matter of revising one's perceptions and adjustments, it isn't like stepping out of one set of clothes into another. Our original perceptions, as we have said, had to be repeated until they crystallized into attitudes and were finally integrated into a vision. We are creatures of habit. We cannot step out of old habits into prefabricated new ones the way we change clothes. The changing of habits, by its very nature, has to be gradual.

However, staying in the old ruts isn't easy either. To persist in the old, diminished vision requires that one must constantly deny all contrary experience and information. One must stubbornly reassert his or her faulty vision in the face of mounting contradictory evidence. This can be strenuous and exhausting. It results over a period of time in considerable inner tension and stress. And the stronger the contrary evidence, the more energy the poor person must expend in the mechanism of denial.

This increased straining to deny, repress, and to keep our security operation intact means that we will be using more and more of our energy in this effort. We will have less and less energy for living, enjoying, and loving. While we may not acknowledge the explicit nature of this contest, we will note that anxiety and nervous symptoms, physical indisposition and fatigue, will become an almost habitual condition. We will become exhausted as a result of defending our imprisoning vision. Such an orientation to life must be labeled: *neurotic* (and painful!). The vision that the poor victim of rigidity tenaciously clings to for peace and security has become the source of considerable unhappiness and insecurity.

When people turn to a psychiatrist or psychologist, it is usually with the hope of an immediate relief. They want to feel better and they want a doctor who will be able to write out a psychological prescription which, when taken three times a day, will anesthetize all pain. If there is a need for "reconstructive psychotherapy," as opposed to "supportive psychotherapy," the result is usually the opposite. Supportive psychotherapy is designed to help a person get through brief periods that are traumatic or very difficult. Therapists help the client to ventilate pent-up emotions, to strengthen existing defenses. Therapists deal only at the conscious and symptomatic level. Their intention is exclusively to relieve temporary distress. Reconstructive psychotherapy, however, is usually needed by people whose symptoms are generally persistent and continual. The therapists attempt to deal, in this case, with the personality structure and the basic vision. When this is done, there is usually an initial period of disorientation or disintegration: chaos.

The person who is trying not merely to get by during a difficult period but to get out of a rutted existence and find the fullness of life will have to revise his or her basic vision. With or without professional help this is reconstructive psychotherapy. As we have been repeating: Our participation in the fullness of life is always proportionate to our vision. Whoever is not living fully is not seeing rightly. However, to give up an old vision in favor of a radically different perspective always involves the limbo of the in-between, the temporary experience of chaos. This is why there is always an initial period of disorientation or disintegration. It is a necessary part of the growth process.

Have you ever tried to cross a stream stepping from one rock to another? While perched on any one rock there is a sense of security. It is safe. Of course there is no movement, no progress, no satisfaction beyond safety. The challenge to move on—to step out to the next rock—is precarious and frightening precisely because of that moment when one is firmly footed on neither rock. The precarious and frightened feeling is comparable to what we feel at the moment an insight beckons and we are tempted to step out of rigidity into a new vision and into a new life. Just as it is foolish to want a dentist or doctor who can always cure us instantly without any discomfort, it is likewise foolish to think that human growth can be accomplished instantly and without pain. There is no painless entrance into a new and fully human life.

What is needed, whether it is accomplished with or without professional help, is a revised view of reality which will take into consideration and accommodate all previous experiences and all available evidence. The revisionist historian goes back and reinterprets, for example, the causes of a war long ended, with an objectivity which would have been impossible while the guns were blazing and the bombs exploding. In a similar manner, individuals who are seeking a new vision must go back, review the evidence of their life experiences, and revise the judgments, evaluations, and interpretations that have been controlling their emotions, their behavior, and their lives. No help is possible until they are willing to attempt this, and no change is real until they have done it.

Now let us turn to a different matter: becoming aware of my present vision. How do I bring my vision into consciousness for the sake of inspection? Before I can review and revise my perceptions, I have to be aware of them. Only then can I proceed to locate and modify the faulty perceptions that are distorting my vision.

The first requirement for finding one's vision and its distortions is a basic disposition of willingness to face the facts, whatever they be. It is a matter of courage and humility. This disposition of willingness will involve a specific willingness to say: "I was wrong." This is not easy for most of us. We are so much in need of approval and respect that we fear anything which might diminish our public image and sense of personal worth, such as admitting our delusions. In a larger dimension, we must be willing to admit a lesser or greater credibility gap between who we really are and who we pretend to be—between a *real* and an *illusory* self. Sometimes this illusory self fools other people. We come off as intelligent, competent, profound, or whatever our pretense is. Sometimes it even fools us. We repress into our subconscious minds the facts we cannot face, along with the fears, hungers, and angers we cannot admit. We stubbornly deny entrance to the truth which keeps knocking on our doors, asking for admittance and recognition. We are afraid to live and we are afraid to die. Ah yes, the first need is for courage and humility.

This willingness is really put to the test when it threatens to unravel a security operation and the consequent selective inattention. By necessity or choice most of us engage in some form of self-deception. We keep our egos afloat by some special ploy and block out of vision the rest of reality. In 1976 a tycoon, reputed to be the wealthiest man in the world, died. His name was J. Paul Getty and his fortune almost uncountable. When a book publisher asked him to write a complete autobiography, Getty unexpectedly agreed and soon sent to the publisher a single line: "J. Paul Getty became a billionaire!" He insisted that this one line was his complete autobiography. One line said it all. Among the legacy of his remembered quotations: "If you can count your money, you are not a billionaire." When reminded that "You can't take it with you!" Getty replied: "Yes, it would be too great a load, wouldn't it?"

I have no inclination to pass judgment on J. Paul Getty, Howard Hughes, or any other deceased billionaires. Human beings are far too complicated for such split-second psychoanalysis. I would simply suggest that if the words "He became a billionaire!" can really be taken literally as Getty's own summation of his total life, he did not live a very full life and he never had the experience of being fully human.

He may have been financially a billionaire, but if this one line really summarizes his life, he was personally bankrupt. Humans and human life are multidimensional. To live huddled in any corner of life, even if it is with an uncountable pile of money, is a life of serious deprivation. Poor Paul Getty. Poor us, if we settle for a security operation and the blindness of selective inattention.

Granted willingness, what then? I think that the next step is indicated in the suggestion of psychiatrist Viktor Frankl: "Let life question you." Dr. Frankl recommends this openness to be questioned by life as a means to find out who we are and what we love. He points out that most of us are forever questioning life: What will this day bring me? Who will love me? Will things go my way today? What will happen to me this year? How will this or that turn out? What has life done for me lately? Of course, no one can help wondering out loud in this way. But there is a deeper wisdom in reversing the process and letting life question us.

It is obvious to me that each new day—along with all the persons and events of that day—does in fact question us, if we will submit to the test. The needy, unattractive person asks me how much I can love. The death of a dear one asks me what I really believe about death and how profitably I can confront loss and loneliness. A beautiful day or a beautiful person asks me how capable I am of enjoyment. Solitude asks me if I really like myself and enjoy my own company. A good joke asks me if I have a sense of humor. A very different type person from a background very dissimilar to my own asks me if I am capable of empathy and understanding. Success and failure ask me to define my ideas of success and failure. Suffering asks me if I really believe I can grow through adversity. Negative criticism directed to me asks me about my sensitivities and self-confidence. The devotion and commitment of another to me asks me if I will let myself be loved.

Yes, every day does, in fact, question us. However, most answers do not pop out automatically, because we have quarantined them out of sight. Selective inattention has buried so many of my memories, thoughts, and emotions in graves of obscurity. My illusory self has served as a self-appointed censor, allowing me contact with thoughts and emotions that are judged to be acceptable, but not permitting me those thoughts and emotions that would threaten my fictitious identity.

Someone has humorously suggested that this repression and selective inattention are governed by three deceitful old witches: Shoulda—Woulda—Coulda. Instead of honestly facing my true thoughts, I am led to deny them by the conviction that I *should* think some other way. I substitute in my conscious awareness the way I should think for the way I do think. I convince myself that I do feel what I *would* like to feel. And what I *could* do becomes my preoccupation rather than addressing myself to what I actually do.

One helpful way to facilitate this process of being questioned by life is a self-analysis of one's emotions. The most fundamental supposition of this book is that our ideas (perceptions) cause our emotions. The patterns of our emotional lives are simple and tangible reflections of the patterns of our perceptual lives. Consequently, my first important effort must be a full, accurate, and conscious awareness of my emotions. I must have and acknowledge my emotions before they can guide me to the perceptions from which they have stemmed. Under every emotion is a definite perception. If I were to live in sensitive awareness of my emotions and be willing to dig for their roots, I would have easy access to the perceptions, to the vision that shapes my life.

I try to work at this in my own life and think of it as "vision therapy." Through emotional awareness and analysis I keep finding out very surprising things about myself and my basic vision. An example. Last summer I was happily driving along a busy Chicago expressway when the car I was using suddenly died. Right there in the middle lane, it died! I had the instinctive presence of mind to coast cautiously over to and through the right lane and onto the shoulder of the road. There was no thought of investigating the mechanical problem myself. The only thing about a car of which I am certain is its color. I did open the hood, but a brisk Chicago wind nearly blew it off. I shut the hood and tried opening the trunk with equally bad results. I knew that I was supposed to tie my handkerchief to the radio aerial, but the aerial of this car was built right into the windshield.

Finally I closed and locked everything and studied the terrain. On the shoulder side of the road, where I was standing, was a deep ravine and no signs of human life or civilization in it. In the other direction were six lanes of speeding traffic. I felt no inclination to try the ravine and an absolute aversion for trying a dash through expressway traffic. I did not know what to do. Finally it occurred to me to hitchhike. I tried to look worried, then pathetic, but no one stopped. In fact, no one even looked at me. I felt rejected. Don't they care?

After fifteen minutes a fine young college student pulled over and asked: "Can I help you?" No words have ever sounded sweeter. As we drove from the scene he told me of his interest in personal growth and I shared with him the mechanics of vision therapy. He asked: "Are you practicing it right now?" So we did it together. We decided that my emotion of the moment had to be called "panic." (I hate to admit it. My illusory self is competent, composed, cool, and always in command.)

In tracing my emotional panic to its perceptual source, I made a surprising discovery. Strangely, it was not danger to life or limb that was found at the roots of my panic. It was not the seeming indifference of the motorists who passed me by. Rather it was the fact that I was not in control of the situation, that I did not know what to do. Apparently I have always entertained the delusion that respectability is somehow forfeited by someone who is at a loss, confused, forced to fumble and improvise. Apparently a part of my own identity and sense of worth has somehow been attached to being in control of every situation. Once I discovered this, I was later able to relate this new awareness to other situations in my past life. By reinterpreting these past events I found that this new insight was strongly reinforced by old evidence. It was always there waiting for me to be ready and willing to recognize it. Being in control of, and knowing what to do immediately in, every situation was apparently part of my security operation. The elimination of this distortion is clearly one condition of my growth as a person and of my fuller participation in the adventure of living.

So the first two requirements for successful vision therapy are a willingness to revise one's interpretations and an openness to be questioned by life. A third requirement would be finding times for silence and solitude. We are all victims of too much noise, too many distractions—victims of what a well-known psychologist has called "stimulus flooding." To come into contact with one's vision, one has to practice some kind of active and sensitive listening to oneself. For such an in-depth effort, silence and solitude are indispensable. "The unreflected life," to requote Socrates, "isn't worth living." The kind of listening I am suggesting here is a peaceful review of the rhythms of one's recent life. It would include a recollection of recent events and one's personal response to those events. Through analysis of the emotional reactions, the perceptions under them will surface. These must be open to inspection and review and, to the extent needed, revision. We shall talk later about how these perceptions are permanently revised. This is the change of vision that alone can bring fuller participation in life. For now, however, we are interested only in locating or becoming aware of that vision. Silence, solitude, and reflection are very necessary to this effort.

An autobiographical illustration of all the above. Some years ago a close friend asked me: "Are you enjoying your life?" Life itself had been asking me that question but I wasn't listening. In answering my friend, I said: "I believe in what I am doing. I find it meaningful. I think I am helping others. I . . . well, no, I don't think I am really enjoying my life." The insight of my answer surprised me. I had been thinking only in terms of commitment, meaningfulness, and service. Strangely, I had not been thinking in terms of personal enjoyment. I began taking my friend's question and my answer into the think tanks of silence and solitude. There it became clear to me that even if a person is doing a fine thing for pure motives, if he or she is not enjoying it, something is wrong. No one should be deprived of joy in one's life and work.

Wanting to understand why I seemed to be experiencing more struggle than joy, I tried to get in touch with the emotional patterns of my life. It was immediately evident that frustration and anger were too dominant in those patterns. Without retelling the dramatic story of my life and how I miraculously came to be saved by startling insights, I must tell you that I did find two faulty perceptions or distortions in my total vision. I think that they were largely responsible for the frustration and anger which I was experiencing at that time. As these distortions have been more and more eliminated I have noticed a proportionate diminution of those negative emotions, and an increase of joy.

The distortions I found were these: (1) I saw myself as responsible for solving the problems of the many people who were coming to me for help. I was perceiving my value and identity as essentially connected with my ability to dictate instant solutions to tangled problems and bring immediate peace to all the sufferers. (2) I found in myself a strong, almost compulsive, need to please others—to meet their expectations. This delusion—that I had to be "for others" and never "for myself"—was truly a ring in my nose by which I was being led around. The discovery of this delusion led to a whole explosion of insights about the need to love oneself in balance with loving other people.

As I began acting on these insights, prompted by the question of a friend and found in solitude and reflection, I began to experience more and more of the joy that had been eluding me. Of course, one has to establish insights as permanent by acting on them. We must "do" the truth as well as believe it. We must continue to act on our lights or the light will fail. The old distortions and emotional syndromes die slowly because we are creatures of habit. New habits must be built from the ground up. However, the more one sees clearly the falseness or distortion of previous perceptions, the more one will be liberated from former tyrants, and will begin to enjoy the fullness of life.

There should be quiet times in every life for such reflection, reevaluation, and reinterpretation. It is also very profitable, if not necessary, to key into emotions—especially negative emotions—while they are being experienced. Memory tends to distort. These emotional reactions can be more accurately traced to perceptual roots and possible distortions if they are inspected while still on the vine.

Such are the requirements of vision therapy. When it has become a way of life, and one is alert to the signals of negative emotions as symptomatic of perceptual distortions, a fuller and more human life cannot be far away. We shall say more of vision therapy in the next two chapters. There we will take up some of the more common distortions found among humans and discuss in detail the mechanics of vision therapy.

Some common misconceptions

> ... the task of logotherapy is to reveal the flaws in improper logical grounds for a world-view and thereby to effect a re-adjustment of that view.
>
> Psychiatrist Viktor Frankl,
> *The Doctor and the Soul*

Most neurotic suffering results from an erroneous outlook. In one way or another the neurotic has acquired a picture of his place in life which simply isn't true. Feeling helpless in the midst of conflicting claims, he allows his life to be molded by circumstances until he feels himself to be little more than a victim of fate.

Can any therapy really serve its purpose if unrealistic views of life are left unchallenged? ... Recognizing how an individual's vision is limited by his own life experience, Frankl perceives the therapeutic task as including the marshaling of arguments to challenge destructive world views.

Psychologist Robert Leslie,
Jesus and Logotherapy

In the last chapter suggestions were made for locating the vision that shapes our lives. Vision therapy, as recommended, is designed to help us find the misconceptions and distortions that lie at the roots of our unhappiness and neurotic suffering. To be successful practitioners of vision therapy we must first ask: What am I feeling? Only then can we move to the causes of our feelings and ask about the perceptions or ideas from which the feelings have resulted. How am I viewing this situation? What is there in my general outlook that this situation should produce these emotions?

To get to the distortions that fester like embedded slivers in the flesh of our emotions, some emotional clearance is usually necessary. After discharging painful emotions, verbally or nonverbally, we can usually think more clearly. Heavy emotions tend to bend the mind out of shape. This emotional clearance is like clearing the air or silencing a deafening noise. An overload of emotions almost always obscures one's vision beyond recognition. This problem is further complicated by what I would like to call a "lifelong buildup" of emotions. Undischarged emotions collect and have a cumulative effect. For example, let us suppose that people who have outranked me (parents, teachers, and the like) have repeatedly called me "stupid." At such times I could never discharge my hurt and anger because these detractors were my parents, had positions of authority over me and could punish me, or were bigger than I.

After years of such accumulation, I might be ripe and ready to overreact. I will probably report a very deep hurt or a furious anger at any suggestion that I have inferior intelligence. In other words, the next time someone calls me "stupid" my reaction will not be directed exclusively at that person. In a very real way my reactions will be directed to the hundreds of people who have, over the years, been in the "firing squad" which assassinated my intellectual self-confidence. I am really reacting to my parents, my teachers, my camp counselor, and the big kid down the block who picked on me.

One of the reasons, no doubt, that Gestalt Therapy has helped many people is that it has provided an acceptable means of ventilating, discharging, and thus defusing many years of emotional buildup. A good scream, a good cry, a good kick at the symbolic pillow, under carefully arranged circumstances in which no one else will get hurt or be manipulated, is probably a very good idea. Having a friend who provides the needed atmosphere for free emotional communication is an invaluable help to vision therapy and personal growth. Only when we exercise our right to have and to express our true feelings do we become capable of finding the vision that lies under those feelings and causes them. Emotions are always an outgrowth of perceptions.

In a book called *Outwitting Our Nerves* (2d edition), two doctors, Jackson and Salisbury, have worked out a cause-effect schematic diagram to illustrate how wrong ideas or misconceptions lie at the roots of unhappy living and social maladjustment. The diagram of the doctors indicates that all hope to restore a person to adjusted and joyful living lies in reversing the formula, in correcting wrong ideas or misconceptions.

Jackson-Salisbury *Diagram for Maladjusted and Unhappy Living*

Lack of adaptation to social environment
    caused by
Lack of harmony within the personality
    caused by
Inappropriate emotions
    caused by
Wrong ideas or ignorance

Working backward, the *cure* naturally would be:

Right ideas
    resulting in
Appropriate emotions
    resulting in
Harmony within the personality
    resulting in
Readjustment to the social environment

Obviously, "wrong ideas or ignorance" in the diagram corresponds to what we have been calling "misconceptions" or "distortions" in one's basic vision. The message is the same: *Health and wholeness begin in the head,* with healthy ideas, energizing attitudes, a vision of vitality. When perceptions get twisted, one's emotional life also gets twisted, and these discordant emotions cause disharmony in the total personality. At this point you've got trouble in River City.

Neurotics wear themselves out trying to cope with the civil war that is going on inside them. They can also be very wearing on others. If neurotics are helped to eliminate the misconceptions or distortions at the bottom of their struggles, this will effect an immediate improvement in their emotional patterns, which in turn will tend to harmonize the whole personality. Such people are then enabled to relate comfortably with others, to enjoy life.

Before our discussion of the misconceptions thought to be most prevalent among human beings, let's try an experiment. It is a homemade little test of one's vision. Relax now. You cannot flunk. Besides, the purpose of this test is primarily to help you become aware of the various dimensions embraced in your vision of reality. It may have some diagnostic value, but that is secondary, and you can decide for yourself its diagnostic validity.

We have already suggested that there are five main categories in the spectrum of a vision: self, other people, life, the world, God. Most students of human nature would probably agree that of these five categories the most important by far is the first: how you see yourself. All ability to love begins with and is conditioned by one's ability to love oneself. If we are to love others and to love life itself, we must have a true love for ourselves, a healthy self-image, a sense of self-appreciation. Consequently, the experts believe that the most harmful and crippling distortions in anyone's vision of reality are usually clustered in this area. Furthermore, the distortions in how we see other people, life, the world, and God are usually traceable to some distortion in the way we see ourselves. However, a check of all areas is in order.

Below you will find some fundamental either/or descriptions under each of the five suggested categories. On a separate sheet of paper, put the numbers from 1 to 100 in a vertical column. After each number draw a straight horizontal line, two or three inches in length. It is important that the lines be directly under one another for the sake of graphing to be done later. Above the first line put the letters A, B, C, D, and E spaced out across the width of the line, with the letter A at the far left and the letter E at the far right. If your answer (judgment, evaluation) verges more to the first of the two given alternatives, put a dot or an X on the line proportionately close to the left end of the line, under or between A or B. If your answer tends more toward the second alternative, indicate this by placing the dot or X proportionately close to the right end of the line, under or between D or E. If you see your answer falling in the middle, then put the dot or X under the C. Here is an example:

1. (I am) Good/Bad

I put the X closer to the left end of the line, under the B, because I see myself as more good than bad. If I saw myself as completely good in every way, I would have put the X under the A. After you have prepared your answer sheet, consider the choices offered below and mark your answer sheet accordingly. Above all else be honest! Don't mark what you *should, would* or *could* think, but in every case what you actually *do* think.

I. Who am I?

1. Good/Bad

2. Compassionate/Unfeeling

3. Generous/Selfish

4. Responsible/Undependable

5. Hardworking/Lazy

6. Capable of personal decisions/Indecisive

7. Authentic/Phoney

8. Involved in social concerns/Uninvolved

9. Interested in others/Interested only in self

10. Loyal/Disloyal

11. Gifted/Ungifted

12. Superior to most others/Inferior

13. Intelligent/Unintelligent

14. Great in potential/Little potential

15. In control of life/Out of control of life

16. Good-looking/Ugly

17. Lovable/Unlovable

18. Many pleasing mannerisms/Few

19. Grateful/Ungrateful

20. Emotionally warm/Cold

21. Deep/Superficial

22. Interesting/Boring

23. Active/Passive

24. Consistent/Inconsistent

25. Independent/Overly dependent

26. Important to others/Unimportant

27. Needed/Not needed

28. Loved by many/Loved by few

29. Supported by many/Supported by few

30. My love wanted by many/Wanted by few

31. Valued highly by many/By few

32. Valued for self/For what I can give

33. Add much to group gatherings/Add little

34. Give much joy to others/Give little

35. Cooperative/Uncooperative

II. Who are other people?

36. Essentially good/Bad

37. Peaceful/Hostile

38. Trustworthy/Suspicious

39. Ready to help me/Disinterested in me

40. Loving/Selfish

41. Generous/Greedy

42. Concerned about others/Only about themselves

43. Honest/Dishonest

44. Compassionate/Unfeeling

45. Loyal/Disloyal

46. Grateful/Ungrateful

47. Similar to me/Unlike me

48. Responsible/Undependable

49. Emotionally warm/Cold

50. Lovable/Unlovable

51. Cooperative/Uncooperative

52. Collaborators/Competitors

53. Balanced/Unbalanced

54. Hurting and needy/In no pain and no need

55. Authentic/Phoney

III. What is life?

56. A pleasant experience/A struggle

57. Important/Doesn't really matter

58. Beautiful/Ugly

59. An adventure/An endurance contest

60. An education/A disillusionment

61. Satisfying/Dissatisfying

62. Challenging/Defeating

63. Meaningful/Meaningless

64. Too short/Too long

65. Exciting/Boring

66. A time for growing/For surviving

67. Perpetually changing and new/Sadly repetitious

68. A time for giving/A time for getting

69. I wouldn't miss it for anything/Sorry I got into it

70. Money is relatively unimportant/Almost everything

71. Tomorrows are eagerly awaited/Dreaded

72. Time is valuable/Worthless

73. Old age is a mellow time/A sad time

74. Suffering can be a time of growth/An evil to be avoided

75. Death is a beginning/A tragedy

IV. What is the physical world?

76. Nature is beautiful/Unimpressive

77. The physical world is important/Unimportant

78. The physical world is fascinating/Dull

79. I have great interest in geography-geology/No interest

80. Animal pets are very enjoyable/A nuisance

81. I enjoy gardens immensely/Never notice them

82. I have much interest in nature-related hobbies/No involvement

83. Solar system is mind-staggering/Is irrelevant to me

84. Archaeology excites great curiosity/Means nothing to me

85. Certain natural scenes are special to me/Have no significance

86. Ecology is a great concern/Excites no interest

87. The animal kingdom is interesting/Is irrelevant to me

88. Stars are breathtaking/Rarely notice them

89. Nature walks are delightful/Silly and boring

90. Seasons are beautiful/A bother

V. Who is God?

91. A father-mother/A tyrant-taskmaster

92. Unconditionally loving/Conditionally loving

93. Forgiving/Angry and unrelenting

94. Interested in me/Not at all interested

95. Near and close/Distant and detached

96. Reassuring/Frightening

97. Comforting/Upsetting

98. Warm/Cold

99. Understanding/Intolerant

100. Affirming/Threatening

After you have completed marking all 100 questions, draw a line after numbers 35 (self), 55 (other people), 75 (life), 90 (world), 100 (God). Then connect all the Xs or dots with straight lines. Your answer sheet should look something like this:

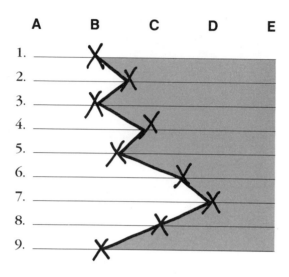

The part on the right side of the line which connects the Xs or dots may be filled in for graphic purposes (as in the illustration). Remember that the primary purpose of this test is not diagnosis but rather an awareness of the dimensions and aspects of a person's total vision. However, it is probably true that the larger the shaded area, the healthier and more human the vision of that person.

Please note well that this last statement is valid only up to a point. First of all, we are never so accurately in touch with our thoughts and perceptions that our answers can be regarded as totally dependable. Second, if we were to put all our marks at the left end of each line, we would certainly be suspected of wearing rose-colored glasses. The fact is that we ourselves, other people, life, and the world are simply not perfect. This is not the best of all possible worlds. Furthermore, our ideas of God are usually distorted by our tendency to humanize God. We make God to our human image and likeness. We tend to project our human limitations upon him. On the other hand, a very small shaded area would probably indicate a very small and painful vision which would result in a small and painful life.

Perhaps it would be interesting and profitable to ask some friend-confidant whose balance, outlook, and judgment seem very sound and reliable to join you in taking this test. If this other person whom you regard as very human and very much alive were to score a profile quite different from your own, it might be helpful to discuss the contrasts, comparing his or her vision with your own. Lastly, if one of the five suggested categories is noticeably different from the others on your test, you might open yourself to be questioned by life in this area. There could well be a cluster of distortions in this area which is limiting your happiness and participation in the fullness of life.

Now let us turn to a review of what some very knowledgeable people regard as the most common and prevalent distortions in the visions of human beings.

Sigmund Freud, as everyone knows, believed that the deepest and most damaging distortions were to be found in the areas of sexual perceptions and aggression (destructive, even violent, behavior directed at others, things, or even self). Freud's onetime disciple, Alfred Adler, proposed that human neurosis is caused by the mistaken belief (misconception) that one must prove his or her personal superiority without regard for the common good.

However, the cognitive approach to human growth and the fullness of life, the development of the misconception hypothesis, and the system of Rational Emotive Therapy is today associated mostly with Albert Ellis (*Reason and Emo-*

tion in Psychotherapy, 1962; and with R. Harper, *A Guide to Rational Living,* 1968). Ellis theorizes that a human being is uniquely rational and irrational. All emotional and psychological problems are traceable to irrational or illogical thinking and ideas. This irrational thinking and the consequent distortion of ideas come mostly from learning experiences in early life, though such experiences are not limited exclusively to childhood. Echoing the ancient Roman philosopher Epictetus (A.D. 50), Ellis maintains that people are not emotionally and psychologically disturbed by events or things but by the views they take of those events or things. For example, being small or sick or bald are not problems in themselves which necessarily result in emotional or psychological disturbance. However, if I distort the significance of these conditions or exaggerate their importance, then I will have painful problems. Consequently, Ellis sees all hope for happiness and a full life in the reorganization of one's thinking.

Though it has not been his main interest to evolve a theory of personality development, Ellis does say that the learning experiences of early childhood have the most profound effect on a person's rational/irrational thinking and behavior. The perpetuation of distorted ideas acquired in childhood is the main source of unhappiness in later life. Since our thoughts or ideas cause our emotions, emotional balance is possible only through the adjustment of one's thinking. It is the faulty interpretation of a situation that leads to emotional and psychological disturbance. Only by disputing the irrational, unrealistic thinking can one be brought to emotional harmony and adjusted behavior.

Ellis rather decisively lists eleven irrational ideas that are most commonly found in emotionally and psychologically disturbed people. The first seven are said to figure most prominently in the development of anxiety. The final four tend rather to produce hostility. I have taken some liberty with the exact choice and order of words used by Ellis. However, the words are almost verbatim, and each idea is substantially that of Ellis. After each of these most common misconceptions I have given a short indication of the distortion found in the idea and a similar indication of a more rational view of the same matter.

1. *I must be loved and approved by everyone in my community, especially by those who are most important to me.*   Any unattainable goal, which leaves one with only the possibility of failure, is an irrational goal. No one will ever be loved and approved universally. The more effort one makes to attain such a goal, the more anxious, frustrated, and self-destructive one will become. A rational orientation in this matter would certainly include the very human desire to be approved and loved. However, I can't get and don't need to have the love and approval of everyone to have a happy and full life. When I am disapproved of, I will examine the validity of the criticism implied in the disapproval to see if the problem is mine or my critic's. If it is mine, I will try to change. If it is my critic's, it is up to him or her to change.

2. *I must be perfectly competent, adequate, and successful in achieving before I can think of myself as worthwhile.*   Another impossible goal is contained in this distortion. It can lead only to constant overexertion in feverish activity, a constant fear of failure, and an inferiority complex. Such compulsive need and striving usually result in psychosomatic sickness and a feeling that I have lost rational control of my life. I have a ring in my nose.

More rationally oriented people want to do well for their own sakes and satisfaction, not in order to be better than others. Rational people also want to enjoy what they undertake, to be led by interest rather than driven by an obsession for success.

3. *I have no control over my own happiness. My happiness is completely in the control of external circumstances.* This distortion is, of course, a lie which I am tempted to tell myself in order to avoid challenge and responsibility. It is sometimes easier to be a martyr—to roll over and play dead—than to reexamine my situation and do whatever I can. The rational person knows that happiness is not determined by outside forces and events. It is rather a matter of attitudes, and these cannot be coerced by outside forces, which at most can be physically afflicting. Happiness or unhappiness is ultimately derived from the way events are perceived, evaluated, and internally verbalized. Happiness does, in fact, come from within, as the sages have been saying for centuries.

4. *My past experiences and the events of my life have determined my present life and behavior. The influence of the past cannot be eradicated.* It is true that we are creatures of habit and that relearning is difficult. The distortion is to believe that it is impossible. This kind of passive acceptance or determinism is often used to avoid the challenge of change. Rational people know the importance of the past and its influences, but they know that they can change by reevaluating those influences, reinterpreting events, and reassessing the perceptions of their original vision. Rational people always remain bigger than their problems.

5. *There is one right and perfect solution to each of my problems. If this is not found, it will be devastating for me.* It is obviously not true that there is one perfect solution for each problem in life. Furthermore, failure to solve a problem with a perfect solution is not catastrophic. We can learn from and grow because of failure. The anxious attitude implied in this misconception will probably produce such anxiety that problem-solving efficiency will be considerably reduced. A rational person knows that there are options and alternatives in the solution to all problems. It is also true that some problems are insoluble. We must live with them and learn the art of acceptance. When a problem-solving decision is upon them, rational people will consider all the options of the moment and choose the solution that seems most feasible.

6. *Dangerous or fearsome things are causes for great concern. I must be prepared for the worst by constantly dwelling on and agonizing over these possible calamities.* The deception involved in this irrational thinking is that worry and anxious anticipation somehow help. In fact, they tend to prevent objective evaluation of the possible danger and will diminish the possibility of effective reaction should the calamity occur. Such anxiety and anticipation may even induce the feared situation. Fear tends to make that which we fear come true. Such worry also tends to exaggerate unpleasant events out of all proportion. Every day becomes doomsday. Rational people know that worry does not help, so they invest their energies in an evaluation of the situation and a decision about what can be done to prevent possible tragedy. Rational people do not presume that tragedy will occur. In the case of crippling fears, they will prudently and gradually dispel them by acting against them.

7. *I should be dependent on others and must have someone stronger than myself on whom I can rely.* This distortion is a gross exaggeration of dependency. It leads a life of "being cared for" in place of independence, self-determination, and self-expression. This kind of dependency has a tendency to escalate; I become more and more dependent. And the more dependent I become, the more I am at the mercy of the person on whom I am leaning. Rational individuals want to be their own persons, to make their own decisions, to take their own responsibility. Of course, rational people are willing to ask for and accept help when they need it, but they will turn over their lives to no one. They are willing to take risks. If they are wrong or fail, it is not the end of the world.

8. *If my life does not work out the way I had planned, it will be really terrible. When things go badly for me, it is a catastrophe.* This is a clearly irrational attitude because things very rarely go exactly as planned. This attitude invites frustration as a normal state. Getting upset does not help, but will make the situation worse. Furthermore, this attitude makes the perfect achievement of one's plans a condition for satisfaction and happiness. This is a good formula for frustration and ulcers. Rational people will try to work at the successful implementation of their plans, but will improvise when things do not turn out. They will develop a tolerance for frustration and learn to enjoy the possibilities for growing, learning, and adjusting in situations of reversal. They stay on top of the situation instead of letting the situation bury them.

9. *It is easier to avoid certain difficulties and responsibilities than to face them.* The irrationality of this idea is that it neglects the fact that avoiding a task or responsibility is often more painful and fatiguing than doing what is required without procrastination. Avoidance always leads to further problems and eventually to loss of self-confidence and self-respect. Rational people spend their energy doing what they can rather than devising escapes. If they fail, they study the causes of the failure and try not to fall into the same traps. Such people know that there is much more pleasure and satisfaction in taking on difficulties and responsibilities than in avoiding them.

10. *Some people are bad, wicked, villainous. They should be blamed and punished.* This distorted idea presumes that we have the ability to judge the responsibility, the conscience, and the knowledge of another. What may appear as evil can be the result of insanity or ignorance. Rational people know they cannot judge persons but only issues. They have no X-ray eyes to see the intention, conscience, or knowledge of another. They confine themselves to an assessment of what is done rather than attempt a judgment of the doer of the deed.

11. *One should be very upset over the problems and disturbances of other people.* The irrationality of this attitude resides in its self-destructiveness and over-eagerness to make the problems of others one's own. This is not to deny a healthy empathy for those who are suffering. However, the only way I am going to be of any help to others is by retaining my own balance and peace of mind. Rational people make a judgment of the situation of their neighbors and try to do whatever they can to help those in need. If nothing can be done, they do not surrender their personal peace to an impossible situation.

Ellis catalogs these eleven major misconceptions into three categories. They are a rough equivalent of the five categories described previously in this book: self, others, life, world, God. Ellis calls these three categories of distortion the "three whines," in each of which something is "awfulized." They are the irrational attitudes that give people trouble.

1. Poor Me! (Awfulizes one's own self.) "Because it would be highly preferable if I were outstandingly competent, I absolutely should and must be; it is awful when I am not, and I am therefore a worthless individual."

2. Poor Stupid Other People! (Awfulizes what others are doing to me.) "Because it is highly desirable that others treat me considerately and fairly, they absolutely should and must, and they are rotten people who deserve to be utterly damned when they do not."

3. Poor Stupid Life and Universe! (Awfulizes what the world is doing to me and my life situation.) "Because it is preferable that I experience pleasure rather than pain, the world absolutely should arrange this, and life is horrible and I can't bear it when the world doesn't."

Albert Ellis,
"The No Cop-out Therapy,"
Psychology Today, 1973

I have combed through the writings of many authors on this subject of distortions in human thinking. The misconceptions they list are almost always contained in one of the eleven listed by Ellis. Anthropologist Margaret Mead, for example, believes that it is a uniquely American distortion to set impossibly high moral standards that can result only in failure and guilt feelings. Psychiatrist Karen Horney thinks that the "idealized self-image" (the illusory self) as opposed to and in conflict with a realistic self-evaluation is at the bottom of much human misery. Psychologist Victor Raimy adds "the special persons complex," usually found in the favorite child of a coddling mother or someone who has received much public attention and praise, and "phrenophobia," the misconception that one is on the verge of insanity. However, I feel that these and other more specific distortions can be found in the general categories of Ellis.

I would like to conclude this chapter with a list of specific distortions or misconceptions that I have found to be at the root of most neurotic suffering in myself and in others. The list is by no means exhaustive. We are all, as Ellis says, uniquely rational and irrational. My distortions are as uniquely mine as my fingerprints. Still, we are all somewhat alike. There is a human unity in our diversity. Consequently, some of these listed misconceptions may look or sound a bit familiar. A study and discussion of these misconceptions might prove personally profitable. It will be a time to practice flexibility and the openness of being questioned by life. I trust that the meaning of and distortion in each of the following will be reasonably clear.

1. I have received so much that I have no right to have any faults.

2. I have only myself to blame.

3. I cannot be angry at anyone but myself.

4. My physical dimensions are the measure of my virility or femininity.

5. Nobody could really love me.

6. I don't deserve to be happy.

7. Loving yourself or admitting your talents is egotistical and conceited.

8. What really matters is *ME!* I am a special person.

9. Self-forgiveness is self-indulgence.

10. I am a born loser.

11. Laughing at yourself is stupid and self-demeaning.

12. I have to bury forever many of my memories; they would make me too angry or sad.

13. If I begin reflecting on my past, it will be like opening a Pandora's box; it is better to leave well enough alone.

14. If I ever begin to release my emotions, I know I will lose control.

15. Keep your mouth shut, and you won't get into trouble.

16. People make me mad or afraid.

17. Stupidity makes me angry.

18. Hurting the feelings of others should always be avoided.

19. My thoughts and feelings would really shock you.

20. Keeping the peace is the most important thing in a relationship.

21. You can't say what you really think and feel.

22. You can't really trust anyone.

23. My parents were ideal in every way.

24. I know that if people get to know the real me, they will not like me.

25. I must play a role in order to be accepted by others.

26. I have to be the center of attention or I don't enjoy myself.

27. Because I play roles in front of people to impress them, I am phoney and therefore no good at all.

28. My parents are to blame for me.

29. Marriage is only a piece of paper.

30. Love does not last.

31. Do your thing, Baby! You're the only one that counts.

32. You can always tell a hypocrite.

33. You have to give in—to compromise yourself—in order to get along with people.

34. If someone comes to me with a problem, I must do more than just listen and discuss the problem.

35. Love is all sweetness and light; when a person has found love, it is the end of all struggle and suffering.

36. What will the neighbors say? We have to look good.

37. Perfect love is the only kind of real love.

38. I do not need others.

39. I know what is best for you.

40. Love is doing whatever the beloved wants.

41. If you want something done, you have to do it yourself.

42. I know your whole trouble.

43. I'll get even if it's the last thing I do.

44. You can't praise others too much; it will go to their heads.

45. Love is blind.

46. I have to please others in order to satisfy their expectations of me.

47. No commitment can be for life.

48. This is the way I am and always will be.

49. I just can't decide.

50. It's no use trying.

51. I just don't have the will power; I can't.

52. It's easier just to give in.

53. Where there's a will there's a way. You can do anything you really want to do.

54. I have to prove myself.

55. Life is one "damn thing" after another.

56. I must win them all. I must be Hertz, not Avis.

57. A true ideal should always be just out of reach.

58. Life is easier if you don't stop to think about it.

59. Good people do not suffer. Virtue always triumphs in the end.

60. Those were the good old days.

61. You only go around once. Grab all you can for yourself.

62. We are for time, not time for us. We must keep moving and producing to justify our existence.

63. You cannot set your sights too high.

64. Whatever you do, you should do it perfectly.

65. Never give up.

66. A thing is either black or white. To make distinctions is always confusing.

67. Beauty is in the eye of the beholder.

68. The world owes me a living.

69. I can't waste time taking a walk, reading a book, or puttering in a garden.

70. Every problem is solvable.

71. The world belongs to the young. Ah, to be young again!

72. Failure is failure and all failure is final.

73. I'm too old to start now.

74. Who needs God?

75. Prayer is for the weak.

A new life through a new vision

Man alone,
of all the creatures of the earth,
can change his own pattern.
Man alone is the architect
of his destiny.
The greatest discovery in our generation
is that human beings,
by changing the inner attitudes
of their minds,
can change the outer aspects
of their lives.

William James,
The Principles of Psychology

Of all the aspects of the misconception hypothesis and the system of Rational Emotive Therapy, certainly the most appealing is its fundamental assumption that *we can change.* Our lives are, to a very great extent, in our own hands. My personal instincts and intuition rebel against the deterministic, fatalistic psychologies which make us passive puppets and make our lives phonograph records playing out a preestablished program. In accepting the misconception hypothesis we accept, to a great extent, personal responsibility for our destiny. We are not prisoners of the past. We are pioneers of an exciting future.

Let us now very briefly review the main principles of the misconception hypothesis and vision therapy.

1. Misconceptions (also called "distortions" or "delusions") are mistaken beliefs, faulty ideas, unrealistic and unhealthy attitudes. They usually come in clusters since one misconception frequently leads to other related misconceptions in the same area. There are five general categories to be considered: self, other people, life, the world, and God.

2. Some misconceptions are relatively harmless, or benign, because they do not noticeably affect emotional or behavior patterns. Other distortions are crippling, or malignant, because they produce painful and negative emotional patterns which are disruptive of the whole personality and of social adjustment.

3. Misconceptions must be identified before one can work at their elimination. When identified properly and adequately, misconceptions are always specific and concrete. For example: "I have to be

approved by everybody or I question my own worth." Vague and unspecified delusions are usually worthless abstractions designed to obscure the real problem. For example: "I think I have a tendency to think too much."

4. A person can find a happy and fully human life only to the extent that these crippling misconceptions are recognized and then modified or eliminated.

5. When a person recognizes one of his or her delusions or misconceptions, it is a moment of insight. What actually happens in such insights is that we see, sometimes very suddenly, the distortion in the way we were interpreting the evidence of personal experience. We see that we were incorrectly putting together the pieces of the reality picture.

6. The more flexible and open people are, the more insights they will acquire. Their emotional patterns and ability to participate in a fully human life will improve and grow with each new insight.

7. Insights can come at any time and under any circumstances. There is no one sure way to acquire new insights, although there are recommended procedures that facilitate insight for most people.

8. The system for eliminating misconceptions through insight which we have devised and are proposing is called "vision therapy." It is a self-help method of growth. It will be described in complete detail in this chapter.

9. The misconception hypothesis and the system of vision therapy do not regard emotions as the

ultimate area of consideration or concentration. Emotions are only indicators. Habitual patterns of negative emotions are always a signal of some underlying misconception. The target of achievement is the elimination of such misconceptions through insight and the acquisition of healthy, realistic attitudes in the place of these misconceptions. It may be that some discharge of pent-up emotions will be necessary before some people are able to come to needed insights.

10. Success at vision therapy is measured by satisfaction and by growth into a fully human and joyful life. Such progress in turn can be more specifically measured by growth in positive, life-giving attitudes toward self, others, life, the world, and God. The composite of all these attitudes is a person's vision, the way he or she sees reality. It is this vision that determines the emotional patterns of one's life. Only if this vision is sound and healthy can a person enjoy a truly happy and fully human life.

Having summarized the main principles of the misconception hypothesis and vision therapy, we return now to the particular system of Albert Ellis, which is based on the misconception hypothesis. When Ellis summarizes his own system of Rational Emotive Therapy, he calls it the ABC system. In every human reaction there is an Activating event, a Belief system through which the event is interpreted and evaluated, and a Consequent set of emotional reactions. Ellis is critical of many other systems of psychotherapy because they seem to concentrate on the A and C, while neglecting the B, which is the central concern of Rational Emotive Therapy. Very simply, the same thing presumably happens to many persons but the results or emotional reactions are often very different. Some people have enormous coping ability and powers of resilience. Others go into a tailspin over trifles. Obviously, something comes into play after the activating event which accounts for the great differences of reaction. This is what Ellis calls a "belief system" and which we have been calling a "vision." Let us look at a diagram:

A: Activating event
   Someone unfairly and harshly criticizes me and professes dislike for me.

B: Belief system
   I must be loved and approved by everybody or I lose all sense of my own worth.

C: Consequent emotions
   Poor me! Depression, sadness.

Ellis has recently filled out his schematic with two more letters, adding that if we are to restore rationality to our belief system and emotional peace to our souls, we must:

D: Dispute the distorted, irrational misconception in the belief system.
   I don't have to please everyone, to be loved and approved, in order to retain a sense of personal worth. My critic has the problem, not I.

E: Event or experience is transformed by reinterpretation and reevaluation, which makes possible the elimination of the misconception.
   Different emotional reaction: continued self-confidence, personal peace, and compassion for the critic.

I would strongly agree with Ellis that not only many systems of psychotherapy but also most people in their daily lives are concerned only with the A (Activated event) and C (Consequent emotions). In the wake of strong and negative emotions most of us do not attempt any kind of a vision-therapy investigation of our belief systems. We make little or no effort to find out what is in us that has caused such emotions to arise. We know that there are probably many other people who would not react as we do to a given stimulus, but we still do not accept the challenge to check our vision. We are tempted to pass it off with a bromide such as: "This is the way I am." Or, "Sorry, but this is me!" Some of us even try to recreate others in our own image and likeness by thinking that everyone really reacts as we do, but some just don't show it.

Remember that every activating event has to flow through the filter system of your own uniquely rational/irrational belief system. The consequent emotions are not determined by the activating event but by the belief system. However, there is always hope, even if the emotional patterns are habitually and painfully negative. It is within our power to dispute our belief systems, locating and eliminating specific misconceptions and consequently transforming the events and experiences of our lives.

Let us look at another diagram:

A: Activating event of failure (at school, in work, in carrying out plans, etc.).

B: Belief that failure indicates something is missing in me. My personal value is undermined and permanently damaged by failure.

C: Consequent sadness, depression, discouragement.

D. Dispute of misconception: I reevaluate and emphatically deny that failure is an exposé of personal worthlessness. Failure does not diminish my person. The only real mistake is the one from which we learn nothing. It is true that my efforts resulted in failure, but I myself am not a failure. Everyone fails. The successful person is one who profits from failure.

E. Event of failure has been reevaluated and transformed into a profitable experience and time of growth. Because of the changed interpretation of the event, the emotional reaction is likewise changed from a "this is the end" depression to a "wait till next time" eagerness and enthusiasm.

Unfortunately, diagraming is easier than doing. Since the main problem in any "doing" is a positive intention and determination, we must now take up the question of motivation. We have already described the counterproductive reluctance that almost everybody feels to challenge his or her own presuppositions. The old vision, for better or for worse, has served long and well. It has given life predictability and given us consistency instead of chaos. The old is always safe even if sad. The new is untested. How are people led to a desire for change and growth? How can they be convinced that the benefits of a new and fuller life through a new and fuller vision are really worth the price demanded?

People who go to professionals for help usually go because their negative emotional patterns have become too painful or because their world seems to be falling apart. The first problem encountered in helping such people is the period of disintegration or disorientation experienced in the stepping from the old into the new. It is a limbo of uncertainty and chaos. Still, pain is very persuasive. Individuals who have had enough struggling, depression, constant anxiety, or smoldering hostility may have hit bottom and be ready to rebound. They may be ready to make the effort, to take the risks of thinking and acting in new ways. However, some people have "low bottoms" and have to fall apart pretty badly before they are willing to put the pieces together in a new and different pattern. Other people have "high bottoms" and are ready for change. They sense that the course they are on will lead only to a sad nowhere. They are ready for reevaluation, for a new vision.

Then there are the children of the new beatitude: Blessed are those who hunger after life in all its fullness! They have no appetite or willingness to settle for mediocrity in any form. These are the pioneer people who write new songs, study new theories, and build better mousetraps. They can be found in offices, schools, factories, or supermarkets, but there is always something of a mountain climber in their blood. They say an expansive "Yes!" to life and "Amen!" to love. They are ready to reexamine their belief systems. They are ready for vision therapy and anything else that promises growth. For them, to stop growing is to stop living. When you're through growing, you're through!

So I suppose that the sales pitch for vision therapy would go something like this: Have you had it with depression, anxiety, loneliness, and hostility? Are you tired of lifelong difficulties and endless struggle? Wouldn't you really rather uncover the roots of your painful emotions than live with them in an endurance contest? If you are the enthusiastic type, do you want to make your life an exciting adventure, to walk into a world of wider dimensions and brighter colors? Are you ready to join the dance and sing the songs of a more human and fuller life? Are you open to the idea that the difference between what you are and what you can be is a matter of ideas, insights, a belief system, a vision? If you are either of these two people, please keep reading.

The journey into a fully human, fully alive existence requires certain supplies and equipment. They are all, in varying degrees, necessary. Please read the list carefully and set yourself to acquire whatever you do not have.

1. *Openness and Flexibility.* You must believe with all your heart that you do not possess all truth in proper perspective. You must be ready to be questioned by life. Of course, every day, every event, and every person that touches your consciousness is questioning you. Do you love yourself? Can you enjoy yourself? What do you think of failure? Have you really recognized humanity and individuality in other people? Have you made the discovery of otherness? Do you like most people, or are they a bother? The first requirement to achieve a new life through a new vision is a readiness to hear and to attempt to answer the questions that life will ask you.

2. *Sensory and Emotional Awareness.* It is necessary that you learn how to listen to your senses, and to register consciously the sights, sounds, smells, tastes, and touches of daily life. You will have to hear what your body is saying: when it is tired and when it is tense. This physical awareness is a prerequisite for emotional awareness because every emotion is a perceptual-physiological reality. In other words, an emotion exists partly in the mind and partly in the body. Fritz Perls, the late and great Gestalt therapist, insisted that "awareness of the new," of sensory input, is "sufficient to solve all neurotic difficulties" (*Gestalt Therapy Now: Theory, Techniques, Application,* edited by Fagan and Shepherd).

It is this sensory awareness that will lead us to our deepest feelings unless we employ some kind of blockage or denial. Jittery nerves, fatigue, and other bodily conditions can become for us direct avenues to emotional awareness. As was said, every emotion by its very nature is partly physiological. The physical reactions are usually like the top of the iceberg, the part that shows.

In whatever way we can, with whatever techniques prove helpful, we must learn to be in touch with our feelings or emotions. This is a complicated achievement, which I have treated at length in two other books and can only touch upon here. (Please see *Why Am I Afraid to Tell You Who I Am?* and *The Secret of Staying in Love,* both published by Tabor Publishing.)

All recent psychological theories of emotion assume that our emotional reactions depend on our interpretation and appraisal of the situation in which the emotions arise. The way we perceive the situation is in fact an intrinsic part of the emotion itself because emotions are mental-physical realities. Consequently, when people explore their deepest feelings, they are simultaneously exploring their deepest thoughts and convictions because emotions are partly perceptual. Even though it may seem difficult to believe, there is no time in a conscious state when we are without any emotions because there is no time when we are not thinking. Much of the time our emotional reactions are so slight that we are not even aware of them. However, a sensitive polygraph (lie-detector) machine would register these constant emotional reactions. Such a machine even picks up physiological reactions to recited words like "mother . . . father . . . love . . . war . . . sex." The point is that if we are to become aware of our belief systems or visions, it is essential that we be attuned to our emotional reactions.

As we have said previously, all negative emotions, but especially anxiety and hostility, are signals of a malignant misconception somewhere in our total vision. We cannot afford to pass over such reactions with a comment that we will probably feel better tomorrow or with a belief that we would be all right if only we could get a good night's sleep. All negative feelings, from the mildest discomfort to the deepest depression, will lead us to a moment of insight if only we will follow.

This is even true in what is called "free-floating anxiety," which is supposedly a state of fearful apprehension without attachment to a definite object of fear. Many psychologists, however, maintain that when a person begins to describe his or her individual experience of this anxiety, a very definite fear and misconception will emerge.

3. *A Friend-Confidant.* A person with whom we can be totally open is for many reasons an absolute requirement for growth into the fullness of life. However, there are special reasons why such a friend-confidant is essential for the successful practice of vision therapy. First of all, you will remember the statement that for many of us some release of pent-up emotional turbulence is necessary before we can quietly review our belief systems and find the troublesome misconception. Only the kind of friend-confidant suggested here will be willing and able to handle the communication of these emotions. A person less close will probably tell us not to cry or become excited. That person would not know us well enough to know what to anticipate. Such a person would be afraid to give us full freedom to have and express our feelings. Only a true friend-confidant will know and love us enough to provide this liberty of experience and expression.

Alfred Adler says that a warm human relationship is necessary to give people the courage needed to face and understand their mistakes. Knowing that someone loves us unconditionally enables us to face and admit our delusions. This is also one of the main principles of Carl Rogers in his theory of counseling. We can understand and accept ourselves realistically only when someone outside ourselves first understands and accepts us. Consequently, Adler and others recommend that if a person does not have and cannot make such a friend, he or she might have to join some kind of a warm and receptive group.

Dialogue and discussion with such a friend-confidant make still another very definite contribution in helping us to locate our misconceptions. We have to organize a problem before we can talk it over with another. Very often, if left to ourselves, we do not go through this organization of the problem and its ramifications. Our problems remain vague and diffuse when kept inside us. With a friend-confidant we must not only organize but also verbalize the problem. This reality of verbalization is extremely important. The way we verbalize a situation often determines how we will evaluate it. Very often our reactions are determined by the words we choose to describe the situation. We think in words, plan our lives with words, and tend to be very much defined by our own verbalizations. This is why some have recommended repeating at regular daily intervals positive words or mottoes such as "I am! I can! I will!" If we are interpreting and verbalizing a given situation in a lop-sided manner, dialogue with a friend will tend to help us back to balance and objectivity.

4. *A Journal.* In her book *Widow,* Lynn Caine has a chapter called "Dear Paper Psychiatrist." The reference is to a journal which she kept after the death of her husband. Recording the events of her life and emotional reactions seems to have helped her in the several ways that it can help all of us. A journal provides an outlet for emotional expression, but it also requires the kind of organization and verbalization described above. For most of us the appearance of a blank piece of paper is less threatening than a human face staring at us, waiting for words. We are less inhibited with a paper psychiatrist than with a real one.

Once we have put down the main activating event of a given day, together with our spontaneous emotional reactions, we can go back either at that time or at a later time of quiet and do a little vision therapy. We can check out and challenge the validity of the belief system or vision between the event and our emotional reaction to it. If people were regularly to practice this kind of gentle but persistent self-examination of their vision, I am sure they would find, as I have, many new insights and an immediate change in the emotional patterns of their lives. Obviously, the more precise and vivid the verbalization in writing of this kind, the greater the likelihood that misconceptions will surface for recognition.

The following is an excerpt from my own attempts at keeping a journal. It may have some illustrative value.

> Tonight, as I was finishing my speech, I was suddenly interrupted by a shouted question. I could hear the

edges of anger on the words of the person speaking. After asking his question the questioner started to leave angrily, but then decided to stay. It was the first time this has ever happened to me. I was flustered, angry and suddenly felt very competitive. It was no longer a sharing situation. This was win/lose. I hate to lose at anything. Adrenalin. The flushed feeling. I never did get to finish my talk. The ending was impressive, too, and might have made a difference. Who knows now? Other questions followed. Some of them were vague but unfriendly questions. I'm not used to this. I almost always get hugs and standing ovations. Failure really stops me cold. And I think that speaking is my greatest talent, too. Afterward, when the adrenalin stopped, I felt like the little boy who stubbed his toe: It hurt too much to laugh but I was too old to cry. Sad. Hurt. Mad. Questioning myself, my intelligence, confidence in my presentation. I needed to and did talk it over with a friend. I couldn't take all those heavy emotions to bed with me. Tomorrow, of course, all the pain will be drained out, though I will remember, maybe angrily. I'm really glad I've got that twenty-four hour shut-off built into my negative emotions. After twenty-four hours, nothing is worth that much anguish. But what is in me? Why do I so hate failure? Was tonight really a failure? Is it that I was speaking about a cause in which I believe with all my heart or was it my pride that I was protecting? Or both?

I think I play at being much more confident in myself than I really am. My illusory self. He's got it made. The "real me" doesn't. That guy who interrupted me was really rude. He must have problems.

Why don't I feel sorry for him instead of angry at him? Apparently, I think I've got to win them all. Success and self-esteem must be welded together in my mind. Failure really rocks my sense of worth. Tomorrow the dust will be settled, and maybe I'll be able to see more clearly. I know that there is some delusion roaming around inside me. I want to find it. Maybe I have already found it. Maybe the answer is in what I have written here. When I reread this later, perhaps I'll know for sure. If I learn something, I will probably be glad that the whole thing happened. Maybe.

Morning after reflections: My sense of self-worth is threatened by any hostile criticism. I still do not distinguish very well, in cases of criticism, whether the problem is mine or that of the other person. I hold people responsible and accountable for what they do and say. I leave small margins for ignorance and irresistible impulses. I take criticisms personally. My person, not my opinions, is attacked. There is a strange identity in my mind between my person and my opinions.

I would strongly recommend the use of such a journal every day but especially on those days when emotions have been vibrating uncomfortably. The journal should be kept strictly private if the thought of sharing it with a friend-confidant would in a way diminish openness and honesty. The much better thing, of course, would be sharing the contents of the journal with a friend. Two heads are always better than one in matters like this. Dialogue has a way of illuminating the darkened corners of consciousness and awareness.

5. *Times of Quiet Reflection.* Those who write on the subject of misconceptions are fairly unanimous in agreeing that it is the presence of "threat" in some form that tends to cause and to camouflage distortions in vision. Confrontation with threat usually constricts vision. When we are threatened, we instinctively throw up defenses, and this almost always means that we will exclude certain evidence being presented to us (selective inattention). This new evidence might force us to reevaluate our vision, and to admit delusion. It might challenge us to begin thinking and acting in a new way. We tend to become more defensive than perceptive.

It would be ideal if a person could reserve some time at the end of each day to relax, review, and reevaluate. Most of us, however, are too much in the clutches of clock and calendar. But there are times such as train rides, while waiting for sleep, walking to and from stores, when we are waiting for someone who has been delayed, and so forth. At these times threat is usually minimal and vision can be expanded to receive new insights. Such times are invaluable for growth into a fuller and more peaceful life.

6. *The Stretch Marks of Risk and Revision.* There is no question that we must act on insights if they are to become the new habits of thinking that will replace our old delusions. Insights demand more than lip service. They demand allegiance. Insights need the support of emotional strength. They must be incorporated into one's life-style. No new truth is ever really learned until it is acted upon. This means some inner crinkling and crunch: stretch marks.

For example, let us suppose that I think of myself as "a problem-solver to the world." It is my vocation. Then I come to the insight that being a problem-solver is irrational. First, it presumes that other people are not big enough, old enough, or smart enough to solve their own problems. Second, to solve another's problem only aids and abets his or her indecisiveness and immaturity. It cultivates in that person an exaggerated sense of dependency on the advice-giver. Lastly, being a problem-solver is an unrealistic and exhausting burden for anyone to carry. It is foolish to play Atlas holding up the whole world.

The true test of change and growth will come the next time some dependent and indecisive person pathetically whimpers: "What should I do? Please tell me." It will take real determination to act on my insight, to step out of the old rut and say: "I don't know what you should do. What do you think you should do?"

There is another aspect of learning and doing. Actual doing obviously completes the learning process. However, it also works in reverse. Doing very often initiates a learning process. Suppose, for example, I am firmly convinced that I cannot give a speech in public or take unsatisfactory goods back to the salesperson. So what should I do? So I should swallow hard and do it! Yes, just do it. I must act against my phobias. Only in doing it will I learn that I *can* do it and thereby dispatch another delusion. Every day we should all do something that will extend us; we should win little victories over our fears that will widen the world and our lives. We will gradually learn in this way about the undreamed-of potentialities which we had all the time but never used.

Is there a person you cannot bring yourself to contradict? Have you really never cried in front of other people? Can you complain (politely, of course) to the landlord? Are there certain decisions you can never make without getting confirmation from another? Is there really some secret and haunting fear which you have never confided to anyone? When the opportune moment occurs, just do it. Win a victory over yourself, widen your vision and your world, walk into a new and fuller life.

I'm sure you know that all the principles and calculations of aerodynamics, as my friend Mark Link has pointed out, deny the bumblebee any right to fly. With his flimsy wings and short wingspread, the experts say, he just shouldn't get his husky body off the ground. It is certainly a good thing that bumblebees don't know this. Believing in limitations without testing them can become a self-fulfilling prophecy. As long as you think you can't, you can't. So don't let anyone else tell you, and above all don't tell yourself, that you can't. Learn that you can by doing it. (Note: I do not mean *flying*.) Practice disbelieving all the old lies and distortions that you have been telling yourself and leaving unchallenged.

7. *Daily Exercise.*   Emotions are most easily recognized and explored while we are experiencing them. Memory is selective. It almost always dulls and distorts. Because emotions are a perceptual-physical reality, our perceptions and our vision are built right into our emotions. Consequently, one's belief system is uniquely available for inspection at the very moment of emotional turbulence. Insights are perhaps more available to us after some emotional clearance and in a setting that is threat-free and conducive to reflection. However, there is a distinct opportunity for insight during the emotional vibration precisely because our emotions are most real and undistorted for us at that moment. It is a valuable time for on-the-spot vision therapy.

I know from personal experience that when practiced with a friend-confidant and in a journal, one can develop considerable facility for this on-the-spot vision therapy. It soon becomes a way of life and its benefits are soon evident. Sensory and emotional awareness, as described, come first. There must be a constantly renewed intention to practice and cultivate such awareness. Then we must go on to a gentle but persistent inspection of the vision or belief system. Remember that there is no time when we are not experiencing some kind of emotional reaction. Consider these reactions:

I feel shy, withdrawn.	Why?
I feel like a failure, guilty.	Why?
I feel attacked.	Why?
I feel strangely sad.	Why?
I really enjoy this attention.	Why?
That remark really hurt me.	Why?

Conclusion: For the average person to continue any practice over a long period of time, he or she must derive a satisfaction or experience a success greater than the price of effort paid. Certainly for extended use of vision therapy, if not for even the most modest beginning, there will have to be some satisfaction or success. I personally very much hunger for the full human life, and of course I want to find the wrinkles of irrationality that diminish my participation in such a life. As I continue to practice what I am here preaching, I am aware of increasing peace and joy in my life. But more immediately and practically I find daily vision therapy very interesting. I have found out that I am interesting, complicated, uniquely rational, and uniquely irrational. I have come to a much deeper understanding of my past and present. I eagerly await the future. And most of all, I have come to like myself much better by being this kind of interested, curious, and helpful friend to myself. I am sure that you will have the same experience.

*   *   *

Suggested Exercises in Vision Therapy

1. Record in writing (a journal?) the strongest negative emotion that you have experienced recently. Describe the activating event and your consequent emotions.

   a. Study your verbalization of the event. For example: Your car has broken down. You can either say: "Well, this is certainly an inconvenience, but I am sure it will all work out." Or you can say: "Oh my God! This is all I need. What a way to ruin a day." Study the relationship between the words you chose to describe the event and your emotional reactions.

   b. Ask yourself what there is in your vision of reality that resulted in your precise emotional reaction. Is there a distortion or misconception in your vision that threw the whole event out of focus?

2. Try this experiment with your friend-confidant. Both of you write what you would guess are your own five basic misconceptions. For example: "I have to be approved and loved by everyone in order to retain a sense of personal worth." Then both of you write what you would guess are the five basic misconceptions of the other person. Finally, share and discuss what has been written. Note:

Do not proceed with this experiment if there is any feeling such as: "I've been waiting a long time to lay this on you!" Review and revise the distortion under that hostility before attempting this exercise. Such guessing and sharing have to be acts of love or they will be counterproductive. Adler and others have found that this exercise of guessing opens a person to the recognition of misconceptions. This has worked very well for me.

3. Take an area of recurrent negative emotions, especially of anger and fear. For example: "I get furious while driving if someone cuts in ahead of me." Or, "When people disagree with me on an important issue, I get very upset and I stay very upset for a long time."

   Ask yourself about your inner vision. What is in you, in your belief system, that makes this situation so disturbing? For example: "I see all other drivers as my competitors. If a man cuts in ahead of me, it is one point for him and none for me." Or, "I think only of myself because I am a 'special person.' I do not consider that he may be on his way to the hospital, to a sick wife or injured child." Or, "When people disagree with me, I always suspect it is because they do not like me. If they liked me, they wouldn't disagree with me."

4. Here are ten principles of full human living. After each principle are questions. Using the techniques of vision therapy, write or describe to a friend-confidant somewhat lengthy answers to the questions. The "Why?" at the end asks you to explain your answers in terms of your basic vision or belief

system. Your answers should come from an examination of that vision.

Principle One: Be yourself. Don't wear a mask
or play a role.

> ***Question:*** In what circumstances do you find
> it most difficult to be honest and open about
> what you think and feel? Why?

Principle Two: Experience fully and express
freely your true emotions.

> ***Question:*** With which emotions are you most
> uncomfortable? Which emotions do you feel
> least free to express? Why?

Principle Three: Do not let fear of hurting another's feelings make your decisions or prevent
you from doing or saying what you think you
should.

> ***Question:*** Are there special persons or types
> of persons or special situations in which this
> fear of hurting another's feelings is crippling and
> painful to you? Why?

Principle Four: Assert yourself. You have a right
to be respected, to think your own thoughts and
make your own choices. You should be listened
to and taken seriously. Insist on this right.

> ***Question:*** When and with whom do you find it
> hardest to be assertive? To demand respect for
> your person and rights? Why?

Principle Five: Do not bend yourself out of shape
trying to please everyone all the time.

Question: Do you feel compelled to please all people or at least certain special people all the time? In certain circumstances? Why?

Principle Six: Do not attempt to make yourself look better by attacking, cutting down, or gossiping about others.

Question: Do you feel threatened by the success of others? Of those with whom you work? Of the same or opposite sex? Do you feel compelled to point out their limitations? Why?

Principle Seven: Look for what is good in others; enjoy and praise others for their good qualities and deeds.

Question: Do you tend to be more aware of others' irritating and obnoxious qualities or their good and pleasing qualities? Do you tend to fix upon the limitations and failures of any particular individual or group? Why?

Principle Eight: Think of yourself in positive terms. Become aware of everything that is good in you.

Question: Are you uncomfortable in describing your achievements or admitting the things you really like about yourself? Within yourself? When talking to others? Why?

Principle Nine: Be gentle and understanding with yourself, as you would like to be with others.

Question: What weakness in yourself most exasperates you? Why?

Principle Ten: Do not judge another's account-ability and subjective guilt. Forgive wherever necessary. Bearing a grudge is self-destructive.

Question: Is there someone you cannot forgive? Why? Is there something that people do which you cannot forgive? Why?

5. Write a verbal portrait of your illusory self, the public image or person you would like others to see, believe in, and be impressed by, but which is not the real you.

Why does this person appeal to you?

6. Evaluate yourself on these five common personality problems by listing them in the order in which you most painfully experience them.

Oversensitivity	Suspiciousness
Resentfulness	Being overly critical
Irritability	

Then take the first two and try to describe, in terms of your basic vision, why you are more troubled by these two problems.

7. What is your basic question or mind-set in approaching life, the persons and events of life? Describe it precisely. For example: "What do I have to fear?" Explain it in terms of your basic vision. *Note:* Do this either in your journal or with a friend-confidant.

8. Do you tend to live (think, daydream) more in the past, present, or future? Why? (See *Note* of number 7.)

9. Describe the person you would like to be. If you were asked why you haven't become this person, how would you answer? What is in your vision or belief system that keeps you from realizing this ideal? (See *Note* of number 7.)

10. Successful vision therapy is based on repetition. Just as we have repeatedly thought the distorted thoughts until they became habitual distortions in our vision, so we must now think the right thoughts, the rational and realistic thoughts, until they become new attitudes replacing the old distortions.

   Go back to your five basic misconceptions (number 2, above) and write out the positive, rational thought that would be an appropriate corrective for each misconception. Try to verbalize these corrective thoughts into a motto or resolution which you can repeat internally on those occasions when the old delusion would have crippled you and destroyed your peace. For example: "I am a good person whether everyone approves of me or not."

CHAPTER EIGHT

Vision therapy and religious faith
An appendix for believers

If you were to take the sum total
of all the authoritative articles
ever written by the most qualified
of psychologists and psychiatrists
on the subject of mental hygiene—
if you were to combine them
and refine them
and cleave out the excess verbiage—
if you were to . . .
have these unadulterated bits
of pure scientific knowledge
concisely expressed
by the most capable of living poets,
you would have an awkward
and incomplete summation
of the Sermon on the Mount.

Psychiatrist James T. Fisher,
A Few Buttons Missing:
The Case Book of a Psychiatrist

One of the main assumptions of the misconception hypothesis and vision therapy is that there is a knowable "reality." We need some version of reality by which we can judge the rationality of our thoughts and to which we can conform our vision or belief system. But who is to say what reality is? Cynics are sure that they are in touch with reality in suspecting everything, trusting no one. Naive persons are convinced that everybody is really a true-blue Boy or Girl Scout at heart. Poets swoon at the beauty of a lake or forest. Others see only a lot of water or lumber. What is reality? Who has conceived it correctly? Who has misconceived it?

Psychologists are reasonable and honest in facing this problem. There are many slightly different solutions. Some suggest that we use a "universal consensus": Reality is that which most people think it is. There are others who offer the pragmatic solution of "what works" as a criterion of reality. There are still others who speak only of an "individual and personal" reality, suggesting that each person has his or her own reality. It is true, of course, that all of us perceive reality, whatever it is, in our own uniquely rational and uniquely irrational ways.

But the practical question persists. How am I to see other human beings? Are we really brothers and sisters in a human family, or are we enemies on a common battlefield? Is there such a thing as a free commitment of love, or are we really determined and predestined to become whatever it is that we will become? Is life governed by the pleasure principle, the power principle, or the programming principle? Is this life all that there is, or is there really a glorious hereafter? Perhaps the answers to these questions would not make a radical difference in my life-style, but they would definitely have some influence on my thoughts, choices, and perspectives. But in these matters, who is to say?

Those who believe in revealed religions have a very definite criterion of reality. They are convinced that God himself has told us in his revelation some very important things about who he is, who we are, about our relationship to one another, about the purpose of life and the significance of this world. There is no logic, of course, either to prove or disprove the authenticity of this revelation of God. Ultimately, the test of faith is always religious experience, which is highly personal and individual. Most believers have at some time felt the touch of God, a conversion-to-faith experience in which they have found a new and distinct peace, power, and presence. The intuition of faith, in this moment, surpasses the reach of all natural logic and scientific knowledge.

This has certainly been my experience, as I have related it in my book *He Touched Me.* Because of my own religious background and personal experience I have accepted the message of Jesus Christ as the master vision of reality. For me the message and person of Jesus are the source of objectification for my own vision of reality. They are the basic norm for my judgments and choices. I have chosen to live my life in the light of this revelation. I want to be God's man and to do God's work: I want to help build a world of love and a human family of mutual understanding.

An evangelist friend of mine told me that when Jesus became real to him as a teenager, he sneaked into his high-school classroom before the start of the school day and printed on the chalkboard in huge letters: JESUS CHRIST IS THE ANSWER! When he returned later with the other students for the beginning of class, he discovered that someone else had printed under his statement: YEAH, BUT WHAT IS THE QUESTION? "Yeah," he thought, "what is the question?"

As his life progressed, my friend found that there isn't only one question. As psychiatrist Viktor Frankl says it should, life asks many different questions of us. Life asks how much we can love, how much we can enjoy and endure. Life asks us if we love ourselves and if we love our fellow human beings. Daily living asks us to distinguish between what is really important and what is unimportant in life: to choose priorities. Life demands that we exercise the judgment of conscience: to choose whatever seems right and to avoid whatever seems wrong. Perhaps the most profound question asked by life is the question of significance and meaning. All of us have to find some purpose or mission in life which will confer upon us a sense of personal distinction and worth. We need to believe that our lives will make a difference for someone or for something.

Of course, there are no patented, simple answers that flow out of automated machines. The German poet Rainer Maria Rilke counsels us to be patient toward all that is unsolved in our hearts. He suggests that we must learn to love the questions themselves while waiting for and working out the answers. Growth is always a gradual process even if there are glittering moments of insight and a divine revelation.

Aleksandr Solzhenitsyn ended his Nobel lecture on literature with the Russian proverb: "One word of truth outweighs the whole world." Saint John, in the prologue of his Gospel, says that the one Word of truth has been spoken by God:

In the beginning was the Word.
The Word was with God.
The Word was God. . . .
All that came to be had life in him.
That life was the light of men,
     a light that darkness could not overpower. . . .
The Word was made flesh.
The Word lived among us.
And we saw his glory . . . full of grace and truth.

My evangelist friend, now an old man, tells me that he now knows much more about the many questions which life asks. Life has questioned him about his values and priorities, about his visions and dreams, about his courage and capacity to love. "But," he said to me, looking over his glasses, "to all the questions life asks: Jesus Christ *is* the answer!"

I am sure that he is right. Of course, this does not imply that the answers which Jesus applied to the problems of his life and times can be imported and applied without any change to the problems of our very different lives and times. Jesus asks us to be as concerned and loving to our world and times as he was to his. However, because all conduct ultimately is the result of a vision, the important thing is to grasp the basic vision of reality that Jesus had, his inner attitudes and belief system. This is the ultimate source of human health and happiness. These Jesus has communicated to us through his message and in his person:

I am the light of the world.
Anyone who follows me
will not be walking in darkness.
He will have the light of life.

                    John 8:12

There is an interesting dialogue between Jesus and his contemporaries recorded in the eighth chapter of John's Gospel. Jesus makes the point that only the truth, the full acceptance of reality, can make a person free.

> If you make my message [vision] the rule of your life, you will then know the truth and the truth will make you free!

When his hearers profess puzzlement at this idea of liberation by truth, pointing out that they have "never been the slaves of anyone," Jesus repeats that he is himself the source of true freedom:

> So if the Son makes you free
> you will really be free!

True health resides principally in one's vision, in one's deepest attitudes; it is not merely the absence of symptoms. Likewise, true freedom has its roots in one's basic vision of reality; it is not merely the absence of coercion from external forces. I see the person of Jesus liberated by a vision that results in a startling freedom: He is free enough to love and to associate with prodigals and prostitutes, and at the end to express a quaking fear and still die freely as an act of love.

> If you make my message [vision] the rule of your life, you will then know the truth and the truth will make you free!

What is the vision of Jesus which lies under his message and manner of life? Whatever else it is, it is certainly a call to the fullness of life.

> I am come that they may have life
> and have it to the full.
> **John 10:10**

At the risk of seeming presumptuous, I would like now to describe some of the central features of the vision of Jesus, as I see them. I think that the message, the life, and the person of Jesus are saying to us:

1. *God is love.*   This means that all God does is love. As the sun only shines, conferring its light and warmth on those who stand ready to receive them, so God only loves, conferring his light and warmth on those who would receive them. This means that God does not have anger in him. He does not punish. When we separate ourselves from God and his love by sin, all the change takes place in us, never in him. He is unchangeably loving. Love is sharing, the sharing of one's self and one's life. God's intention in creating us in this world was to share himself and his life with us. In fathering this life in us, God calls us to be his human family, to become a community of love, each wanting and working for the true happiness of all.

2. *You are loved by God, unconditionally and as you are.*   God has assured you through his prophets and through his Son that even if a mother were to forget the child of her womb, he would never forget you. Your name is carved in the palms of his hands, inscribed indelibly in his heart. You do not have to win or earn or be worthy of his love. It is a "given." Of course, you can refuse to accept it. You can separate yourself from God's love for a while or even for an eternity. Whatever your response, all during your life and at every moment of your life he will be there offering his love to you, even at those times when you are distracted or refusing it.

Wherever you are in your development, whatever you are doing, with a strong affirmation of all your goodness and good deeds, with a gentle understanding of your weakness, God is forever loving you. You do not have to change, grow, or be good in order to be loved. Rather, you are loved so that you can change, grow, and be good. Your realization of this unconditional love is extremely important. You must remember people like:

> **Peter the Rock,** who was often a sandpile, a loudmouth, a man who had denied even knowing the one who had loved him most.

> **Zacchaeus,** who was a runt, who offered to collect taxes for Rome from his own people for a "kickback" from the take.

> **Mary Magdalene,** who was a "hooker."

> **James and John,** who were mama's boys and pretty ridiculous at times, such as the time when they wanted to destroy a whole town which had given them a poor reception. The "Sons of Thunder," they were laughingly called.

> **Andrew,** who was pretty naive. He thought five loaves and two fish were enough for five thousand people.

> **Thomas,** who was an all-star bullhead.

> **Martha,** who was a twitch, worrier, and complainer.

> **The woman taken in adultery,** who was pretty frightened until Jesus saved her life and forgave her sin.

> **The thief on the cross,** who said what might have been his first prayer and was promised immediate paradise.

The blind man, who didn't know who Jesus was but only that he himself was blind and now he could see!

The paralyzed boy, whose body needed healing but who first needed to have his sins forgiven.

The prodigal son, who was pretty heartless but who came home when he was hungry into his father's open arms and open heart.

Saul of Tarsus, who was hellbent on destroying Christianity until he took that road to Damascus and found a loving Lord.

God was in Jesus, loving them, affirming them, forgiving them, encouraging them, challenging them all the way into greatness, peace, and the fullness of life: and millions more like them, and like us.

3. *The providence of God rules the world. Jesus is the Lord of human history.* At times you may experience the feeling that everything is falling apart. You wonder: What is the world coming to? What am I coming to? How will I make ends meet? Who is going to push my wheelchair? You do not consciously define or defend the thought, but sometimes you may be tempted to imagine God with his back to the wall, furious and frustrated at the fact that everything has gotten out of hand. "King Christ, this world is aleak; and lifepreservers there are none" (e. e. cummings). In the words of Saint Paul: "Jesus is the Lord!" You must remember that this world, the course of human history and human destiny are in his hands. He is in charge of this world. He alone has the game plan, total knowledge of the human situation and the power to turn things around completely. Do not try to make yourself the Messiah to all people or caretaker to the world. You are not equipped to cover so much territory or bear such a burden. Reflect upon these words until they have formed a new insight in you and have become deeply embedded in your vision:

> Then Jesus said to his disciples, "That is why I am telling you not to worry about your life and what you are to eat, not about your body and how you are to clothe it. For life means more than food, and the body more than clothing. Consider the birds of the air. They do not sow or reap; they have no storehouses and no barns; yet God feeds them. And how much more are you worth than the birds! Can any of you, for all his worrying, add a single cubit to his span of life? If the smallest things, therefore, are outside your control, why worry about the rest? Think of the flowers; they never have to spin or weave; yet I assure you, not even Solomon in all his regalia was robed like one of these. Now if that is how God clothes the grass in the field which is there today and thrown into the furnace tomorrow, how much more will he look after you, you of little faith! But you, you must not set your hearts on things to eat and things to drink; nor must you worry. It is the pagans of this world who set their hearts on all these things. Your father well knows you need them. No; set your hearts on his kingdom, and these other things will be given to you as well."
>
> **Luke 12:22-31**

4. *You are called to love: your God, your self, and your neighbor.*   God, who is love, has made you in his image and likeness. Love is your calling and destiny. It is

the perfection of your human nature. Love is also a gift of God, the highest gift of God's Spirit. It is necessary that you realize the importance of loving yourself. There has to be some kind of logical, if not chronological, priority to loving yourself. If you do not love yourself, you will be filled with pain, and this pain will keep all your attention riveted on yourself. Agony constricts our consciousness. If you do not love yourself, you cannot truly love either God or your neighbor. So you must learn to do the same things for yourself that you would do in loving others: You must acknowledge and affirm all that is good in you. You must gently try to understand all that is weak and limited. You must be aware of and try to fulfill your needs: physical, psychological, and spiritual. As you learn to love yourself, you must also learn to balance concern for yourself with concern for others. "Whatever you do for the least of my brothers and sisters you do for me." But remember that your success in loving will be proportionate to your openness in accepting the love and affirmation of God. It will likewise be proportionate to the love that you have for yourself. In the end, the success of your life will be judged by how sensitively and delicately you have loved.

5. *I will be with you.* God says: I am covenanted, committed forever to love you, to do whatever is best for you. I will be kind, encouraging and enabling, but I will also be challenging. At times I will come to comfort you in your affliction. At other times I will come to afflict you in your comfort. Whatever I do, it will always be an act of love and an invitation to growth. I will be with you to illuminate your darkness, to strengthen your weakness, to fill your emptiness, to heal your brokenness, to cure your sickness, to straighten what may be bent in you, and to revive whatever good things may have died in you. Remain united to me, accept my love, enjoy the warmth of my friendship, avail yourself of my power, and you will bear much fruit. You will have life in all its fullness.

6. *Your destiny is eternal life.* God says: By all means join the dance and sing the songs of a full life. At the same time, remember that you are a pilgrim. You are on your way to an eternal home which I have prepared for you. Eternal life has already begun in you but it is not perfectly completed. There are still inevitable sufferings. But remember that the sufferings of this present stage of your life are nothing compared to the glory that you will see revealed in you someday. Eye has not ever seen, nor ear ever heard, nor has the mind ever imagined the joy prepared for you because you have opened yourself to the gift of my love. On your way to our eternal home, enjoy the journey. Let your happiness be double, in the joyful possession of what you have and in the eager anticipation of what will be. Say a resounding "Yes!" to life and to love at all times. Someday you will come up into my mountain, and then for you all the clocks and calendars will have finished their counting. Together with all my children, you will be mine and I will be yours forever.

*   *   *

This is, as I see it, the basic vision proposed in the Gospels (the good news) of Christians. It offers a perspective of life and death—a vision of reality—that is reassuring and at the same time challenging. It provides a needed sense of security, but also meaning and purpose in life. It gives us a basic frame of reference to understand ourselves, our brothers and sisters in the human family, the meaning of life and the world, and God as our loving Father. For the believer it offers a vision of reality or belief system through which all the activating events of our human lives can be interpreted and evaluated. It is a reassurance of what reality is by the Maker of all that is.

This vision of religious faith remains for some people a sweet but mere construct, only a pair of lovely rose-colored glasses to tint and tone down the harsh demands of reality. Again, the decisive factor is personal religious experience, the touch of God. One must be actively engaged with and educated by the Holy Spirit, who alone can make a person a believer. Faith is not a matter of logical reasoning or a natural acquisition. It is a matter of experience. Only God's Spirit can provide the needed religious experience. Only the touch of grace can make the Christian message more than a code of conduct and comfort for pious and plastic people.

It cannot be repeated too often that a living faith is not a human skill or acquisition. We do not pick up "believing" as we would learn, for example, to play the piano. We must be touched by the Spirit of God. The difference in one who has been touched in this way is so profound that Saint Paul calls this person a "new creation." Such a one is, as we say, a new person. Paul calls a life which has not been touched and transformed by the Spirit "life according to the flesh." The life of a person who has been renewed by the Spirit lives a "life according to the Spirit."

Jesus says that it is the Spirit who gives us a certain instinct or intuition that we are affirmed by God. It is through the Spirit that we know we are his beloved children. It is the Spirit who calls out of our hearts the tender and loving words: "Father!"

Even if we did once know Christ in the flesh, that is not how we know him now. And for everyone who is in Christ, there is a new creation; the old creation has gone, and now the new one is here. It is all God's work. It was God who reconciled us to himself through Christ and gave us the work of handing on this reconciliation. In other words, God in Christ was reconciling the world to himself.

2 Corinthians 5:16-19

Paul himself is so deeply moved by the reality of this complete transformation that he expresses his personal experience in the line: "I live, now no longer I, but Christ lives in me!" (Galatians 2:20).

We have said that we need a vision when we look out at reality through the eyes of our mind. When we perceive ourselves, other people, life, the world, and God, we have to make some kind of an interpretation or evaluation. We need some kind of order and predictability because we cannot abide chaos. It is the touch of the Spirit that provides the kind of focus and clarity that we need in order to see clearly and to live fully.

In the first words of the first book of the Bible, Genesis, the Spirit of God is depicted as bringing the order of creation out of the primordial chaos.

In the beginning God created the heavens and the earth. Now the earth was a formless void [chaos]; there was darkness over the deep, and God's spirit hovered over the water.

Genesis 1:1-2

It is by this Spirit that confusion and chaos are transformed into the loveliness of creation. Eight chapters later, in the narration of the Flood, it is the same Spirit of God that causes the waters of the flood to subside. Again he restores the order of creation out of the watery confusion and chaos. Through the prophet Joel, God promises that "it will come to pass that I will pour out my Spirit upon all humankind" (Joel 3:1; quoted in Acts 2:17).

It is this same Spirit of God who comes on the day of Pentecost to transform the disciples of Jesus from cowardly and confused men into clear-headed and convinced apostles. The chaos of their confusion is replaced by great clarity of purpose. It is the Spirit of God who directs the Christians of the early Church. His action appoints leaders, heals the sick, melts hearts, and enables people to love one another in an overwhelming release of power that will renew the face of the earth.

This touch of the Spirit transforms everything in a person and in his or her world. The person is indeed a new creation. The revelation of God, which might otherwise seem to be a fiction, is clearly a fact: a vision of reality. The touch of the Spirit results in a deep harmony, peace and order, replacing a kind of primordial chaos in a human being's inner vision of reality. Consequently, all the emotional and behavioral patterns of the person touched by the Spirit are deeply affected. There is a new sense of integration and wholeness. The person experiences that "unity which has the Spirit as its foundation and peace as its binding force" (Ephesians 4:3). As a new creation, this man or woman is enabled by the Spirit to walk into the beautiful world of God and into the fullness of the life to which God has called his children.

God's Grandeur

The world is charged with the grandeur of God.
It will flame out, like shining from shook foil;
It gathers to a greatness, like the ooze of oil
Crushed. Why do men then now not reck his rod?
Generations have trod, have trod, have trod;
And all is seared with trade; bleared,
    smeared with toil;
And wears man's smudge and shares
    man's smell: the soil
Is bare now, nor can foot feel, being shod.

And for all this, nature is never spent;
There lives the dearest freshness deep down things;
And though the last lights off the black West went
Oh, morning, at the brown brink eastward, springs—
Because the Holy Ghost over the bent
World broods with warm breast and with
    ah! bright wings.

                           Gerard Manley Hopkins, S.J.

Acknowledgments   *Continued from page ii*

Quotation of Rudolf Dreikurs reprinted with permission of Macmillan Publishing Co. Inc., from *Contemporary Psychotherapies,* edited by Morris I. Stein. Copyright © 1961 by The Free Press of Glencoe, Inc.

From "Sex and Society," by Margaret Mead. Reprinted by permission of *The Catechist.*

From *Revolt of the Masses,* by José Ortega y Gasset. Copyright 1932 by W. W. Norton & Company, Inc., copyright renewed 1960 by Teresa Carey.

From *Jesus and Logotherapy,* by Robert Leslie. Copyright © 1965 by Abingdon Press.

From "The No Cop-out Therapy," by Albert Ellis. Copyright © 1973 by Ziff-Davis Publishing Company. REPRINTED BY PERMISSION OF PSYCHOLOGY TODAY MAGAZINE.

From *A Few Buttons Missing: The Case Book of a Psychiatrist,* by James T. Fisher and Lowell S. Hawley. Copyright © 1951 by J. B. Lippincott. Reprinted by permission of J. B. Lippincott Company.

From "God's Grandeur," by Gerard Manley Hopkins. *Poems of Gerard Manley Hopkins.* Copyright © 1970 by Oxford University Press.

THE
Fully Alive
EXPERIENCE

The Fully Alive Experience by John Powell, S.J., and Loretta Brady is a unique program to help you (1) clarify and evaluate life goals and values, (2) explore pathways to a closer relationship with God, and (3) develop a deeply human and Christian life.

This program includes a practical combination of input talks by John Powell and personal exercises by Loretta Brady. The complete program can be implemented by large or small groups in ten two-hour sessions.

The complete kit (#25318) includes:
- 11 Audiocassettes
- 1 Guidebook
- 1 Personal Notebook

The kit, as well as additional Personal Notebooks in packs of ten (#25335), is available from Tabor Publishing, One DLM Park, Allen, Texas 75002.

JOHN POWELL, S.J.

Why Am I Afraid ^{TO} Tell You Who I Am?

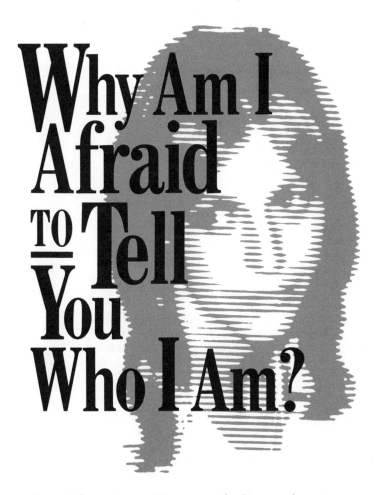

Insights into Personal Growth

P U B L I S H I N G

Allen, Texas

Book Design: Chris Schechner Graphic Design

Cover Design: Debbie Allen

Calligraphy: Sue Bohlin, Bob Niles, Faith Scarborough,
   Chris Schechner

Photo Credits:
   C. David Edmonson: Pages 6, 23, 26, 31, 37, 44, 49, 56, 67, 74, 80, 118
   Jean-Claude Lejeune: Pages 10, 15, 20, 62, 92, 99, 104, 110, 139, 154

Send all inquiries to:
Tabor Publishing
One DLM Park
Allen, Texas 75002

Library of Congress Catalog Number 70-113274

Printed in the United States of America

ISBN 1-55924-279-5

   2 3 4 5   94 93 92 91 90

Contents

1

Understanding the Human Condition

"How beautiful, how grand and liberating this experience is, when people learn to help each other. It is impossible to overemphasize the immense need humans have to be really listened to, to be taken seriously, to be understood.

"Modern psychology has brought it very much to our attention. At the very heart of all psycho-therapy is this type of relationship in which one can tell everything, just as a little child will tell all to his mother.

"No one can develop freely in this world and find a full life without feeling understood by at least one person. . . .

"He who would see himself clearly must open up to a confidant freely chosen and worthy of such trust.

"Listen to all the conversations of our world, between nations as well as those between couples. They are for the most part dialogues of the deaf."

—Dr. Paul Tournier, M.D.
Swiss psychiatrist and author

Then the Lord God said, "It is not good for man to be alone." Genesis 2:18

Our word *communication* refers to a process by which someone or something is made common, that is, it is shared. If you tell me a secret, then you and I possess the knowledge of your secret in common, and you have communicated it to me.

But you have much more to communicate to me, if you wish to, than merely one of your secrets. You can tell me who you are, just as I can tell you who I am.

THE "REAL" PERSON

In our society today, we have placed a great stress on being authentic. We have talked about placing masks over the face of our "real" selves, and of playing roles that disguise our true and real selves. The implication is that somewhere, inside you and inside me, lurk our real selves.

Supposedly, this real self is a static and formed reality. There are moments when this real self of mine shines out of me, and there are other moments when I feel compelled to camouflage my real self.

There is perhaps some justification for this manner of speaking, but I think that it can be more misleading than helpful. There is no fixed, true, and real person inside you or me, precisely because *being a person* necessarily implies *becoming a person, being in process.* If I am anything as a person, it is what I

> think
> judge
> feel
> value
> honor
> esteem
> love
> hate
> fear
> desire
> hope for
> believe in
> and
> am committed to.

These are the things that define my person, and they are constantly in process, in the process of change. Unless my mind and heart are hopelessly barricaded, all these things that define me as a person are forever changing.

My person is not a little hard core inside of me, a little fully formed statue that is real and authentic, permanent and fixed. My person rather implies a dynamic process. In other words, if you knew me yesterday, please do not think that I am the same person that you are meeting today.

I have experienced more of life, I have encountered new depths in those I love, I have suffered and prayed, and I am different.

Please do not give me a "batting average," fixed and irrevocable, because I am "in there" constantly, taking my swings at the opportunities of daily living. Approach me, then, with a sense of wonder, study my face and hands and voice for the signs of change; for it is certain that I have changed. But even if you do recognize this, I may be somewhat afraid to tell you who I am.

THE HUMAN CONDITION

Consider the following conversation:

Author: "I am writing a book, to be called *Why Am I Afraid to Tell You Who I Am?*"

Other: "Do you want an answer to your question?"

If I expose my nakedness
as a person
to you,
do not make me feel shame.

Author: "That is the purpose of the book, to answer the question."

Other: "But do you want *my answer?*"

Author: "Yes, of course I do."

Other: "I am afraid to tell you who I am, because if I tell you who I am, you may not like who I am, and it's all that I have."

This short excerpt was taken from an actual conversation, unrehearsed and from life as it really is. It reflects something of the imprisoning fears and self-doubt which cripple most of us and keep us from forward movement on the road to maturity, happiness, and true love.

In a previous effort, entitled *Why Am I Afraid to Love?* (Tabor Publishing, 1967), I have tried to describe something of the human scars and pains that block the way to true love. They are the same scars, the same inner fears and pains, that block the way to true self-communication, on which love is built. Since that other publication, to which this is intended to be a sequel, is still available from Tabor Publishing, there is no need here to review the psychological dilemmas and distress that are a part of the human condition.

Nevertheless, as a progression from that earlier work, I do want to describe here something of how these scars, as well as the defenses that we use to protect ourselves from further vulner-ability, tend to form patterns of action and reaction. These patterns eventually become so self-deceptive that we forfeit all sense of identity and integrity. We act out "roles," wear "masks," and play "games."

None of us wants to be a fraud or to live a lie; none of us wants to be a sham, a phony. But the fears that we experience and the risks that honest self-communication would involve seem so intense to us that seeking refuge in our roles, masks, and games becomes an almost natural reflex action.

After a while, it may even be quite difficult for us to distinguish between what we really are, at any given moment in our development as persons, and what we pose as being. It is such a universally human problem that we might justifiably call it "the human condition."

It is, at least, the condition in which most of us find ourselves and the point of our departure toward growth, integrity, and love.

TRANSACTIONAL ANALYSIS

The well-known California psychiatrist Dr. Eric Berne, in his best-selling book *The Games People Play*, speaks of "transactional analysis," by which he means an analysis of the social transaction when two people meet in a given situation. In such a situation, there is the "transactional stimulus" (for example, a sick child asking for a glass of water) and the "transactional response" (the mother bringing it). Transactional analysis attempts to diagnose the so-called "ego states" of the interacting persons (the stimulator and the respondent) at the time of the transaction. The supposition of transactional analysis is that, in various interactions, we may well be acting in a different role or ego state.

These ego states can be divided into three categories: the *Parent* (a collection of all the messages stored in us from infancy and child-hood), the *Adult* (the real me, capable of thinking my own thoughts and making my own decisions), and the *Child* (a storehouse of all the emotional responses of my life: the fears, angers, guilt complexes, and also the joys). None of us remains permanently fixed in any of these ego states, but we may fluctuate from one to another, depending on the situation at hand and our needs of the moment.

For example, the man who can at times function as a Parent to his child, or as an Adult to his wife or business associates, is also capable of assum-ing (either consciously or unconsciously) the ego state of a Child. While getting ready to escort his wife to the theater, where he will most probably assume the ego state of a Parent or an Adult, he may say impetuously to his wife, "Mama, will you please find my cuff links for me?" The Child (in this case, impatience and frustration) that is in him is suddenly activated because of his need of the moment. Of course, he may quickly revert to one of the other ego states, depending on his physical or emotional needs.

It may also happen that the respondent in the example given is inclined to avoid any responsibilities, and the Child in the wife may come to the surface. "Gee whiz, Daddy, if you can't find them, I'm sure that I certainly can't." The "vector line" is strictly horizontal in this transaction: Child is relating to Child. Emotions are in control in both persons.

HOW WE ARE "PROGRAMMED" TO CHOOSE EGO STATES

Clinical experimentation, applying these theories, has operated on the assumption that all of us are capable of these various ego states, and that we have been programmed by our individual, psychological histories to react as Parent, Adult, or Child, in given life situations. This "programming" is a result of the composite of previous influences in our lives (social programming) and our reaction to them (individual programming). The stimuli of these previous influences and reactions are recorded indelibly inside us.

*I can help you to accept and
open yourself
mostly by accepting and
revealing myself to you.*

As human organisms we carry within ourselves something like a portable tape recorder, which is always playing softly but insistently inside us. On the tape of this recorder there plays the message of Mother or Father (or other). Mother may still be saying: "Nothing is too good for my little Darling. I'll do the dishes and make the beds. You just run along and play, Honey." If the reaction of "Honey" was to accept this message and act out the role of the perpetual child, you may see her (supposed by now to be an adult) running right by you someday, on her way to play. She is still expecting others to do everything for her, and is unwilling to take any responsibility. She is reassured by her parent-tapes.

Or Daddy's thunder may be the parent-message on the tape recorder: "You're no damned good, you Louse!" If the child in this case has reacted in a docile manner, he is likely to be sullen and discouraged when he passes you. He will probably be mumbling to himself: "I'm no damned good . . . I'm no damned good!"

Social programming and individual programming tend to crystallize in patterns of action and reaction. These patterns can often be predicted in most of us with high accuracy. Depending on our habits and habitual reactions, we tend to play the same roles, the same "games." And the "game" always follows the "program." If you want to understand the game correctly, it helps to know the program.

PROGRAMMING: WHO WILL DOMINATE IN THE PSYCHODRAMA?

Inside each of us, there is a tape recorder that plays the sound track of a psychodrama that is continually being enacted. On the stage is the Parent, the Child, and the Adult. The Mother or Father is delivering a message to the Child. The Child is reacting emotionally to the message. When the Adult hears the message and sees the reaction of the Child, he or she has to step in and corroborate or deny the message. The Adult has to be assertive, because if not, the whole future of the person involved will be nothing more than a living out of the programming of the past. The Parent and/or Child will dominate such a life.

For example, if the Parent is saying, "You'll never amount to anything," the Adult has to step in and deny this message. "Stop telling this child that he or she is no good!" Only when the message is expunged by the intervention of the Adult can the person act and feel worthwhile. The balance can and has to be tipped. Life has to be more than simply a living out of the programming of the past, and it can be if the Adult in us will intervene.

When we speak or act, sometimes the Parent in us is in control, is speaking (the parental message is indelible and always operative). Sometimes the Child in us takes over. Our emotions begin to make our decisions for us. Sometimes we get plugged into the Adult. There are times, too, when the Parent in us interrupts the Child, as, for example: "It is such a nice day outside and I would like to go out and play (Child), but you can't always be doing what you want to (Parent)." At this point the intervening Adult may be assertive and decide: "But I need some fresh air and I need it now, so I'm going out."

There is in each of us not only a variety of ego states but also an *acculturated self* and a *deliberated self*. This distinction is essentially the same as the distinction between the programmed self and the intervening Adult self. The culture or subculture in which we live is one of the sources of our programming. It sets us up to react to certain situations in certain ways. When we oblige others with the expected reactions, or when we fall into patterns that have been pretty much determined by our past, it is the *acculturated* self that is acting. As a person becomes more and more adult (mature) the *deliberated* self, which acts out of personal integration and conviction, takes over. The fully human being is gradually extricated from his or her programming and turns from being a "reactor" to being an "actor." The person becomes "his own man" or "her own woman."

RESORTING TO GAMES

"Games" in this context are not really fun. They are our patterned reactions to life situations, programmed for us somewhere back in our personal, psychological history. Sometimes these games are extremely grim affairs, because everyone is playing to win—to win something. In order to achieve the honest communication of ourselves to others, to experience the reality of others, to become integrated and to grow, it helps very much to be aware of these patterned reactions—the games we play. If we become consciously aware of these games, we may give them up.

These games are almost always little maneuvers on our part, which we employ to avoid self-realization and self-communication. They are little shields, which we carry in front of us as we enter the battle of life. They are designed to protect us from being hurt and to help us win some little trophy for our egos. Eric Berne calls these little gains "strokes," little victories or successes that bring us protection or recognition. The games are various because psychological histories and programming are always unique. The games also vary because there are three ego states in which we may choose to cast ourselves, depending on the needs of the moment and the life situation.

"BUT IF I TELL YOU
WHO I AM,
YOU MAY NOT LIKE
WHO I AM,
AND IT IS ALL
THAT I HAVE."

The one thing that all of these games have in common is this: They defeat self-knowledge and destroy all possibility of honest self-communication with others. The price of victory is costly; there is little chance for game players to experience true interpersonal relationships, which alone can put them on the path to human growth and the fullness of human life.

Most of us play games with others in our habitual behavior. We set others up to react to us in the way that we want them to react. For example, we may not ever grow into authentic persons because we have settled for being children, inadequate and in need. We send out our "pity signals" in the sound of our voices and in the expressions on our faces. We attempt to condition others to react very gently to us. We sound and look as helpless as any child; most people are obliging enough to follow our stage directions.

Others of us, who are messianic in our assumed role, insist on wanting to save others at all times. We want to be "the helper" and to make everyone else to whom we relate "the helped." Sometimes the perpetual child marries the messiah, and they make a lifelong game of it together. Since these two games mesh, things will go very well, and neither of them will ever have to grow up. However, if one of them decides to "grow up," there will be sparks of conflict.

It is our fears and insecurity that prompt us to assume various ego states and play various games. However, if we try to be in honest touch with our emotions and to report them truthfully, the patterns of "pity signals" or "messianic mystique" will become obvious even to us. And that is the moment of change.

The perpetual child would find that she never relates well to others except when she is bringing her problems and helplessness to them. The self-styled savior would discover that he never relates well to others unless the other is troubled and helpless . . . and needing him. Being honest with one's self in this way is no easy matter, because it involves letting one's repressed emotions rise to recognition for what they really are. It also demands reporting these emotions to others, as we shall see later.

It is doubtful that there is anyone who does not play these or other games. Therefore, if I really want to "see it like it is . . . and tell it like it is," I must ask myself some difficult questions about the patterns of action and reaction that emerge in my conduct, and I must ask myself what these patterns reveal to me about myself.

Do I subconsciously develop problems in order to get attention? Do I insist on relegating all those with whom I relate to the category of "those who need my help"? Do I present myself as delicate in

*I can only know
that much
of myself
which I have had
the courage to
confide to you.*

order to insure gentle treatment from others? Am I using other people as conquests to provide a transfusion of life for my limping ego? Am I seeking to impress others with my self-sufficiency, precisely because I doubt my adequacy as a person? Hard and probing questions, aren't they?

The final section of this book is a partial listing of some of the more common roles that people assume for either permanent or occasional use. It could be called a "catalog of games and roles." This catalog, however, is not intended at all to be the "entertainment" section. All of us experience the "human condition" of fear and hiding. We all know something of what was meant by: "But if I tell you who I am, you may not like who I am, and it is all that I have."

What you and I really need is to come to a moment of truth and to develop a habit of truth with ourselves. We have to ask ourselves in the quiet, personal privacy of our own minds and hearts: What games do I play? What is it that I am trying to hide? What is it that I hope to win?

My willingness to be honest with myself and these questions will be the decisive factor and the essential condition for growth as a person.

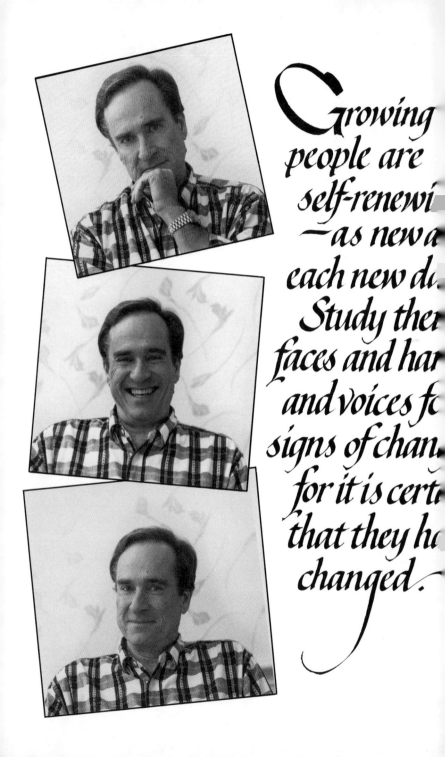

Growing people are self-renewi —as new a each new da Study ther faces and har and voices fc signs of chan for it is cert that they ha changed .

2

Growing as a Person

In these pages there are frequent references to "growth as a person," and much will be said about the necessity of self-communication and interpersonal encounter as a means to this growth. It is both intriguing and difficult to try to describe what this "growth" implies. It is impossible to cite an example of the full-grown person because each of us has to grow into his or her own person, not become "like" anyone else.

What kind of a person are we trying to become? Carl Rogers calls this person "the fully functioning person" (*Psychotherapy: Theory, Research, and Practice*, 1963) and certainly, since becoming a person is a lifelong, dynamic process, growth will have to be defined largely in terms of functions. The late Abraham Maslow, the famous psychologist from Brandeis University, calls this person "the self-actualizing person," and "the fully human person."

INTERIORITY AND EXTERIORITY

The fully human person preserves a balance between "interiority" and "exteriority." Both the extreme introvert and the extreme extrovert are off balance. Introverts are almost exclusively concerned with themselves; they become the center of gravity in their own universe. Because of their preoccupation with self, introverts are distracted from the vast world outside. Extreme extroverts, on the other hand, pour themselves out, move from one external distraction to another. Their lives are not very reflective, and consequently they experience little interior deepening. As Socrates said, "The unreflected life isn't worth living." Thus the first condition of growth is balance: a balance of interiority and exteriority.

"Interiority" implies exploration and experience of self. People who have explored and experienced themselves are aware of the vitality of their senses, emotions, mind, and will. They are neither a stranger to, nor afraid of, the activities of their body and emotions. Their senses bring them both beauty and pain, and they refuse neither. They are capable of the whole gamut of human emotions: from grief to tenderness. Their minds are alive and searching; their wills reach out for an ever greater possession of all that is good and at the same time savor that which is already in their possession. They have listened to

themselves, and they know that nothing which they hear is evil or frightening.

"Interiority" implies self-acceptance. The desired interiority means that fully functioning, self-actualizing, fully human people not only are aware of physical, psychological, and spiritual hungers and activities, but also accept them as good. Such people are "at home" with their bodies, their tender as well as hostile emotions, their impulses, thoughts, and desires.

Not only are fully human people "at home" with what they have already experienced within themselves, but they are open to new sensations, new and deeper emotional reactions, changing thoughts and desires. They accept their inner condition as forever changing, since growth always involves change. Their ultimate destiny as human beings, that is, what they will become at the end of their lives, is delightfully unknown. No human growth patterns can be prestructured for all. These people do not ambition to turn out like anyone else, because they are themselves. Their potential selves, newly actualized every day by new experiences, cannot possibly be defined at any one stage of their growth.

Fully human people accept what they are, physically, emotionally, and intellectually. They know that what they are, as far as it is known to them, is good; they know that their potential selves are even greater. They are, however, realistic about their limitations; they do not dwell in dreams of what they *want* to be and spend the rest of their lives convincing themselves that they *are* these things. They have listened to, explored, and loved what they actually are. And each new day this experience of themselves will be as new as the day itself because they are forever changing, always new persons, revealed in a constantly changing, self-renovating personality. They trust their own abilities and resources, confident that they can adapt to and cope with all the challenges that their lives will present.

This kind of self-acceptance empowers people to live fully and confidently with all that goes on inside them. They are afraid of nothing that is or could be a part of themselves.

"Exteriority" implies an openness not only to the self within but to the environment from without. Fully human people are in deep and meaningful contact with the world outside of them. They listen not only to themselves but to the voices of their world. The breadth of their own individual experience is infinitely multiplied through a sensitive empathy with others. They suffer with the suffering, rejoice with the joyful. They are born again in every springtime, feel the impact of the great mysteries of life: birth, growth, love, suffering, death. Their hearts skip along with the "young lovers," and they know something of the

The greatest kindness
    I have to offer you
is always:
        THE TRUTH.

exhilaration that is in them. They also know the ghetto's philosophy of despair, the loneliness of suffering without relief. The bell never tolls without tolling in some strange way for them.

"Create in me, O God, a listening heart," the psalmist prays.

The opposite of this openness is a kind of "defensiveness." This defensiveness hears only what it wants to hear, according to its own preconceived structure and bias. It sees only what it wants to see. Defensive people cannot be growing people because their world is no bigger than themselves, and the circle of their horizons is tightly closed.

"Exteriority" reaches its peak in the ability to *"give love freely."* Dr. Karl Stern, a psychiatrist of deep insight, has said that the evolution of human growth is an evolution from an *absolute need to be loved* (infancy) toward *a full readiness to give love* (maturity), with all sorts of stages in between. Dr. Stern said: "In our primary state of union (at the beginning of our growth as persons) we are selfish, and I am, of course, not using the word in its usual moral connotation. The infantile self is still *id* (Freud's term for our drives and ambitions) without differentiation of *ego* (that which, in the Freudian system, adapts and harmonizes personal drives with reality); the *id* of the infantile self is all-engulfing without proper

awareness of its own borders. The acts of union of the mature personality are *self-less.*"*

Fully human beings can go outside of themselves, can be committed to a cause; and they do this *freely.* Of course, fully human beings must be free. There are many philanthropists among us who give of their goods or their time addictively or compulsively. There seems to be some driving need that leaves them restless, some guilt or anxiety that becomes an obsessive ring in the nose, leading these people from one good deed to another. Fully human beings go out to others and to God, not by a kind of compulsive-obsessive neurosis, but actively and freely, and simply because they have chosen to do so.

The philosopher Martin Heidegger, in discussing the unions of love, points out two pitfalls that can stifle human growth: a complacent satisfaction that settles for that which already is, and, at the other extreme, a restless activity that goes from distraction to distraction in search of something beyond. The result, says Heidegger, is always self-estrangement. In love we must possess and savor that which is, and simultaneously reach out to possess (to love) the

*Institute of Man Symposium on *Neurosis and Personal Growth*, Duquesne University, Pittsburgh, Pa., November 18, 1966.

good more fully. This is the balance achieved by fully human beings. It is the balance between "what is" and "what is to come."

Fully human beings, in their love, do not identify themselves with what they love, as though these loved things were extensions of themselves. Gabriel Marcel, in his book *Being and Having*, laments that our civilization teaches us how to take possession of things, when it should rather initiate us in the art of letting go. There is neither freedom nor real life without an apprenticeship in dispossession.

Balanced "interiority" and "exteriority" is what is meant by integration of personality. Human nature, contrary to much that has been implied about it, is basically reasonable. Carl Rogers insists that this is his certain conclusion, based on twenty-five years of work in psychotherapy. A person is not a forest of irrational desires and impulses. If this were so, people would not want to be fully human. We are all of us capable of exaggeration. We can turn too much inward or outward. We can become slaves to our sense pleasures without reflection on our peace of soul or on our social need to love and to give to others. Or we can exaggerate by becoming prisoners of "intellect," alive only from the neck up.

When people live fully in all of their faculties, and harmonize all of their powers, human nature will prove constructive and trustworthy. In other words, as Rogers points out, when we function freely, our reactions may be trusted; they will be positive, forward moving, constructive. This is a great act of faith in human nature that too few of us ever make: If people are truly open to all that they are, and if they function freely and fully in all of their powers (senses, emotions, mind, and will), their behavior will harmonize all the data of their powers, and will be balanced and realistic. They will be on the path to growth, and that is our human destiny, not perfection but growth.

ACTING VS. REACTING

The fully human person is an actor, not a reactor.
Sydney Harris, the syndicated columnist, tells the story of accompanying his friend to a newsstand. The friend greeted the newsman very courteously, but in return received gruff and discourteous service. Accepting the newspaper that was shoved rudely in his direction, the friend of Harris politely smiled and wished the newsman a nice weekend. As the two friends walked down the street, the columnist asked:

"Does he always treat you so rudely?"

"Yes, unfortunately he does."

"And are you always so polite and friendly to him?"

"Yes, I am."

"Why are you so nice to him when he is so unfriendly to you?"

"Because I don't want *him* to decide how *I'm* going to act."

The suggestion is that "fully human" people are "their own persons," that they do not bend to every wind which blows, that they are not at the mercy of all the pettiness, the meanness, the impatience and anger of others. Atmospheres do not transform them as much as they transform their atmospheres.

Most of us, unfortunately, feel like a floating boat at the mercy of the winds and waves. We have no ballast when the winds rage and the waves churn. We say things like: "He made me so mad." "You really get to me." "Her remark embarrassed me terribly." "This weather really depresses me." "This job really bores me." "The very sight of him saddens me."

Note that all these things are *doing something to me and to my emotions.* I have nothing to say about my anger, depression, sadness, and so on. And like everyone else we are content to blame others, circumstances, and bad luck. Fully human people, as Shakespeare puts it in *Julius Caesar,* know that "the fault, dear Brutus, is not with our

your slightest look
easily will unclose me
though i have closed myself as fingers,
you open always petal by petal
myself as spring opens
(touching skillfully, mysteriously)
her first rose

e.e. cummings

stars, but with ourselves." We must learn that we can rise above the dust of daily battle that chokes and blinds so many of us. This is precisely what is asked of us in the process of growth as a person.

There is nothing implied here that suggests *repression* of emotions or that denies the fullness of life in our senses and emotions. The suggestion is rather of *balance* and *integration* of emotions. In fully alive human beings, there can be no such thing as either deadening or unconditionally surrendering to the senses or emotions.

Fully alive people listen to, are attuned to their senses and emotions. However, surrendering to them would imply abdication of intellect and choice. These are the precise powers that make human beings more than brute animals, though a little less than the angels. We will say more of this reconciliation of senses, emotions, intellect, and will in the next chapter (see "Rule three").

3

Interpersonal Relationships

Harry Stack Sullivan, one of the more eminent psychiatrists of interpersonal relationships in our times, has propounded the theory that all personal growth, all personal damage and regression, as well as all personal healing and growth, come through our relationships with others. There is a persistent, if uninformed, suspicion in most of us that we can solve our own problems and be the masters of our own ships of life. The fact of the matter is that by ourselves we can only be consumed by our problems and suffer shipwreck. What I am, at any given moment in the process of my becoming a person, will be determined by my relationships with those who love me or refuse to love me, with those whom I love or refuse to love.

It is certain that a relationship will be *only as good as its communication*. If you and I can honestly tell each other who we are, that is, what we think, judge, feel, value, love, honor and esteem, hate, fear, desire, hope for, believe in, and are committed to, then and then only can each of us grow. Then and then alone can we be what we really are, say what we really think, tell what we really feel, express what we really love. This is the real meaning of authenticity as a person, that my exterior truly reflects my interior. It means I can be honest in the communication of my person to others. This I cannot do unless you help me. Unless you help me, I cannot grow, or be happy, or really come alive.

I have to be free and able to say my thoughts to you, to tell you about my judgments and values, to expose to you my fears and frustrations, to admit to you my failures and shames, to share my triumphs, before I can really be sure what it is that I am and can become. I must be able to tell you who I am before I can know who I am. And I must know who I am before I can act truly, that is, in accordance with my true self.

THE SUBJECT-OBJECT RELATIONSHIP VS. THE "ENCOUNTER"

In the language of existential psychology, "encounter" describes a special relationship between two persons. It implies that a communion or communication of persons has been achieved. One existence is communicating to another existence, is sharing with another. Gabriel Marcel calls this kind of relationship an "ontological communion," a real fusion of two people. To illustrate what this means, Marcel explains that very often our emotions and sympathy do not spring to life at all when we encounter the suffering of others in our daily lives. Somehow, Marcel goes on, I just cannot respond to them; they are just "not there" for me. But if we should open a letter from a friend many miles away telling us of some great disaster or sickness, we are at once with that friend, suffering with him or her; we are together without any qualification.

In the words of Martin Buber, the Jewish philosopher of interpersonality, it is in the *encounter* that the other individual no longer is a person of impersonality, a "he" or "she," but becomes for my "I" a sensitized, correlative "Thou." (See Martin Buber, *I-Thou* [New York: Scribner, 1958].) The other person becomes, in some mysterious and almost undefinable way, a special being in my eyes, a part of my world, and a part of my self. Insofar as it is possible, I enter into the world of the other's reality and he or she enters into the world of my reality. There has been some kind of fusion, even though each of us always remains a distinct self. As e. e. cummings writes:

"One's not half two. It's two are halves of one."

My friend of encounter is no longer someone "out there somewhere" who serves my purposes, or who belongs to my club, or who works with me. Ours is no such subject-object relationship; we have experienced that mysterious but certain communion of togetherness. It is this that the existential psychologists call "encounter." And the stuff of which encounter is made is honest communication.

Where true encounter exists, and we are saying that it is absolutely essential for growth as a person, the concern of the persons in such an encounter is not so much with the problems and their solutions as with the communion, the sharing. I open myself and my world to you for your entry, and you open yourself and your world to me for me to enter. I have allowed you to experience me as a person, in all the fullness of my person, and I have experienced you in this way. And for this, I must tell you who I am and you must tell me the same about yourself. Communication is the only avenue to communion.

This is why psychologists such as Erich Fromm say that we cannot love anyone without loving everyone more. If I can communicate with you and you with me only on a "subject-object" level, we will probably both communicate with others, and even with God, on this same level. We will remain isolated subjects; others and God will remain merely "objects" in our world, but not experiences. Unless we have been opened up by such an encounter, we will have so-called friendships, and will perhaps retain a so-called religious faith (a kind of relationship with God), mostly because these are things that are somehow expected of us. These relationships with others will be social amenities and nothing more. There will be no personal meaning in them.

The world of people in subject-object relationships is a world of objects, things to be manipulated, to serve as distractions or sources of pleasure. The possessions of such people may be beautiful and expensive or common and cheap, but these people will be lonely. They will come to the end of life without ever having really lived. The dynamic process of personhood will become a static thing like debris floating on stagnant waters. When the process of personhood is stifled, all of life becomes a terrible bore. If the edges of reality for a humanly isolated person are sharp, life can be very painful. There will seem to be need for those artificially induced but short-lived stimuli called "kicks." These kicks are little attempts to run away from life, short "trips," in an effort to escape the inexorable intrusion of reality and the essential loneliness of the person without true friends.

Human life has its laws, one of which is: We must *use* things and *love* people. People whose whole lives are lived on the subject-object level

To refuse the invitation
to interpersonal encounter is
to be an isolated dot in the
center of a great circle
—a small island in a vast ocean.

find that they love things and use people. It is the death warrant for happiness and human fulfillment.

INTERPERSONAL ENCOUNTER AND THE FIVE LEVELS OF COMMUNICATION

Someone has aptly distinguished five levels of communication on which persons can relate to one another. Perhaps it will help our understanding of these levels to visualize a person locked inside of a prison. The prisoner in our example is a man, but he represents every human being. He is urged by an inner insistence to go out to others and yet afraid to do so. The five levels of communication, which will be described a little later, represent five degrees of willingness to go outside of the self, to communicate the self to others.

The man in the prison—and he is everyone—has been there for years, although ironically the grated iron doors are not locked. He can go out of his prison, but in his long detention he has learned to fear the possible dangers that he might encounter. He has come to feel some sort of safety and protection behind the walls of his prison, where he is a voluntary captive. The darkness of his prison shields him from a clear view of himself. He is not sure what he would look like in broad daylight. Above all, he is not sure how the world, which he sees from behind bars, and the people whom he sees moving about in that world, would receive him. He is fragmented by an almost desperate need for that world and for those people, and, at the same time, by an almost desperate fear of the risks of rejection he would be taking if he ended his isolation.

This prisoner is reminiscent of what Viktor Frankl writes, in his book *Man's Search for Meaning*, about his fellow prisoners in the Nazi concentration camp at Dachau. These prisoners yearned desperately for their freedom. Yet some of them had been held captive so long that when they were eventually released, they walked out into the sunlight, blinked nervously, and then silently walked back into the familiar darkness of the prison. They had been accustomed to this darkness for such a long time.

This is the visualized, if somewhat dramatic, dilemma that all of us experience at some time in our lives and in the process of becoming persons. Most of us make only a weak response to the invitation of encounter with others and our world because we feel uncomfortable in exposing our nakedness as persons. Some of us are willing only to pretend this exodus, while others somehow find in themselves the courage to go all the way out to freedom. There are various stages in between. These stages are described below, under the headings of the five levels of communication. The fifth level, to be considered first, represents the least willingness to communicate ourselves to others. The successive, descending levels indicate greater and greater success in the adventure.

Level Five: Cliché Conversation. This level represents the weakest response to the human dilemma and the lowest level of self-communication. In fact, there is no communication here at all, unless by accident. On this level, we talk in clichés, such as: "How are you?" "How is your family?" "Where have you been?" We say things like: "I like your dress very much." "I hope we can get together again real soon." "It's really good to see you." In fact, we really mean almost nothing of what we are asking or saying. If the other party were to begin answering our question "How are you?" in detail, we would be astounded. Usually and fortunately, the other party senses the superficiality and conventionality of our concern and question. People usually oblige by simply giving the standard answer, "Just fine, thank you."

This is the conversation, the noncommunication, of the cocktail party, the club meeting, the neighborhood laundromat, and so on. There is no sharing of persons at all. Everyone remains safely in the isolation of his or her pretense, sham, sophistication. The whole group seems to gather in order to be lonely together. It is well summarized in the lyrics of Paul Simon's "Sounds of Silence," used so effectively in the movie *The Graduate:*

"And in the naked night I saw
Ten thousand people, maybe more,
People talking without speaking,
People hearing without listening,
People writing songs that voices never shared.
No one dared
Disturb the sounds of silence."

Level Four: Reporting the Facts about Others. On this fourth level, we do not step very far outside the prison of our loneliness into real communication because we expose almost nothing of ourselves. We remain contented to tell others what so-and-so has said or done. We offer no personal, self-revelatory commentary on these facts. We simply report them. Just as most of us, at times, hide behind clichés, so we also seek shelter in gossip items, conversation pieces, and little narrations about others. We give nothing of ourselves and invite nothing from others in return.

Level Three: My Ideas and Judgments. On this level, there is some communication of my person. I am willing to take this step out of my solitary confinement. I will take the risk of telling you some of my ideas and reveal some of my judgments and decisions. My communication

Most people tend to overcompensate . . . .

**PEOPLE WHO ARE
RIDDLED WITH DOUBTS
TEND TO BE
DOGMATISTS
WHO ARE NEVER WRONG.**

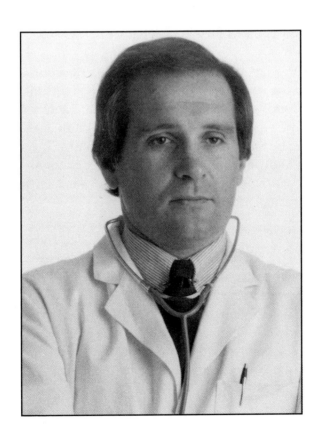

usually remains under a strict censorship,
however. As I communicate with you, I will be
watching you carefully. I want to test the
temperature of the water before I leap in. I want
to be sure that you will accept me with my ideas,
judgments, and decisions. If you raise your
eyebrow or narrow your eyes, if you yawn or
look at your watch, I will probably retreat to
safer ground. I will run for the cover of silence or
change the subject of conversation. Or worse, I
will start to say things I suspect that you want
me to say. I will try to be whatever pleases you.

Someday, perhaps, when I develop the courage
and the intensity of desire to grow as a person, I
will spill all of the contents of my mind and heart
before you. It will be my moment of truth. It may
even be that I have already done so, but still you
can know only a little about my person, unless I
am willing to advance to the next level of self-
communication.

Level Two: My Feelings (Emotions)—"Gut Level."
It might not occur to many of us that, once we
have revealed our ideas, judgments, and
decisions, there is really much more of our
persons to share. Actually, the things that most
clearly differentiate and individuate me from
others, that make the communication of my
person a unique knowledge, are my *feelings*
or *emotions.*

If I really want you to know who I am, I must tell you about my stomach (gut level) as well as my head. My ideas, judgments, and decisions are quite conventional. If I am a Republican or Democrat by persuasion, I have a lot of company. If I am for or against space exploration, there will be others who will support me in my conviction. But the *feelings* that lie under my ideas, judgments, and convictions are uniquely mine. No one supports a political party, or has a religious conviction, or is committed to a cause with my exact feelings of fervor or apathy. No one experiences my precise sense of frustration, labors under my fears, feels my passions. Nobody opposes war with my particular indignation or supports patriotism with my unique sense of loyalty.

It is these feelings, on this level of communication, that I must share with you if I am to tell you who I really am. To illustrate this, I would like to put in the left-hand column a judgment, and in the right-hand column some of the possible emotional reactions to this judgment. If I tell you only the contents of my mind, I will be withholding a great deal about myself, especially in those areas where I am uniquely personal, most individual, most deeply myself.

Judgment	*Some possible emotional reactions*
I think that you are intelligent.	. . . and I am jealous.
	. . . and I feel frustrated.
	. . . and I feel proud to be your friend.
	. . . and it makes me ill at ease with you.
	. . . and I feel suspicious of you.
	. . . and I feel inferior to you.
	. . . and I feel impelled to imitate or compete with you.
	. . . and I feel like running away from you.
	. . . and I feel the desire to humiliate you.

Most of us feel that others will not tolerate such emotional honesty in communication. We would rather defend our dishonesty on the grounds that it might hurt others. Having rationalized our phoniness into nobility, we settle for superficial relationships. This occurs not only in the case of casual acquaintances but even with members of our own families; it destroys authentic communion within marriages and families. Consequently, we ourselves do not grow, nor do we help anyone else to grow. Meanwhile we have to live with repressed emotions—a dangerous and self-destructive path to follow. Any relationship that is to have the nature of true personal encounter must be based on this honest, open, gut-level communication. The alternative is to remain in a prison of isolation, to endure inch-by-inch death as a person.

We will say more of this level of communication, after describing the first and deepest level of communication between persons.

Level One: Peak Communication. All deep and authentic friendships, and especially the union of those who are married, must be based on absolute openness and honesty. At times, gut-level communication will be most difficult, but it is at these precise times that it is most necessary. Among close friends or between partners in marriage there will come from time to time a complete emotional and personal communion.

In our human condition this can never be a permanent experience. There should and will be, however, moments when encounter attains perfect communication. At these times the two persons will feel an almost perfect and mutual empathy. I know that my own reactions are shared completely by my friend; my happiness or my grief is perfectly reduplicated in him or her. We are like two musical instruments playing exactly the same note, filled with and giving forth precisely the same sound. This is what is meant by level one, peak communication. (Cf. A. H. Maslow, *Religions, Values, and Peak Experiences,* 1964.)

"RULES" FOR GUT-LEVEL COMMUNICATION

If friendship and human love are to mature between any two persons, there must be absolute and honest mutual revelation. This kind of self-revelation can be achieved only through what we have called "gut-level" communication. There is no other way, and all the reasons that we adduce to rationalize our cover-ups and dishonesty must be seen as delusions. It would be much better for me to tell you how I really feel about you than to enter into the stickiness and discomfort of a phony relationship.

Dishonesty always has a way of coming back to haunt and trouble us. Even if I should have to tell you that I do not admire or love you emotionally, it would be much better than trying to deceive you and having to pay the ultimate price of all such deception, your greater hurt and mine. And you will have to tell me things, at times, that will be difficult for you to share. But really, you have no choice. If I want your friendship, I must be ready to accept you as you are. If either of us comes to the relationship without this determination of mutual honesty and openness, there can be no friendship, no growth. Rather, there can be only a subject-object kind of thing that is typified by adolescent bickering, pouting, jealousy, anger, and accusations.

The classic temptation in this matter, and it would seem to be the most destructive of all delusions in this area of human relations, is this: We are tempted to think that communication of an unfavorable emotional reaction will tend to be divisive. If I tell you that it bothers me when you do something you are accustomed to doing, I may be tempted to believe that it would be better not to mention it. Our relationship will be more peaceful. You wouldn't understand, anyway.

So I keep it inside myself, and each time you do your thing my stomach keeps score—2 . . . 3 . . . 4 . . . 5 . . . 6 . . . 7 . . . 8 . . . Then one day you do the same thing that you have always done and all hell breaks loose. All the while I was feeling annoyed, I was keeping it inside and somewhere, secretly, learning to hate you. My good thoughts were slowly turning to gall.

When it finally erupted in one great emotional avalanche, you didn't understand. You thought that this kind of reaction was totally uncalled for. The bonds of our love seemed fragile and about to break. And it all started when I thought: "I don't like what she [he] is doing, but it would be

*To reveal myself
openly and honestly
takes the
rawest kind of courage.*

better not to say anything. The relationship will be more peaceful." That was all a delusion, and I should have told you in the beginning. Now there has been an emotional divorce. Our relationship is strained or ruptured. And all because I wanted to keep the peace between us.

Rule one: Gut-level communication (emotional openness and honesty) must never imply a judgment of the other. I am simply not mature enough to enter into true friendship unless I realize that I cannot judge the intention or motivation of another. I must be humble and sane enough to bow before the complexity and mystery of a human being. If I judge you, I have only revealed my own immaturity and ineptness for friendship.

Emotional candor as such does not ever imply a judgment of you. In fact, it even abstains from any judgment of myself. For example, if I were to say to you, "I am ill at ease with you," I have been emotionally honest and at the same time have not implied in the least that it is your fault that I am ill at ease with you. Perhaps it is my own inferiority complex or my exaggerated concept of your intelligence. I am not saying it is anyone's fault, but simply giving a report of my emotional reaction to you at this time.

If I were to say to you that I feel angry or hurt by something you have done or said, I have not judged you. Perhaps it is my own self-love that has made me so sensitive, or my inclination to paranoia (a persecution complex). I am not sure, and in most cases, I can never be sure. To be sure would imply a judgment. I can only say for sure that this has been and is my emotional reaction.

If I were to tell you that I am annoyed by something you do, again I cannot be so arrogant as to think that your action would annoy anyone. I do not even mean that your action is in any way wrong or offensive. I simply mean that here and now I experience annoyance. Perhaps it is my headache or my indigestion or the fact that I did not get much sleep last night. I really do not know. All that I know is this, that I am trying to tell you that I am experiencing annoyance at this moment.

It would probably be helpful in most cases to preface our gut-level communication with some kind of a disclaimer to assure the other that there is no judgment implied. I might begin by saying, "I don't know why this bothers me, but it does . . . I guess I'm just hypersensitive. I really don't mean to imply that it is your fault, but I do feel hurt by what you are saying."

Of course, the main thing is that there is *in fact* no judgment. If I am in the habit of judging the intentions or motivation of another, I should try very hard to outgrow this immature habit. I simply will not be able to disguise my judgments, no matter how many disclaimers I make.

On the other hand, if I am really mature enough to refrain from such judgments, this too will eventually be apparent. If I really want to know the intention or motivation or reaction of another, there is only one way to find out: *I must ask the person.* (Don't pass this by lightly. You don't have X-ray eyes either!)

Perhaps a word should be inserted here about the difference between judging a person and judging an action. If I see someone stealing another's money, I can judge that this *action* is morally wrong, but I cannot judge *the person.* It is for God, not for you or me, to judge human responsibility. If, however, we could not judge the rightness or wrongness of an action in itself, it would be the end of all objective morality. Let us not fall into this, that there is nothing objectively wrong or right, that it is all in the way you look at it. However, to judge the responsibility of another is playing God.

Rule two: Emotions are not moral (good or bad). Theoretically, most of us would accept the fact that emotions are neither meritorious nor sinful. Feeling frustrated, or being annoyed, or experiencing fears and anger does not make one a good or a bad person. Practically, however, most of us do not accept in our day-to-day living what we would accept in theory. We exercise a rather strict censorship of our emotions. If our censoring conscience does not approve certain emotions, we repress these emotions into our subconscious mind. Experts in psychosomatic medicine say that the most common cause of fatigue and actual sickness is the repression of emotions. The fact is that there are emotions to which we do not want to admit. We are ashamed of our fears, or we feel guilty because of our anger or our emotional and physical desires.

Before we can be liberated enough to practice "gut-level communication," in which we will be emotionally open and honest, we must feel convinced that emotions are *not moral* but simply *factual.* My jealousies, my anger, my sexual desires, my fears, and so on, do not make me a good or bad person. Of course, these emotional reactions must be integrated by my mind and will. But before they can be integrated, before I can decide whether I want to act on them or not, I must allow them to arise and I must clearly hear what they are saying to me. I must be able to say, without any sense of moral reprehension, that I am afraid or angry or sexually aroused.

Before I will be free enough to do this, however, I must be convinced that emotions are not moral, neither good nor bad in themselves. I must be convinced, too, that the experience of the whole gamut of emotions is a part of the human condition, the inheritance of every human being.

Rule three: Feelings (emotions) must be integrated with the intellect and will. It is extremely important to understand this next point. The nonrepression of our emotions means that we must experience, recognize, and accept our emotions fully. It does not in any way imply that we will always *act on* those emotions. Allowing our feelings or emotions to control our lives would be tragic and the worst form of immaturity. It is one thing to feel and to admit to myself and to others that I am afraid, but it is another thing to allow this fear to overwhelm me. It is one thing for me to feel and to admit that I am angry, and another to punch you in the nose.

Will

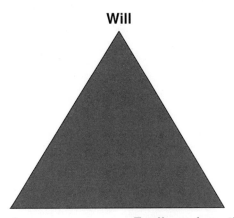

Intellect   **Feelings (emotions)**

In the triangle above we see the three human faculties that must be integrated, that is, brought into one harmonious wholeness, if one is to advance in the process of becoming a person. If the meaning of this integration is clear, it is

The behavior
of the fully human being
is always unpredictable —
simply because it is free

apparent that the mind judges the necessity or desirability of acting upon certain emotions that have been fully experienced. Then the will carries this judgment into effect. For example, I may feel a strong fear of telling you the truth in some given matter. The fact is, and it is neither good nor bad in itself, that I am experiencing fear. I allow myself to feel this fear fully, to recognize it as such. My mind makes the judgment that I should act not out of this fear but in spite of it, and that I should tell you the truth. The will consequently carries out the judgment of the mind. I tell you the truth.

However, if I am seeking a real and authentic relationship with you, and wish to practice "gut-level" communication, I must tell you something like this: "I really don't know why . . . maybe it's my streak of cowardice . . . but I feel afraid to tell you something, and yet I know that I must be honest with you . . . This is the truth as I see it . . ."

Or, to take another example, maybe I feel very tender and loving toward you. As Chesterton once remarked, the meanest fear of all is the fear of sentiment. Perhaps it is our cultural heritage or maybe it is the fear of rejection, but we often experience a great reluctance to be externally tender and loving. Perhaps in this case my mind will pass the judgment that it is right to act on this impulse of feeling, and again my will carries the judgment into execution. It should be obvious that in the integrated person, emotions are neither repressed nor do they assume control of the whole person. They are recognized (What is it that I am feeling?) and integrated (Do I want to act on this feeling or not?).

Rule four: In "gut-level" communication, emotions must be "reported." If I am to tell you who I really am, I must tell you about my feelings, whether I decide to act upon them or not. I may tell you that I am angry, explaining the fact of my anger without inferring any judgment of you, and not intending to act upon this anger. I may tell you that I am afraid, explaining the fact of my fear without accusing you of being its cause, and at the same time not succumbing to the fear. But I must, if I am to open myself to you, allow you to experience (encounter) my person and tell you about my anger and my fear.

It has been truly said that we either *speak out* (report) our feelings or we will *act them out.* Feelings are like steam that is gathering inside of a kettle. Kept inside and gathering strength, they can blow the human lid off, just as the steam inside of the kettle will blow off the lid of the kettle.

We have already referred to the verdict, handed down by psychosomatic medicine, that repressed emotions are the most common cause of fatigue and actual sickness. This is part of the "acting out" process. Repressed emotions may find their outlet in the "acting out" of headaches, skin rashes, allergies, asthma, common colds, aching backs or limbs. They can also be acted out in the tightening of muscles, the slamming of doors, the clenching of fists, the rising of blood pressure, the grinding of teeth, or in tears, temper tantrums, acts of violence. We do not bury our emotions *dead;* they remain *alive* in our subconscious minds and intestines, to hurt and trouble us. It is not only much more conducive to an authentic relationship to report our true feelings, but equally essential to our integrity and health.

The most common reason for not reporting our emotions is that we do not want to admit to them for one reason or another. We fear that others might not think well of us, or actually reject us, or punish us in some way for our emotional candor. We have been somehow "programmed" not to accept certain emotions as part of us. We are ashamed of them. Now we can rationalize and say that we cannot report these emotions because they would not be understood. We might reason that reporting them would disturb a peaceful relationship or evoke an emotionally stormy reaction from the other. But all of our reasons are essentially fraudulent, and our silence can produce only fraudulent relationships. Anyone who builds a relationship on less than openness and honesty is building on sand. Such a relationship will never stand the test of time, and neither party to the relationship will draw from it any noticeable benefits.

Rule five: With rare exceptions, emotions must be reported at the time that they are being experienced. It is much easier for most of us to report an emotion that is past, a matter of history. It is almost like talking about another person when I can talk about myself a year or two years ago, and admit that I was very fearful or very angry at that time. Because they were transient emotions and are now gone, it is easy to dissociate these feelings from my person here and now. It is difficult, however, to recapture a feeling once it has passed into my personal history. We are very often puzzled by such previous emotions. "I don't know why I ever got so excited." The time to report emotions is the time when they are being experienced. Even temporary deferral of this report of emotions is unwise and unhealthy.

All communication must obviously respect not only the transmitter of the communication but also the receiver who is to accept the communication. Consequently, it could occur that in the integration of my emotions, my judgment may dictate that this is not the opportune moment to report my emotional reaction. If the receiver is so emotionally disturbed that he or she could hardly be in a receptive mood, and my report

Whatever my secrets are,
remember
when I entrust them to you,
—they are part of me.

would only be distorted somehow by the receiver's turbulent emotional state, it may be that I will have to defer this report.

But if the matter is serious enough and the emotions strong enough, this period of deferment cannot be too long nor can I be frightened or bullied into complete repression of emotions. Please note that this period of deferment should never be a long one. It would seem that in most cases shelving emotions even temporarily should be a rare thing.

However, it would seem to be a valid exception to this rule to defer or eliminate this report in the case of a passing incident with a chance acquaintance. The gruff manner of a bus driver may irk me, without this being the occasion for me to tell the driver about my emotional reactions to him or her. In the case of two people, however, who must work or live together or who want to relate deeply, this emotional reporting at the time of the emotions is seriously and vitally important.

THE BENEFITS OF "GUT-LEVEL" COMMUNICATION

The obvious and primary benefit of "gut-level" communication will be real and authentic relationship and what we have called a true "encounter" of persons. Not only will there be mutual communication of persons and the

consequent sharing and experiencing of personhood, but "gut-level" communication will result
in a more and more clearly defined sense of self-
identity for each of the parties in the relationship.

Today, many of us are asking: "Who am I?" It
has come to be a socially fashionable question.
The implication is that I do not really know my
own self as a person. We have said that my
person is what I think, judge, feel, and so on. If I
have communicated these things freely and
openly, as clearly as I can and as honestly as I
can, I will find a noticeable growth in my own
sense of identity. I will also experience a deeper
and more authentic knowledge of my person. It
has come to be an accepted psychological truism
that I will understand only as much of myself as I
have been willing to communicate to another.

The second and very important result of such
communication is that, having understood
myself because I have communicated myself, I
will find the patterns of immaturity gradually
changing into patterns of maturity. I will change!
Anyone who sees the *patterns* of his or her
reactions, and is willing to examine them, may
come to the realization that these are patterns of
hypersensitivity or paranoia. At the moment the
realization penetrates, he or she will find the
pattern changing. Notwithstanding all that we
have said about emotions, we must not believe
that emotional patterns are purely biological or

inevitable. *I can and will change my emotional patterns;* that is, I will move from one emotion to another if I have honestly let my emotions arise for recognition and, having honestly reported them, judge them to be immature and inappropriate.

For example, if I consistently and honestly report the emotion of "feeling hurt" by many small and inconsequential things, it will become apparent to me in time that I am hypersensitive and that I have been indulging myself in self-pity. The moment that this becomes clear to me, really hits me, I will change.

In summary the dynamic is this: We allow our emotions to arise so that they can be identified; we observe the patterns in our emotional reactions and then we report and judge them. Having done these things, we instinctively and immediately make the necessary adjustments in the light of our own ideals and hopes for growth. We change. Try this and see for yourself. It works.

As has been said, our emotional reactions are not biological or psychological necessities. We can move from one emotion to another if we want to. Many examples could be added here. I can feel viciously competitive, but if I allow the emotions under my spirit of competition to surface for recognition, I may discover that it is only my sense of inferiority, my lack of belief in myself, that propels me into competition. It is strangely mysterious how, when these emotions are allowed to illuminate our inner selves, they can tell us things we never knew about ourselves. And this kind of self-knowledge is the beginning of growth.

Or I might be laboring with a destructive emotion like despair. If I allow it to arise for inspection, my despair will show itself to be merely an attempt at self-punishment. Much "depression" is simply self-punishment. Further self-investigation may show me that I have a guilt complex, and that I need this punishment to atone for my guilt feelings. I am on a course of self-destruction. When I can recognize these emotions as negative and self-destroying, it is then within my power to move to a new emotional reaction—from self-pity or self-punishment to love, from anger to empathy, from despair to hope.

If all this is true, and you have only to experience it to know its truth, it is obvious that the little phrase we have used so conveniently, "I'm sorry, but that's the way I am," is nothing more than a refuge and delusion. It is handy if you don't want to grow up; but if you do want to grow up, you try to rise above this fallacy.

The third benefit of "gut-level" communication is that it will evoke from others a responsive honesty and openness, which is necessary if the relationship is to be interpersonal, mutual. A psychiatrist friend of mine somewhat boastfully claims that he can gain instant access to the deepest parts of anyone within a matter of minutes. His technique is not to begin by probing with questions. This would only make the insecure person more defensive. The theory of this psychiatrist is that if we want another to be open with us, we must begin by opening up ourselves, by telling the other very honestly and openly of our feelings.

Person is resonant to person, psychologist Josef Goldbrunner insists. If I am willing to step out of the darkness of my prison, to expose the deepest part of me to other persons, the result is almost always automatic and immediate: The other persons feel empowered to reveal themselves to me. Having heard of my secret and deep feelings, others are given the courage to communicate themselves. This, in the last analysis, is what we meant by "encounter."

4

Dealing with Our Emotions

We have said that fully human people do not repress their emotions, as far as this is under their control, but allow them to rise to the surface of recognition. They experience the fullness of their emotional life; they are "in touch with," attuned to their emotions, aware of what their emotions are saying to them about their needs and their relationships with others. On the other hand, we have also said that this does not imply surrender to the emotions. In fully human people, there is a balance of senses, emotions, intellect, and will. The emotions have to be integrated. Though it is necessary to "report" our emotions, it is not at all necessary that we "act on" them. We must never allow our emotions to control our decisions.

The critical importance of all this will be clear to you if you will reflect for just a moment on the following: (1) Almost all the pleasures and pains

Most of us feel that others will not tolerate such emotional honesty in communication. We would rather defend our dishonesty on the grounds that it might hurt others. Having rationalized our phoniness into nobility, we settle for superficial relationships.

of life are deeply involved with the emotions. (2) Most human conduct is the result of emotional forces (even though we are all tempted to pose as pure intellects, and to explain on rational, objective grounds all of our preferences and actions). (3) Most interpersonal conflicts result from emotional stresses (for example, anger, jealousy, frustrations), and most interpersonal encounters are achieved through some kind of emotional communion (for example, empathy, tenderness, feelings of affection and attraction). In other words, your emotions and how you deal with them will probably make you or break you in the adventure of life.

The mechanics of "awareness," "reporting," and "integration" of the emotions may be illustrated as follows.

Situation: You are having a discussion with a member of your family or a friend. There are several differences of opinion, and very gradually voices and blood pressures rise. You are beginning to feel the stress of strong feelings. What should you do?

HEALTHY

1. Be aware of your emotions. Turn your mind briefly away from the argument and pay direct attention to your emotional reaction. Ask yourself: What am I feeling? Is it embarrassment (because the other person's arguments sound better)? Is it fear (the other person is pretty big and is getting more angry by the minute)? Superiority (because you're ahead on points, and he or she knows it)?

2. Admit your emotion. Turn your full awareness toward the emotion. Take a good look so that you can identify it. Estimate, too, how strong it is. It is anger, for example, and it is pretty high voltage, too.

3. Investigate your emotion. If you really want to find out a lot about yourself, ask your anger how it got there, and where it came from. Trace the origin of your emotion. You may not be able to uncover the whole family tree of your present emotion, but you just may get a glimpse of an inferiority complex to which you have never admitted.

UNHEALTHY

1. Ignore your emotional reaction. It has nothing to do with the argument anyway. Better yet (if you want to make the worst mistake), tell yourself that you're not getting upset at all. If you are perspiring, tell yourself that it's just warm in the room. Keep your anger down in the pit of your stomach, where your head can't notice it. Feeling emotions during an intellectual discussion is unworthy of you anyway.

2. Keep denying your emotions. Tell yourself and tell others, "But I'm not mad at all." Emotions are more easily ignored if you keep your mind fixed on the argument. Don't let your emotions distract you. You can take Alka Seltzer later, when your stomach calls you a liar.

3. Keep combing through your mind for rebuttal materials. The person with the right moves and bright lines is going to break this thing wide open. It's strictly win-lose now. Slow the words down; you're starting to sputter. But keep up a steady flow, or the other person will get in there and make a point. Keep your mind on the argument, and keep moving toward the jugular vein.

HEALTHY

4. Report your emotion. Just the facts now. No interpretations or judgments. "Let's cool it for a minute. I'm getting too worked up, and I'm starting to say things I really don't mean." It is very important not to accuse or judge in this report. Do not tell the other person that it is his or her fault that you got so angry. It really isn't, you know. It's something in you. Don't blame the other person even to yourself.

5. Integrate your emotion. Having listened to your emotion, and having questioned it and reported it, now let your mind judge what is the right thing to do, and let your will carry out the judgment. For example, "Let's start again. I think I've been too defensive to listen to you. I'd like to try again." Or, "Would you mind if we dropped the subject? I'm afraid I'm getting too touchy to discuss anything."

UNHEALTHY

4. If you should blow your cool completely and become incoherent, blame it on the other person. And be sure to include some deep personality defect in your indictment. For example, "It's impossible to discuss anything with you. You're too damned arrogant. You never (generalizations like this are good, too) listen. You think you're God, don't you?" (Make sure he or she knows that the question is rhetorical.)

5. Since you haven't even admitted to having an emotion, you won't have to go through the trouble of trying to learn from your emotional reactions or integrating them. Repressed emotions, however, have a way of acting up, so walk out in a huff, and take a couple of aspirins—and keep your mind on how unreasonable the other person was.

To tell you my *THOUGHTS*
is to locate myself
in a category.

To tell you about my
feelings is to tell
you about *me.*

REFLECTIONS ON "ESTRANGEMENT" AND "ENCOUNTER"

In spite of our unwillingness and reluctance to tell others who we are, there is in each one of us a deep and driving desire to be understood. It is clear to all of us that we want very badly to be loved, but when we are not understood by those whose love we need and want, any sort of deep communication becomes a nervous and uncomfortable thing. It does not enlarge and enliven us. It becomes clear that others cannot really love us effectively unless they really understand us. People who feel that they are understood, however, will almost certainly feel that they are loved.

If there is no one who understands me, and who accepts me for what I am, I will feel "estranged." My talents and possessions will not comfort me at all. Even in the midst of many people, I will always carry within me a feeling of isolation and aloneness. I will experience a kind of "solitary confinement." It is a law, as certain as the law of gravity, that those who are understood and loved will grow as persons; those who are estranged will die in their cell of solitary confinement, alone.

There are many things inside every one of us that we would like to share. All of us have our own secret past, our secret shames and broken

dreams, our secret hopes. Over and against this
need and desire to share these secrets and to be
understood, every one of us must weigh fear and
risk. Whatever my secrets are, they seem, more
than anything else, to be deeply and uniquely a
part of me. No one has ever done the precise
things that I have done; no one has ever thought
my thoughts or dreamed my dreams. I am not
sure that I could even find the words to share
these things with another, but what I am even
less sure of is this: How would they sound to
another?

   People who have a good self-image, who really
and truly accept themselves, will be greatly
helped at this time of dilemma. It is not very
likely, however, that those who have never really
shared themselves could have the support of a
good self-image. Most of us have experienced
and done things, have lived with sensations and
feelings, that we feel we would never dare tell
another. To the other, I might appear deluded or
even evil, ridiculous or vain. My whole life could
appear as a hideous deceit.

   A thousand fears keep us in the solitary confinement of estrangement. In some of us there is
the fear of breaking down, of sobbing like a child.
Others of us feel restrained by the fear that the
other person will not sense the tremendous
importance that our secret has for us. I usually
anticipate how deep the pain would be if my

secret were met with apathy, misunderstanding, shock, anger, or ridicule. My confidant might become angry or reveal my secret to others for whom it was not intended.

It may have happened that, at some point in my life, I took some part of me out of the darkness and placed it in the light for the eyes of another. It may be that this other person did not understand, and I ran full of regrets into a painful emotional solitude. Yet, there may have been other moments when someone heard my secret and accepted my confidence in gentle hands. I may remember what that person said to assure me, the compassion in his or her voice, the understanding look in his or her eyes. I remember what those eyes looked like. I remember how the individual's hand took mine. I remember the gentle pressure that told me I was understood. It was a great and liberating experience, and in its wake I felt so much more alive. An immense need had been answered in me to be really listened to, to be taken seriously, and to be understood.

It is only through this kind of sharing that we come to *know ourselves.* Introspection of itself is helpless. We can confide all of our secrets to the docile pages of a personal diary, but we can know ourselves and experience the fullness of life only in the sharing with another person. Friendship becomes a great adventure. There is a continuously deeper discovery of myself and my friend as we continue to reveal new and deeper layers of ourselves. It opens my mind, widens my horizons, fills me with new awareness, deepens my feelings, gives my life meaning.

Yet the barriers are never permanently broken. Friendship and mutual self-revelation have a newness about them with each new day, because being a human person involves daily change and growth. You and I are growing, and our differences are becoming more apparent. We are not growing into the same person, but I am growing into my own person and you into yours. I discover in you other tastes and preferences, other feelings and hopes, other reactions to new experiences. I discover that this business of telling you who I am cannot be done once and for all. I must *continually* tell you who I am and you must *continually* tell me who you are, because both of us are continually evolving.

It may be that the very things that first attracted me to you now seem to work against communication. In the beginning, your sentiment seemed to balance off my more intellectual inclinations; your extroverted ways complemented my introversion; your realism counterbalanced my artistic intuition. It seemed like such an ideal friendship. We seemed like separate halves that needed each other to become one whole. But now, when I want you to share my intellectual

Fully human people are in deep and
meaningful contact with
the world outside of them.

They listen not only to themselves
but to the voices of their world.
The breadth of their own individual
experience is infinitely multiplied
through a sensitive empathy with others.
They suffer with the suffering,
rejoice with the joyful.
They are born again every springtime,
feel the impact of the great mysteries of
life: birth, growth, love, suffering, death.
Their hearts skip along with the "young
lovers,"and they know something
of the exhilaration that is in them.
They also know the ghetto's philosophy
of despair, the loneliness of suffering
without relief. The bell never tolls
without tolling in some strange way
for them.

vision, I am annoyed that you take no interest in my objective arguments of reason. Now, when I want to show you that you are not logical in your sentiment, it does not seem to matter at all to you. In the beginning we seemed to fit together so well. Now your desire to go out to others and my more introverted inclinations to seek solitude seem to be divisive.

Of course, our friendship can still be. We are standing within arms' reach of that which is most humanly rewarding and beautiful. We must not turn back now. We can still share all the things we once shared with such excitement, when first I told you who I was and you told me who you were. Only now our sharing will be deeper because we are deeper. If I will continue to hear you with the same sense of wonder and joy as I did in the beginning, and you will hear me in this way, our friendship will grow firmer and deeper roots. The tinsel of our first sharing will mellow into gold. We can and will be sure that there is no need to hide anything from each other. We will have shared everything.

I am continually experiencing the ever-growing, ever-new reality of you, and you are experiencing the reality of me. And through each other, we are together experiencing the reality of God, who once said that "it is not good for man to be alone."

your slightest look
easily will unclose me
though i have closed myself as fingers,
you open always petal by petal
myself as spring opens
(touching skillfully, mysteriously)
her first rose

e. e. cummings

5

Human Hiding Places: Methods of Ego-defense

Before proceeding to a catalog of various roles and games, it seems necessary to say something about the methods of ego-defense, which are always somehow involved in these roles and games. In brief, these ego-defenses are compensations cultivated to counterbalance and camouflage something else in us which we consider a defect or a handicap.

The great Alfred Adler first became interested in *compensation* as a psychological phenomenon when he noticed how human nature tends to make up for bodily deficiencies. One kidney takes over the function of two if one fails to function. The same thing is true of lungs. A bone fracture that heals properly makes the place of the fracture become stronger than normal.

It is also true that many famous people have developed some skill to an extraordinary degree precisely because they were trying to overcome some handicap. Glenn Cunningham, the first of the famous American mile runners, probably became such a great runner trying to strengthen his legs which were seriously crippled at age seven in a fire that almost took his life. Wilma Rudolph contracted polio as a small child and finally learned to walk without braces. She later began to run, and at the 1960 Olympics in Rome she became the first woman to receive three gold metals in track and field. There is also what is called "vicarious compensation," by which a person handicapped in one way learns to excel in another. Whistler, the famous painter, flunked out of West Point and forfeited his desires for a career in the military, but learned to excel as an artist by developing his talents in that field.

REACTION FORMATION

The "reaction formation," which we are considering here, is an overcompensation by exaggerating or overdeveloping certain conscious trends. It is developed as a defense against unconscious tendencies of an opposite and unapprovable character, which threaten to break into conscious recognition. Extremely dogmatic people, who are absolutely sure of everything, consciously cultivate this posture of certainty because of demoralizing doubts in their subconscious mind. Their self-image isn't strong enough to live with these doubts. People who are overly tender, to the point of exaggerated sentimentality, are usually suspected of assuming this attitude in compensation for harsh and cruel tendencies that have been repressed into the subconscious mind.

Prudishness, in an exaggerated form, is usually an overcompensation for repressed normal sexual desires with which the prude cannot live in comfort. The person who seems to exert an exaggerated concern for the health of an aged parent probably does so to compensate for the subconscious desire to be freed of responsibility for that parent by the death of the same.

Please note well that we cannot suspect every good inclination of being a psychological cover-up for opposite inclinations. The thing about reaction formation is that it is always an over-compensation, an exaggerated reaction. Compensatory attitudes are a leaning over backward to avoid tipping forward. This kind of compensation, once set in motion, always results in an exaggeration or excess. It is, consequently, only exaggerated behavior of any kind that is suspect of being compensatory "reaction formation." The dogmatist is never wrong. The prude is hyperchaste. The reformer-type, preachy and self-righteous, viciously hates sin and sinner alike without any recognition of normal human weakness.

It is socially fashionable
to ask: Who am I?
There is no little
"real self"
inside of me.
I am what I am committed to.

The conclusion is this: *Exaggerated behavior* in a person usually means *just the opposite* of what it implies. Very often we accuse dogmatists of pride and feel "called" to help them learn sweet humility. In fact, they are not at all sure of themselves, and the more we try to defeat them, to cultivate doubts in them and expose their errors, the more they have to compensate. Their dogmatism will probably become even more extreme and obnoxious.

DISPLACEMENT

A second ego-defense mechanism is called "displacement." It usually refers to the indirect expression of an impulse that the censoring conscience (Freud's *superego*) prohibits us from expressing directly. For example, a child may develop a seething hostility toward his or her parents. Our social programming usually will not allow direct expression of this hostility. I mean, you can't hate your own parents. So, not in touch with the hostility that the child felt forced to repress, he or she smashes public property, bullies younger children, or does something equally irrational. The apparent homicidal-minded boxing fan, who stands up at ringside and vociferously yells "Murder the bum!" as a helpless, senseless boxer is sinking to his knees, obviously harbors some subconscious hostility. The anger had to be repressed because the person just couldn't live with it or express it.

"Scapegoating" is a common form of displacement. We react with uncalled-for violence when
someone looks at us the wrong way, because
there is a hostility in us that we cannot express
directly. For some reason the person to whom we
would like to express hostility seems too
formidable to us. A man with a violent temper in
the office may well be expressing the hostility he
feels for his wife or for himself but cannot bring
himself to express it at home. Or the woman who
has been unjustly upbraided by her employer (of
whom she is afraid because her job is at stake)
may come home and take out her hostility on her
husband and children. Prudes, who cannot admit
to their sexual drives directly, will take great
interest in "scandals" of a sexual nature. Lonely,
isolated individuals, who cannot admit directly
to their need for love and affection, will profess
to be "madly in love" with someone else (whom
they do not really love at all).

A second meaning of "displacement" is the
device of disguising unpleasant realities to which
we cannot admit (and therefore repress) by
consciously stressing something else which is not
so embarrassing to the ego. We profess to worry
about some triviality to conceal some greater fear
to which we cannot honestly admit. Or let us say
that I am jealous of you, but I cannot really admit
it, not even to myself. So I "zero in" on some
trivial annoyance, like the quality of your voice. I
find it very grating. The husband and wife who

have come to despise each other, but cannot openly admit to the real sources of their mutual agony, usually bicker about trivialities with great vehemence.

The man whose mother dominated his father is usually programmed to treat his own wife as an inferior. However, he cannot admit to his resentment for his mother and her treatment of his father, or that he definitely wants his wife "under" him. So he will usually complain about small and inconsequential habits of hers. He will deny the value of her opinions and the wisdom of her actions. He will bitterly criticize her for the "stupid way" she plays cards.

PROJECTION

Another ego-defense mechanism is called "projection." All of us tend to disown things in ourselves and to "project" them into others. We try to rid ourselves of our own limitations by attributing them to someone else. Adam explained his sin to God by saying, "The woman tempted me." Eve ascribed the whole calamity to the serpent. It is also projection when we blame other things for our own failures, like the circumstances, the tools we had to work with, the position of the stars. We are tempted to ask, "Why don't you look where you're going?" when we bump into people.

It is a very common human inclination (projection) to dislike most in others what we cannot accept in ourselves. The real mystery of this projection is that we don't recognize these things in ourselves. They have been repressed. We can therefore strongly condemn in others what we cannot admit in ourselves. The stronger and the more exaggerated the dislike of anything or any quality is manifested, the more it might be suspected as projection.

When we get a bug on "hypocrisy," and often condemn it, and proclaim that it is widespread among the human race, it is most probable that we must repress all conscious recognition that we ourselves are hypocritical. Vain people, who can't admit to their own inclinations, suspect everybody of wanting attention and publicity. Ambitious men and women, who cannot honestly admit (and therefore repress) their own driving ambitions, usually feel that "everybody is out for No. 1; all that most people want is fame and money."

Then there are the paranoids (persecution complex victims) who project their own self-hatred into other people and feel that others don't like them. Prudes think that every attractive person of the opposite sex is making improper advances; they project their own concealed (repressed) longings into others. People with an uneasy conscience feel that others are suspicious of them, watching them. Very often, too, when someone puts a finger on a weakness in us, for example, being too temperamental, we counter by charging, "You're the one who is too temperamental!"

INTROJECTION

"Introjection" is the ego-defense by which we attribute to ourselves the good qualities of others. Introjection is prominent in what we call "hero worship." We identify with our heroes. Also, we identify our possessions with ourselves. We take great pride when someone praises our home, or we think that we are "big time" because we come from a famous city, belong to a well-known fraternity, or have traveled to many places. Many women identify with the tragic heroines of soap-opera programs on television. A Manhattan psychiatrist noticed that very many of his women patients had relapses after becoming addicted to these shows. They identified with all the unhappiness of the suffering characters in these melodramas. This kind of identification provides an easy access into a world of fantasy and provides romance in our lives. However, often the result of this ego-defense is neither very profitable nor very consoling.

RATIONALIZATION

The most common form of ego-defense is "rationalization." As a technique for self-justification, it is hard to beat. We find some reason for our action that justifies it. We "think" (rationalize) our way to a preordained conclusion. Very often there are two reasons for everything we do: the alleged good reason and the real reason. Rationalization not only results in self-deceit but eventually corrupts all sense of integrity (wholeness). We rationalize our failures; we find justification for our actions; we reconcile our ideals and deeds; we make our emotional preferences our rational conclusions. I say that I drink beer because it has malt in it. The real reason is that I like it; it helps me feel uninhibited and secure with others.

As with all ego-defense mechanisms, there is always something that I cannot admit in myself, something that I would like to do which appears wrong, or something that would make me feel better if only I could just believe it. Rationalization is the bridge that makes my wishes the facts. It is the use of intelligence to deny the truth; it makes us dishonest with ourselves. And if we cannot be honest with ourselves, we certainly cannot be honest with anyone else. Rationalization consequently sabotages all human authenticity. It disintegrates and fragments the personality.

Insincerity, as an interior state of mind, is a psychological impossibility. I can't tell myself that I do and don't believe something at the same

To understand people,
I must try to hear
what they are <u>not</u> saying,
what they perhaps
will never be able to say.

time. Choosing evil as evil is also a psychological impossibility, because the will can only choose the (apparent) good. Consequently, to deny the truth I cannot admit, and to do the deed I cannot approve, I must necessarily rationalize until the truth is no longer true and the evil becomes good.

Did you ever ask yourself the surprisingly difficult question: How does one choose evil? How do we commit sin? The will can choose, by its very nature, only that which is somehow good. I am personally convinced that the exercise or use of free will in a given situation of guilt is this: The will, desirous of some evil that has good aspects (if I steal your money, I will be rich), forces the intellect to concentrate on the good to be acquired in the evil act. The will impels the mind to turn away from the recognition of evil. And so the intellect must rationalize that which was originally recognized as evil. While I am doing something wrong (in the act of doing it), I cannot be squarely facing its evil aspect; I must somehow be thinking of it as good and right. Consequently, free will seems to be exercised in the act of coercing the intellect to rationalize rather than in the execution of the act itself.

CAUTION: HUMAN BEINGS

In all of these ego-defense mechanisms, please notice that there is something that people who operate the mechanism have felt the necessity of repressing. They cannot live with some realization. In one way or another, they keep their psychological pieces intact by some form of self-deception. They just couldn't live comfortably with the truth, so they repressed it.

Therefore, and this is extremely important, the vocation of putting people straight, of tearing off their masks, of forcing them to face the repressed truth, is a highly dangerous and destructive calling. Eric Berne warns against disillusioning people about their "games." It may be that they just can't take it. They sought out some role, began playing some game, took to wearing some mask, precisely because this would make life livable and tolerable.

So we must be very careful, extremely careful in fact, that we do not assume the vocation of acquainting others with their delusions. We are all tempted to unmask others, to smash their defenses, to leave them naked and blinking in the light of the illumination provided by our exposé. It could be tragic in its results. If the psychological pieces come unglued, who will pick them up and put poor Humpty Dumpty Human Being together again? Will you? Can you?

THE GREATEST KINDNESS: THE TRUTH

All that has been said in these pages would urge us to be open and truthful about ourselves, our thoughts and emotions. It has urged us to be honest with ourselves and with others. Nothing is taken back here. But it is absolutely necessary to realize that nothing in these pages asks me or justifies me in becoming a judge of others. I can tell you who I am, report my emotions to you with candor and honesty, and this is the greatest kindness I can extend to myself and to you. Even if my thoughts and emotions are not pleasing to you, it remains the greatest kindness to reveal myself openly and honestly. Insofar as I am able, I will try to be honest with myself and communicate myself honestly to you.

It is another thing to set myself up as judge of your delusions. This is playing God. I must not try to be the guarantor of your integrity and honesty: that is your work. I can only hope that my honesty with and about myself will empower you to be honest with and about yourself. If I can face and tell you my faults and vanities, my hostilities and fears, my secrets and my shames, perhaps you will be able to admit to your own and confide them to me, if and when you wish.

It is a two-way street. If you will be honest with me, report your triumphs and tragedies, agonies and ecstasies to me, it will help me to face my own. You will help me to become a real person. I need your openness and honesty; you need mine. Will you help me? I promise that I will try to help you. I will try to tell you who I really am.

"It costs so much to be a full human being that there are very few who have the enlightenment, or the courage, to pay the price. . . . One has to abandon altogether the search for security, and reach out to the risk of living with both arms. One has to embrace the world like a lover. One has to accept pain as a condition of existence. One has to count doubt and darkness as the cost of knowing. One needs a will stubborn in conflict, but apt always to total acceptance of every consequence of living and dying."

Morris L. West
in *The Shoes of the Fisherman*

NO ONE ELSE CAN
DECIDE HOW
YOU ARE GOING
TO ACT.

YOU MUST MARCH
TO YOUR
OWN DRUMS.

6

Catalog of Games and Roles

There is no logical order in this partial listing of the roles and games that are very common patterns in human relations. Nor are there any restrictions as to sex or age. Anyone can play one or more of these games. The ones you and I become proficient at or employ most often will depend upon our "programming" and needs.

These games have one thing in common, no matter how different they may seem; they mask and distort the truth about the one most important thing that I could share with you: myself. I must ask myself: Which of these games do I play? What am I seeking? What am I hiding? What am I trying to win?

ALL HEART

What Freud called "reaction formation" is thought to be responsible for the excessively tender and sentimental concern of these people. It is a subconscious compensation for their sadistic (cruel) tendencies. We all have cruel inclinations at times, but these people are particularly horrified by theirs.

The one thing about compensation is that once it is set in motion, it nearly always results in overcompensation. Somehow their programming has rendered these people unable to be in touch with themselves. "All Hearters" just can't admit to their hostile inclinations, and they spend most of their energy denying the truth they cannot admit. These people are likely to be excessively tender to pets, overindulgent with children, excessively demonstrative in showing affection and tenderness.

"All heart" people follow the heart in all matters, to the point that others wonder if the head is operative at all. The heart decides everything. They can show all kinds of soft emotions, but will rarely if ever report harsher emotions precisely because they are afraid of such emotions and must keep them repressed. Women are more inclined to this "reaction formation" because our society programs them to believe that hostile or cruel emotions are particularly horrifying in a woman.

ALWAYS RIGHT

These people rarely if ever lose an argument. Even when the evidence begins to stack up against them, they can salvage respect for their position. They do not listen well and give the appearance of expecting to learn little if anything from others. Basically, their self-esteem is threatened. Their dogmatism, like excessive tenderness, is a result of reaction formation. They act doubly certain in order to guard against demoralizing doubts that stir in their subconscious and tend to undermine their certainty. Their behavior indicates the opposite of what seems to be true. They have deep, if subconscious, doubts about themselves and their opinions.

BODY BEAUTIFUL, THE

Usually physical vanity is a compensation for a gnawing sense of inferiority as a person. The beautiful or handsome people who play this game keep staring into the mirror on the wall and into the mirror of the eyes of others (or in any shiny surface), looking for their own reflection. They do this because they cannot find any deeper consolations. There is a sadness that hangs over vanity of this sort. Life is obviously over at thirty-five. In the extreme, these people identify their person with their body. They would answer the question "What are you?" with the response "I'm good-looking." And if they could be honest and open, they would add: ". . . nothing more, just good-looking."

BRAGGART, THE

This game is a childish attempt to assert one's superiority. It is one of the various manifestations of arrested emotional development. The braggart is usually a bully, too, if the situation allows. Braggarts want to dominate others, either by words or, if they feel sure of themselves, by physical strength. The indication is lack of self-esteem. They want to feel important and discover nothing in themselves that satisfies this need. We sometimes are tempted to ask them: "Are you trying to convince us or yourself?" The answer is: both.

The games we play always follow the program.

CLOWN, THE

Compulsive clowns are, like most of us, seeking some sort of recognition and attention. The sadness is that they think they can gain notice only by playing the fool for others. Deeper than this, it may be that they identify with their act and try to escape reality by taking nothing seriously. Clowning is sometimes an escape device. Clowns don't know how to handle themselves in a serious situation or how to react to sorrow, so they adopt an attitude of irresponsible gaiety. In dealing with others, their clowning serves as an adequate defensive mask (like the mask of the circus clown) to prevent others from knowing who they really are. They would rather laugh and joke than face the grim realities of life. They would rather put their act on the stage than lay their person on the line.

COMPETITOR, THE

Our American culture has programmed most of us to accept competition as a part of some divine plan. Competitors must win at whatever they do. They make everything a "win-lose" situation. They don't discuss; they debate. The triumphs that they seek, so often at the expense of others ("Nice guys finish last!"), may be the outgrowth of emotional deprivation or lack of approval earlier in life. The resultant insecurity causes them to question their worth, and they are consistently trying to prove this worth in competition and rivalry. Their need for recognition intensifies the drive to "get ahead." Competitors feel hostility toward anyone they feel is standing in their way or surpassing them. Sooner or later, they will be overcome by a sense of failure since the appetite for victory becomes increasingly voracious. They have, in the end, failed to prove their superiority and end up in frustration. Basically, the problem is that they cannot distinguish between themselves as persons and their accomplishments, between being and having. (See "Inferior and Guilty," below.)

CONFORMIST, THE

This game is called "peace at any price," and the price is surrender of all individuality to others. It usually begins with domineering authority and guilt feelings. Conformists won't or can't risk the nonacceptance of others. They are often praised for their willingness to "go along," but they pay a high price in repressed emotions for the pittances of praise that they receive. Their unwillingness to disagree with the established or fashionable opinion renders them an anonymity to others. They usually develop some sort of psycho-somatic symptoms because their subconscious mind eventually becomes overloaded with all that they have had to repress in order to be "the good guy/gal who goes along with anything." (See "Inferior and Guilty," below.)

CRANK, THE

The neurotic tendency that characterizes the crank is a low frustration tolerance. Cranks don't do very well in situations of strain and stress. Usually their programming, like that of competitors, involves early emotional deprivation, resulting in feelings of hostility. Cranks feel deprived of personal security. They feel less sure of themselves when things go wrong and nurse a long list of pet peeves, which they publish for others from time to time. Those in their vicinity know that any one of these can send them into orbit, and this is the game aspect. Others are warned in various ways that they must not frustrate cranks.

CYNIC, THE

The excessive expectations of life often collapse and result in the cynic game. People who are programmed to think that the universe should be tailored to their comfort often suffer a painful collision with reality. At this point, they strike back with their cynicism. Basically, cynics are demoralized unrealists. Things have failed to turn out the way they wanted them, and so cynics take their pains of disillusion out on everyone. You can't trust anyone. The whole system is corrupt. As long as they persist in their role as cynic, they won't have to take an honest look at themselves and their world nor go through the pains of adjustment to reality. Their facile wit is usually a symptom of submerged antagonism; they have not found life as they wanted it. They have never learned empathy or tolerance, and they have never experienced a true affection for others. Consequently, they are very lonely people behind their sardonic "smirks."

DELUDED BY GRANDEUR

This game usually grows out of a mistaken sense of personal importance. Players have been programmed to portray to others a sense of importance. They are name-droppers and tend to be "I-centered" in conversation. Like braggarts, these people play a game of compensation for inadequate self-esteem. There is always some effort to protect the wounded ego from further humiliation. They are attracted to dramatic deeds—a grandstander. They resent insignificance. They usually dream about some magnificent memento by which the world will remember them when they are gone. The delusional system tries to afford them a sense of importance denied in reality. Obviously, it is difficult to be honest with them about themselves.

DOMINATOR, THE

This game is often characterized by an
exaggerated desire to control the lives of others
as well as their thought processes. Like most
people who exaggerate their importance or
wisdom, dominators are bothered by subconscious feelings of inadequacy. It is strange
that very often such people are so determined to
feel adequate that they are distracted from the
fact of their domineering ways. They usually
explain their domination as necessary, reasonable, and justifiable. Dominators are very often
troubled by feelings of hostility. These feelings,
which they repress, find expression in selfishness
and thoughtlessness in dealing with those they
are supposed to love.

It is a law of human life,
as certain as gravity
To live fully, we must
learn to use things and love
people... not love things
and use people.

DREAMER, THE

This game is clearly an "escape" game. Dreamers are intent upon flight from reality. They achieve great things in a fantasy world, where they receive recognition and honor. Very often their dreams are a substitute for achievement and represent some kind of compensation for their lack of success with and in the real world. Dreamers usually like movies and stories because such flights of fancy stoke their imaginations with new settings and materials for future reveries. Eventually, they create a comfortable world in which they can become "somebody." Very often dreamers have ambitioned more than their abilities could reach, and they have to compensate themselves in fantasy for their disappointment in reality. This is sometimes called "neurotic fiction." Dreamers have an alibi to explain every actual failure. They can't bring their ambitions into line with their abilities. What they need most is the courage to accept themselves as they are.

DRINKER, THE PROBLEM,
AND DOPE ADDICT, THE

The dreamer escapes from reality on the magic rug of fantasy; the drinker tries the route of narcosis. Those who are most vulnerable to stress are usually most in need of an escape. Addiction to drink or narcotic drugs is usually found in those who react poorly to deprivation, who are most easily overcome by defeat, and who are most self-conscious and ill at ease with others. This is not to deny, of course, that addiction is or can be genetic.

The momentary release and the experience of freedom, enjoyed under the sedation of excessive drink or dope, are usually followed by heightened anxiety and deeper depression when the haze clears. This, of course, brings on further need of sedation to deaden anxiety, the sense of guilt, and depression. Drinking and dope as a "way out" are definitely limited in their capacity to do the job. Leaving reality, while the narcosis lasts, only makes it more difficult to return to reality and to live with it. The name of the game is a "crutch" for sociability, self-expression, the concealment of embarrassment, and the possibility of forgetting one's troubles.

FLIRT, THE

The "flirting game" is basically an attempt to gain for the ego some kind of recognition. It is usually played by those who have never cultivated any real emotional depth. Only deeper relationships can result in security for the ego. Such relationships effect this security by promoting better self-knowledge and self-acceptance. Flirts, however, refuse to take the gamble of these more self-revealing relationships; they keep running.

Flirting is possible only when the emotions are trivial and superficial, though no one wants to admit this about his or her emotions. Stable and deeper human relationships can never be built on such emotions. The flirting game also assumes that when one tires of one conquest, he or she can move on to another. This is, of course, a rather selfish kind of sport, in which there are many injuries. No one wants to admit to being a flirt (or to playing any one of these games), but it is the first step to real emotional growth when we admit the tendency in order to hold it in some kind of check.

In all of these games, we must ask ourselves what it is that we really want, why we want it (which will always tell us something about ourselves), and why it would be better to give up our game. While flirting can bring some passing gratification to the ego, little fleeting infatuations often complicate life considerably. They lead us into subterfuges, the invention of excuses, deceits, and preoccupation with self. Sexual and emotional development starts with narcissism (self-fascination) in the child, but with growth as a person, one should become more and more capable of altruism (love of others). Flirts have been somehow fixated in an adolescent, self-centered state, and their growth has been arrested.

FRAGILE—HANDLE WITH CARE

Fragile people give many advance signals to others that they are delicate and need to be handled with great caution. Others are reluctant to confront people who have ready-to-go tear ducts and are capable of instant depressions. No one wants to deliver bad news to them, to ask them to accept responsibility (it is much easier to take it on yourself), or to offer them honest criticism. Fundamentally, this game grows out of a neurotic feeling of inability to cope with life. Fragility players exhibit a great sensitivity, too, to the estimate of others. Their ego is tender; remarks or gestures are often misinterpreted. Fragile people are hypersensitive precisely because they place very little value on themselves. This, however, will usually not be clear to themselves or to most others.

Fragility represents a regression to childhood, to a state of need and helplessness. If the game is played successfully, the players will never have to grow up or face the blood, sweat, and tears of real life. Fragile people express with their sudden tears and traumas what children say with their tantrums and screaming. The demand is for the preferential treatment children so often require.

GOSSIP, THE

Participants in the gossip game, like most game players, are in there for sensitive, personal stakes. Unable to make the full use of their own abilities, and being defeatists at heart and sorry for themselves because they cannot measure up to their own ego ideal, they choose to elevate their own self-esteem by undermining the esteem of others. Adler calls it the "derogatory critique." It is much easier to tear down others than to lift one's self up by achievement. Superiority and inferiority being relative terms, lowering others seems to raise one's own status.

Benjamin Franklin once said that if you want to know someone's faults, praise the person to his or her peers. Gossiping can also be a salve for sensitive guilt feelings. We like to recite the misdeeds of others so we won't have to feel so bad about our own misdeeds. This accounts for our eagerness to learn the latest scandals from newspapers, magazines, and so on. The media readily oblige and comfort the gossip. After reading about vicious murders, for example, our own sarcasm and anger do not seem to be such terrible evils. The gain of the game: elevation of self and greater ease in living with one's regrets.

HEDONIST, THE

"My pleasure before all" type people try to hide their emotional immaturity under various euphemisms ("just for 'kicks!'"), but the immaturity surfaces quickly in relationships. It is characteristic of the child and the neurotic (the emotional child) that they must have their pleasure and have it immediately. They will not inhibit for long any impulse to indulge themselves. They are not able to suspend their grasping for pleasure even long enough to look at the implications of their actions.

The inability to postpone pleasure eventually leads hedonists to seek their pleasure in all things, at anyone's expense. When the stimulus of pleasure-to-be-had is registered, the response is automatic. Habits of hedonism are very often acquired as compensatory for the difficult aspects of life. "I was overlooked or misunderstood, so now I can overeat or masturbate." (Such logic is almost never examined consciously.)

I . . . I . . . I

It is almost a universal law that the extent of
egocentrism in any person is proportionate to the
amount of pain in him or her. It is a question of
attention. We cannot give a great deal of
attention to ourselves and to others simultaneously. We have only a limited amount of
attention that we can confer. The destructive or
diminishing part of pain is that it magnetizes
attention to ourselves and to the area of our pain.
Those who are suffering anything from a
toothache to the loneliness of old age tend to
egocentrism. Preoccupation with self often
evolves into hypochondria (overconcern with
health) or paranoia (persecution complex).

People cannot fashion themselves to be the
center of the universe and then live comfortably
with the fact that others do not accept them as
such. Whatever pains our past programming has
left in us (guilt, inferiority, anxiety, and so on),
these pains will inevitably lead us into all the
pitfalls of egocentrism. Egocentrics do not mind
what the conversation is about as long as it is
about them. Eventually, they will fall into
emotional depression because living in such a
restricted world is living in a prison. They will
suffer even more than the others who must live
or work with them.

INDECISIVE AND UNCERTAIN

It has been said that the greatest mistake a person can make is to be afraid of making mistakes. Indecision and uncertainty are ways of avoiding mistakes and responsibility. If no decision is made, nothing can go wrong. The inclination to avoid decisions is sometimes manifested by dragging out as long as possible the ones we actually must make. The only real mistake is not to learn from our mistakes.

The basic problem here is self-esteem and the protection of self-esteem. People who are indecisive fear that they will lose respect if their decision turns out to be wrong. Only little people, someone has said, are never wrong. We learn more from our mistakes than from our successes. But indecisive people are so focused on their own egos and personal value that they do not see the validity of all these truths. The name of the game is safety and self-protection; the motto: Nothing attempted, nothing lost.

Very often, too, indecisiveness results in people who have been programmed by multitudinous (and sometimes contradictory) instructions and moralizing, or who have been reproached and embarrassed for past mistakes. Finally, indecisiveness can result in people who attempt to support more emotionally burdening problems than they can solve. They usually become rattled and can solve none of them.

INFERIOR AND GUILTY

Psychoanalytic literature distinguishes between inferiority feelings and guilt feelings, though both are manifestations of conflict between the actual self and the ideal self. The inner struggle is between what one actually is and what one would like to be, between what one actually does or feels and what one thinks one should do or feel. The fundamental difference is that in *inferiority* feelings, there is a recognition of weakness and inadequacy. People who suffer from inferiority feelings usually provoke competition and aggression. They seek to eradicate their feelings of inferiority by showing their superiority in some form of rivalry. *Guilt* feelings, on the contrary, can be verbalized: "I am not much good. Most of what I want to do (my desires) and have done (my deeds) seem mean and evil. I really deserve contempt and punishment for my failures." Guilt feelings inhibit the competitive spirit. They are reactions to the hostile and aggressive impulses that one feels within the self.

To get rid of such guilt feelings, we usually try to renounce competition, while inferiority feelings usually invite us to a competitive attitude. Guilt feelings usually persuade us to subordination; they usually surface in self-depreciation and even self-punishment. People generally try to free themselves from inferiority feelings by ambition and competition, by trying to get revenge or the upper hand. The extrication from guilt feelings is usually attempted through submission and the avoidance of any hostile or aggressive behavior. Inferiority feelings tend to produce *rebels;* guilt feelings tend to produce *conformists* with modest and submissive ways.

Ambition and competition remain restricted to the imagination and the phantasy life of guilt-ridden people. They are usually retiring, nonconspicuous types, who assiduously avoid contradictions. They have a tendency to minimize their own abilities. After behaving in a way that their consciences cannot approve, the people with guilt feelings usually resolve that they will never again do the same thing. People with inferiority feelings more often react by asking, "Why not? Why not do these things? I'm not going to give in to external or interior pressures on my conduct!" (See Franz Alexander, *Fundamentals of Psychoanalysis,* 1964.)

INFLAMMABLE—
HANDLE WITH CAUTION

It is hard for most of us to believe this, but people who have "short fuses" and give forth loud noises are frequently reacting to some supposed grievance. But the supposed grievance is not what is really bothering them. As they cannot discuss openly the real source of anger, they are simply letting off steam and their explosions can rarely be taken at face value. What is smoldering in their subconscious is a buried hostility. People are usually much more hostile than they realize. We usually repress our real resentment because our society has conditioned us to believe that hostility is unbecoming in socialized, civilized human beings.

Karl Menninger, in *Love Against Hate,* describes the chain reaction of parents with hidden hostilities frustrating their children and building up in them more repressed hostilities. Then the children grow up into frustrated parents who in turn frustrate themselves and their children. More hostilities! The first step in breaking this chain reaction, Menninger submits, is *to recognize the sources and extent of our aggression and hostility,* of which we are very often unconscious. They are hidden (repressed) because we are led to feel that we can't be angry (especially at our own parents, who have "done so much" for us). After recognizing our true source of hostility, we should try to neutralize these recognized resentments by deepening our understanding or by releasing them in nondestructive ways (athletic competition). It also helps to talk them out. Meanwhile we should be aware that we are often most inflammable with those we love because it is usually against them that we bear the most hostility, since our dealings with them have been longer and more intense.

INTELLECT, THE—
ALIAS THE EGGHEAD

Our social programming often makes it much easier for us to be intellectual and to scorn fuller human reactions, especially insofar as they are emotional. Usually, the role of the "intellect" is assumed by people who are afraid of their emotions or are uncomfortable with them for one reason or another. Perhaps they were programmed not to show them, to think that sentiment was weakness. Sometimes, too, people find themselves unable to relate easily with others, to enjoy friendship, and so they resort to their pose of intellectualism.

The ivory tower of such intellectualism is also a common refuge from the competition involved in human relations. In themselves the learning processes are not as threatening to most of us as are other people. The classroom is preferable to the cold, cruel world we have been taught to fear. More timid souls would rather read about life than try to live. Library stacks can be a retreat from the headaches of daily living, and they can provide the solace of isolation and the prestige of being a scholar. They can also be an escape from social responsibilities.

People programmed for isolation are usually more inclined to scholarly work than to meaningful relations with others. Rather than admit that they are hermits, shut off from society, the players of this game insist that they are dedicated to higher learning. Incidentally, this game frees us from social responsibilities, organizations, committees, paying dues, and making friends. (Please note: This is definitely not intended as an indictment of scholars. The true scholar makes a valuable contribution to society, but no one is called to be a scholar at the expense of being a truly human being, a fully functioning person.)

LONER, THE

There is another escape pattern, or game, which is very much like the ivory tower of intellectualism described above; it is the isolation game. Loners shut themselves off from others, live alone, and try to convince themselves that they like it this way. By entering this kind of solitary confinement, they succeed in evading all the most difficult challenges of human life and society. Loners assume the attitude of smugness; they smirk at organizations, laugh at the poor "joiners," whom they look upon with a pretended attitude of superiority and condescension. They keep telling themselves that they are above this sort of nonsense.

Neurotics are torn between their inner need to push toward and pull away from people. Loners are neurotics who opt in favor of the pulling away from people. They retreat, and since they cannot relate easily to others, they play their game to avoid failures in human relationships. The ultimate effects are conditioned by what is inside of loners, the reasons for their withdrawal tendencies. If it is hostility that is predominant, it could eventually erupt into violence, as with Lee Harvey Oswald. If it is anxiety, it could result in compulsive-obsessive neurotic habits (for example, repeatedly washing hands). If it is paranoia, it will deepen the gulf between themselves and the rest of the human race. The escapist pattern always ends in some kind of lonely tragedy.

MARTYR, THE

The persecution complex (paranoia) of "the
martyr" is an emotional disorder characterized
by many false suspicious beliefs. Paranoid trends
are observed in one kind of schizophrenia, a
mental disorder in which the sick person is
separated from reality. In neurotic paranoiacs the
outstanding characteristic is suspicion. They
suffer from what psychologists call "delusions of
reference." Such delusions convince paranoiacs
that everyone is talking about them, that it rains
on the day of their parade because God is
holding something against them personally, and
so on. It is a feeling of being abused.

It should be said that something of this feeling
is in all of us at times; very normal people at
times suffer from delusions. In the normal
person, however, these delusions are not so
irrational, so extreme, or so crippling. Paranoiacs
often find themselves in the same predicament as
liars, who must invent stories to justify their mis-
representation of the facts. Eventually these
delusions become systematized, and paranoid
individuals tend to hang on to them in spite of all
the apparent inconsistencies.

The persecutory delusions usually grow out of
an inferiority complex. Individuals with such
delusions hate their own inadequacy and project
their thinking into the minds of others; they

conclude that others hate them too. They cannot establish satisfactory relationships with others and are generally oversensitive. Their egos are very tender. In feeling rejected by others, they gradually withdraw into themselves and become increasingly estranged and alienated from them. Then they are unable to check their imagined interpretations of the facts that they are misjudging. They feel that they were not suspicious enough of other people, and that others took advantage of them. Now they are too suspicious and feel that they cannot trust anyone.

Normal social relations are impossible to sustain with such an attitude of mind. All of us are somewhat suspicious. The opposite of this normal awareness would be gullibility or naiveté. Paranoiacs have gone much too far. They implement their game by blaming other people for their mistakes. This habit, called "passing the buck," is a normal part of the paranoid delusion. Paranoiacs cannot evaluate properly their own responsibility as distinguishable from the role of others in causing their problems. Their own self-deceptions seem absolutely clear and true to them.

The martyr complex grows out of an unstable self-evaluation and a failure to maintain a satisfactory degree of faith in others. Its expression is to blame others for our unhappiness. Paranoiacs are also aware of their own hostile feelings, but rationalize them with their delusions. Their desire is to attack others because they feel persecuted. Delusions in this way are simply attempts to create an imaginary situation in which the symptoms experienced within can appear rational and acceptable. Paranoiacs' capacity for rationalization is often remarkable, and sometimes they succeed in convincing others of the rationality of their behavior.

MESSIAH, THE

This game calls for a little imagination (and a subconscious need to feel important). Messiahs fancy themselves saviors of the human race. It could well be a reaction formation to the fear of insignificance. They think of themselves as the "helper" and others as the "helped" in almost all of their relationships. Instead of urging others to use their own strength and wisdom, messiahs dutifully lend out theirs. They relate to very few people as equals. If people are attracted to messiahs because of their good qualities that are not completely submerged by their assumed role, it will be easier for these people if they have a problem or need. It will be an admission ticket.

The gain of the game is a rather large, expansive feeling and a long, well-memorized list of those who have been helped. Basically, messiahs have inferiority feelings and seek to free themselves from these by dominating others emotionally.

When I repress my emotions, my stomach keeps score.

MOMMY, THE

The overprotective mother (or, more rarely, a father) plays a very harmful game. Mommies usually produce little monsters, utterly selfish people who demand their own way in everything. Such children are tragically unprepared for a world that is simply unwilling to baby them and accede to their every whim. Psychological studies done on soldiers in wartime show that those who "crack up" most often and most severely are the products of overprotective mothers. The most often requested song of soldiers, when Bing Crosby visited the South Pacific troops in World War II, was Brahm's "Lullaby."

This game is not motivated by a genuine, healthy, and mature love. There are three possible causes: (1) *Neurotic anxiety.* The insecure mother is fearful that her children may suffer some harm unless she does everything for them. This fear is usually transmitted to her children. Such a mother does not enjoy her children and only worries about them. (2) *Hostility.* Strange as this may seem, maternal overprotection is sometimes an overcompensation (reaction formation) for a subconscious hostility toward her children. She atones for her personal dislike of her children by conscientious devotion to them. (3) *Frustrated marital relations.* The mother who is unhappy with her husband frequently pours her pent-up feelings of affection on her children. Under such circumstances the children bear the brunt of the unsatisfied love life of the mother. (See David Levy, *Maternal Overprotection* [Columbia University Press, 1966].)

PEACE AT ANY PRICE

(See "Inferior and Guilty.")

PONCE DE LEON

This is the game of people who are aging and simply cannot adjust to the fact. Frequently, middle-aged people feel that they are losing their physical attractiveness. Baldness, the middle-age spread, wrinkles around the neck—all symbolize declining prestige among the opposite sex. To compensate for this deterioration of age, those who have never developed as true persons and who have never developed deeper emotional ties with others usually begin looking for a young lover. In addition to the physical evidence, which shows in the mirror, these people also compensate for an emotional "slump," which is evidenced in loss of ambition, fatigue, and more frequent fits of depression. Biologically, this can be due to insufficient hormone production.

The tragedy of this game is that these people have suffered emotional arrest and have never learned to relate meaningfully as persons; they have very little left for consolation in middle age. They have prized their "sex appeal" and fear that it is waning. Sadly, they try to hide their double chins, varicose veins, the wrinkles, gray hair, and so on. They keep trying to think and act young. Sex appeal has never been and could never be the key to the finer things in life. It certainly does not sustain us in the process of aging.

POOR MOUTH, THE

This game is played by those who appear to be self-depreciating. The players talk themselves down, perhaps in search of reassurances that assuage their "guilt feelings." (See also "Inferior and Guilty.")

POUTER, THE

The pouting game is played by emotional children. Pouters cannot sit down and openly discuss interpersonal problems, usually because their position or grievance is irrational and they secretly know it. They can scourge others emotionally by their silence, sad looks, and so on, without having to tell these people what is bothering them. They can sulk without accepting the responsibility of having to explain why they are acting this way. A full explanation might sound so silly that they know (peripherally) that the other person might even laugh. However, they can derive their needed satisfaction and indulge their own self-pity without having to work out difficult situations through communication. (See also "Fragile—Handle with Care.")

PREJUDICE AND BIGOTRY

This game is the outgrowth of a social neurosis that flourishes chiefly among the insecure. Prejudiced people need some kind of vent for their emotional hostilities. The personal development of the chosen scapegoat in this situation will certainly not be helped if he or she is abused in this way. Gordon Allport, in *The Nature of Prejudice*, suggests that prejudice arises from our anxieties. We feel insecure, and so we form around us an in-group as a kind of buffer of protection. Those outside of my in-group are thought to be a threat and menace. I lash out at them because I am somehow threatened by them. I cannot logically suggest why (though many reasons are adduced), but anyone who is not in my in-group is necessarily a threat to me if I am highly anxious and insecure.

Prejudice is an emotional delusion. Still, wherever it exists, it is never recognized as such by those who are afflicted by it. Bigots will inevitably try to explain their prejudice in intellectual terms. They could hardly admit the irrationality of their position. But the very term *prejudice* means a premature judgment, a judgment made before all the evidence is considered.

Society very often helps us with the work of the rationalization needed to explain our prejudices;

most bigots therefore don't have to work out their own rationalized, logical explanations. They can just recite well-rehearsed lines.

PROCRASTINATOR, THE

The "mañana" game attempts to evade reality by postponing the things that should be done—that should be done here and now. Procrastinators have to deceive themselves by unrealistic assurances, like, "I'll cut down on my smoking as soon as I can go on a vacation." "I'll start exercising when the weather gets better." "I'll start going to church again when I settle down and have my own family and children." Escaping into vague and unrealistic tomorrows is only one of the many varieties of evasion of reality that we commonly seek. (See "Indecisive and Uncertain.")

RESENTFULLY YOURS

When born-loser types look for a scapegoat for their own failure, they very often blame someone or something else: the establishment, life, the breaks. They resent the success and happiness of others because their own lives, by comparison, are unhappy. They have been somehow deprived. We are all tempted to make our own failures understandable by explaining them in terms of something other than our own inadequacies. Unfair treatment by others, injustice, the conspiracy of circumstances, and so on, make it easier for us to face our failures.

Resenters use up all their energies resenting, and therefore they usually accomplish very little. Sometimes it seems that the most vicious critics of anything (national government, school, church) are very often the ones that do nothing for the institutions they criticize so vocally. Resentful people are forever trying to bring their case before the court of life, hoping that the jury of others will acquit them of their failures.

Resentment comes from the Latin *resentire* ("to feel all over again"). Resenters are always rehearsing and rehashing the past. They insist on reliving past battles they cannot win, and they often persist in this game for a lifetime. Resentment becomes an emotional habit. No one's feelings are caused by others. Our feelings are caused by our own emotional response, our own choices and reactions. Resenters are reactors, not actors, and eventually, when they realize this, they are left with no vestiges of self-respect. They have spent their lives employing a failure mechanism, and they somehow know it. Resentment is a cop-out.

SEX BOMB AND
PREDATORY MALE, THE

Barring the sick condition of the nymphomaniac
who is obsessed with sex, most girls who play
the "sex bomb" game do so not because they
really enjoy genital sexuality or because they are
"highly sexed." It is rather because they feel they
have nothing else to offer but a provocative
body. They want to gain male attention, and they
desire to be popular. The ruse of this game
usually pays off, but the emotionally arrested
males it attracts are always very regrettable
conquests. Besides this sad motive of reaching
out for affection and attention, sometimes the
"sex bomb" is trying to reject her parents, to spite
them.

   "The predatory male" is usually an ego-hunter,
looking for some new trophy of conquest. His
inferiority feelings (see "Inferior and Guilty") are
deep, and he wants to compensate for them by
trying to make conquests of the opposite sex.
Sometimes, successful "ladies' men" are merely
neurotics who are industriously engaged in an
attempt to cover up their personal insecurity.
They are more to be pitied than censored.

   The sadness of both "sex bomb" and
"predatory male" is that they are seeking some
kind of human intimacy or nearness. Because
personal closeness takes a long time and

demands much honesty (gut-level communication), and because these people feel totally
inadequate to pay this price of true personal
intimacy, they substitute physical for personal
intimacy. They are not equipped, they feel, to do
any better. People are not attracted to the useless
side of life, Alfred Adler says in his book *What
Life Should Mean to You*, unless they fear that they
will be defeated if they remain on the useful side.
Those who play this game are usually so
emotionally undeveloped that the Don Juan
pattern claims them for life. They are unable to
confer their love lastingly on anyone, if, indeed,
they are capable of love at all.

STRONG, SILENT TYPE, THE,
VS. WILLING AND WORDY

There are two ways to keep from communicating
yourself to others, and because of various fears,
most of us are reluctant to let others know who
we really are. The two very effective techniques
to prevent communication are (1) to say very
little. People may think that you are profound if
you don't open your mouth. An old saw says
that "still waters run deep." The other way is (2)
to say so much that no one can possibly sort it all
out and figure out anything about you. You can't
say a great deal, using this buckshot technique of
obscurity, without giving a lot of contradictory
indications. No one can possibly accuse you of
not doing your part to communicate. Only the
sharper members of the group will realize that
they don't know what the devil you've been
talking about.

SUFFERING IS THE
SPICE (PRICE) OF LIFE

Some neurotics have been so conditioned that
they feel guilty for enjoying anything in life. As
Abraham Lincoln once said, "People are about as
happy as they decide that they are going to be."
This masochistic game calls for renewed penance
for every pleasure. These people rarely spend
money on frivolous things; they do not really
enjoy an evening if the price of admission is high.
They tend to get involved in love situations that
are hopeless and become infatuated by someone
who is totally beyond their reach. If they do catch
themselves having a good time, they will devise,
like a contrite sinner, some manner of punishing
themselves for it. Material gains seem futile and
meaningless, and such sufferers rarely realize
that the deficiency is really inside themselves.

Fundamentally, the problem is often buried
guilt feelings. These people don't think that they
deserve to have pleasant thoughts or to enjoy
good times. People who are programmed for this
game tend to paranoia. They project their self-
hatred into others, believing that others must feel
about them as they themselves do. Such people
are also very concerned to please others and
dread disapproval. They are not able to relate
deeply to many people, if any at all, because their
basic self-hatred sabotages all their relationships.

WORRIER, THE

Rollo May, in his book *The Meaning of Anxiety*, says that normal anxiety is proportioned to the objective threat or danger to the existence of an individual as a person. Neurotic anxiety, however, is *disproportionate* to the objective danger. The most common cause of disproportionate anxiety is the insecurity an individual has experienced as an infant and child. If infants are not given the needed sensations of security—if they are not held in secure arms, rocked tenderly to sleep, and so on—and if children are not sure of their parents' love, their level of anxiety will probably be high. The game always follows the program.

As a game, worry is an immature way to handle difficulties. Worriers usually get on a treadmill, go over the same ground again and again, getting nowhere. (In the end, however, they get ulcers.) They repeat useless statements of their problem, rehearse alternatives without reaching any decision. They calculate all the possible consequences of possible decisions again and again. Worriers would probably feel guilty for not doing anything constructive, so they do something: they worry. (Got a term paper coming up?)

Psychologically, worry is related to anxiety, which results from supercharged *repressed (hidden) emotions* (for example, hostility) with or without any external threats. It is therefore possible for chronic worriers to feel ill at ease without knowing what is actually bothering them. The internal pressures of repressed emotions do not always need external stimuli to produce this uncomfortable feeling. It is one of the high prices we pay for emotional repression.

"Sorry,
   but that is the way I am...
I was like this in the beginning,
   am now, and ever shall be..."
   is a handy motto and delusion
      to have around you if you
don't want to grow up.

JOHN POWELL, S.J.

UNCONDITIONAL

Love

Love without Limits

TABOR ®
PUBLISHING

Allen, Texas

Acknowledgments

Excerpt from Viktor E. Frankl, *Man's Search for Meaning,* translated by Ilse Lasch. Copyright © 1959 by Viktor Frankl. Reprinted by permission of Beacon Press.

Specified excerpts from pages 41–42 and 126 from *The Art of Loving* by Erich Fromm. Volume 9 of World Perspective Series, planned and edited by Ruth Nanda Anshen. Copyright © 1956 by Erich Fromm. Reprinted by permission of Harper & Row, Publishers, Inc., and Allen & Unwin Ltd., London.

Robert Frost, "The Road Not Taken," from *The Poetry of Robert Frost,* edited by Edward Connery Latham. Copyright 1916, © 1969 by Holt, Rinehart and Winston. Copyright 1944 by Robert Frost. Reprinted by permission of Holt, Rinehart and Winston, Publishers; the Estate of Robert Frost; Jonathan Cape Ltd., London.

Excerpt from Carl Jung, *Memories, Dreams, Reflections,* recorded and edited by Aniela Jaffe, translated by

Continued on page 124

Photo Credits

Algimantas Kezys, S.J.   8, 12, 17, 51, 62, 72, 100, 104

Jean-Claude Lejeune   iv, 5, 21, 24–25, 29, 39, 42, 46, 54, 59, 66, 80, 86, 93, 96, 113, 120

Cover design: Karen McDonald

Calligraphy: Bob Niles

Tabor Publishing
One DLM Park
Allen, Texas 75002

Library of Congress Catalog Card Number 78-74154

Printed in the United States of America

ISBN 1-55924-282-5

   2 3 4 5   93 92 91 90

Contents

CHAPTER ONE

A life principle

**Most of all,
let love guide your life.**
Colossians 3:14

Socrates said that the unexamined life is not worth living. Sooner or later we all ask deep within ourselves: What is life for? It is an important and sometimes painful question. But it is a question that must be asked.

When I ask myself this question, I try to direct it to my stomach rather than to my head. My poor head has memorized so many ideal answers, and these rote responses are ready to come tumbling out as soon as someone presses the right button.

The late and great psychologist Abraham Maslow saw us in pursuit of our human goals and needs according to a definite hierarchy: a ladder with many rungs. The lower rungs of the ladder are the fundamental drives for food, shelter, safety from external threats. The middle rungs are the more precisely human set of needs and goals—the "higher order" needs of dignity, belongingness, love. At the summit of Maslow's ladder are the highest human aspirations: independence and excellence. He calls this state "self-actualization." Of course, we never reach the top, but it is precisely this that keeps us going. Maslow was convinced that we function best when we are striving for something we don't have. I think that, for the most part, this is true.

So I ask you to make with me what Dag Hammarskjold once called "the longest journey, the journey inward" to the center of your being, where answers are not memorized but are very much alive.

It is a reluctant journey to which I invite you. Carl Jung, the renowned psychiatrist, once wrote:

> Wherever there is a reaching down into innermost experience, into the nucleus of personality, most people are overcome by fright, and many run away. . . . The risk of inner experience, the adventure of the spirit, is in any case, alien to most human beings.
>
> ***Memories, Dreams, Reflections***

I invite you to reflect with me: What is life for?

Perhaps it would be good if each of us were to sit down and to write out a script for our lives-to-come. Try it sometime. You have a blank check. You can fill in all the amounts of success-failure, tears-laughter, long life-short life, agony-ecstasy. You have complete control over pleasure, power, money, fame, relationships. What would you consider the ideal life? What do you really want most?

Or it may help to write out a description of your "perfect day," or a list of the ten activities you enjoy most. When you reflect on what you have written, you may find your deepest needs and longings in clearer perspective. For example, if you find that during your perfect day or in the activities you enjoy most you are alone, perhaps there is some need, buried deep inside you, for solitude or even a desire to avoid relationships.

The question is: What is life for—for you?

To Win a Place in Heaven

I remember a time, many years ago, when I was in Germany trying to master the language of the "natives." I was privileged to serve for a while as a chaplain in a remote Bavarian convent. The dear little Sister who was assigned to care for my room was eighty-four years old. Every time I left my room, even for a moment, she cleaned it. And I don't mean a superficial cleaning. She would wax the floors, polish the furniture, and so forth. On one occasion when I left my room for a short walk, I came back to find "Schwester" on her knees, putting a final sheen on her waxing job. I laughingly teased her:

> *"Schwester, Sie arbeiten zuviel!"* ("Sister, you work too much!")

The dear and devoted little Sister straightened up (still kneeling) and looked at me with a seriousness that bordered on severity. She said:

> *"Der Himmel ist nicht billig!"* ("Heaven isn't cheap, you know!")

*Of course, we never reach the top,
but it is precisely this that keeps us going.*

God bless her. She was no doubt educated to believe, and she believed with all her heart, that life was supposed to be an ordeal, the price of eternal bliss. Heaven must be bought, and it is not cheap. I feel sure that heaven now belongs to that dear soul, who lived so faithfully according to her lights. (In fact, I think that there must be a roped-off section for special souls like "Schwester.") But I can't believe that this kind of joyless purchase of a place in heaven is really the life to which God is calling us. I do not believe that he intends that we should crawl through a dark tunnel on bleeding hands and knees to have a so-called "pie in the sky when we die." God is not a Shylock, demanding his pound of flesh for eternal life. In fact, I believe that, theologically speaking, eternal life has already begun in us because God's life is already in us. We should be celebrating this. We are the branches to Christ's vine (*see* John 15:5).

Do you remember, as I do, the famous *Salve Regina* prayer? It describes a very sad and forlorn version of human life: ". . . to thee do we cry, poor banished children of Eve, to thee do we send up our sighs, mourning and weeping in this valley of tears." I have often thought that if someone really believed this, life would be very bleak. What Jesus said was: "I have come that you might have life, life to the fullest" (John 10:10). "I have told you these things, that my joy may be in you, and your joy may be perfect" (John 15:11).

A Personal Inventory

You and I must open ourselves to the question: What is life for? We should get right down into the fabric of our daily lives. What am I doing? Is my life a series of deadlines . . . meetings . . . clearing my desk . . . answering phones . . . moving from one crisis to the next? Do I look forward to the stretch of life that is ahead of me? To next week? To the coming year? Is mine a hand-to-mouth existence? Is it a matter of "getting by"? When I wake up in the morning, is my first reaction: "Good morning, God!" or "Good God, morning!"? Am I in a survival contest? Do I feel trapped? Am I just hanging on? Am I asking: How much longer can I take this?

Some of us are afraid, as Carl Jung says, to face these questions because of what the answers might imply. We rather anticipate that someone who really doesn't understand will use our answers to tell us that we have to change our lives—to give up our present jobs, to leave our families, to move to a sunnier climate, and so forth. Of course, it may be that you or I should change something in our lives, but I think it is much more realistic and important to change something in ourselves. It may be that the parasites which are eating away inside us, depriving us of the deeper joys and satisfactions of life, should become the object of our attention.

For example, if I am a "compulsive pleaser" of others, living or dying according to the approval I get for my person or my work, then no change of life, job, family, or climate can possibly help me. No matter where I would go or what I would do, the problem would be with me. I would still be asking those torturous questions: Did that look mean that he didn't like me? . . . She didn't smile. I guess she is unhappy with my performance . . . (A thousand et ceteras.)

The same would be true of the "compulsive perfectionist," who can never experience satisfaction because nothing is ever completely perfect. Such a person is, at least internally, a ruthless critic of everything and everyone. (This person, upon entering heaven, will no doubt suggest to God that he spend a few bucks to fix up the place.)

We should comb through our patterns of action and reaction to locate these or similar distortions in our attitudes, and we must then work at revising those attitudes where necessary. But the more universal and more important reality to be investigated is what I would call a "life principle."

The question is: What is life for—for you?

The Meaning of
a Life Principle

A life principle is a generalized, accepted intention of purpose that is applied to specific choices and circumstances. For example, "Good must be done and evil avoided." If this is one of my life principles, whenever I come to a specific choice involving good and evil, my principle directs me to choose that which is good and to avoid that which is evil.

I would like to suggest that everyone has one dominant life principle. It may be difficult to lure it out of the dark, subconscious regions to face examination in the light, but it is there. There is in each of us a set of needs, goals, or values with which we are psychologically preoccupied. There is something, in all the zigs and zags of daily living, which dominates all our other desires. This life principle runs through the fabric of our choices like the dominant theme in a piece of music: it keeps recurring and it is heard in different settings. Of course, only you can answer for yourself, just as only I can answer for myself: What is my life principle?

For example, some people are above and before all else seeking *safety*. They avoid all places where danger might lurk, even if opportunity could be waiting in the same place. They will take no risks, make no gambles. They stay home at night and reveal their deepest selves to no one. It is better to be safe than sorry, they say. The same kind of thumbnail sketch could be made of a person whose primary concern and life principle is *duty, recognition, money, fame, need, success, fun, relationships, approval of others,* or *power.*

Practice Makes a Perfect Habit

Having a life principle is a matter of psychological economy. It diminishes the wear and tear of having to make all decisions from the ground up. For example, if my life principle is *fun,* then whenever I come upon a choice or receive two invitations for the same evening, I simply have to apply my life principle: Where will I have the most fun? My fundamental option or choice is having fun. I have already, consciously or unconsciously, accepted that as a life principle. The specific options or choices are easy. I don't have to go searching through my soul to find out what it is that I am really looking for in life. I already know that. The only uncertainty with which I must deal is: Where will I have the most fun? Having such a life principle, as we said, is a matter of psychological economy.

It is very important to realize that we are creatures of habit. Every time we think a certain

way, seek a certain good, use a given motive, a habit is forming and deepening in us. Like a groove that is being furrowed, each repetition adds a new depth to the habit. (Have you ever tried to break a habit? Then you know what I am trying to say.)

And so it is with a life principle, whatever it be. With each use it becomes a deeper and more permanent habit. And in the twilight of life our habits rule us. They define and dictate our actions and reactions. We will, as the old saying goes, die as we have lived. People who in old age prove quite self-centered and demanding, as well as those who are "mellow" and tolerant, did not become so only in their last years of life. Old cranks have practiced all their lives, just as old saints have likewise practiced all their lives. They just practiced different life principles. What you and I will become in the end will be just more and more of what we are deciding and trying to be right now. There is a fundamental choice, a life principle, which will one day possess us in the marrow of our bones and the blood in our veins. It is a certainty that we will die as we have lived.

"Heaven isn't cheap, you know!"

The Life Principle of Jesus

In the so-called temptation narratives which are recorded in Luke 4:1–13, we find Jesus, at the beginning of his public life, clarifying his own life principle. More specifically, we find him rejecting three life principles suggested to him by the devil. Jesus waited until he was thirty to begin his public life, because that was the acceptable age for a man to begin his practice as a rabbi (teacher). At this time, before beginning what we call his public life, Jesus was led by the Spirit into the desert.

> Then Jesus, full of the Holy Spirit, left the Jordan River, being urged by the Spirit out into the barren wastelands of Judea, where Satan tempted him for forty days. He ate nothing all that time, and was very hungry.
>
> Satan said, "If you are God's Son, tell this stone to become a loaf of bread." But Jesus replied, "It is written in the Scriptures, 'Other things in life are much more important than bread!' "
>
> Then Satan took him up and revealed to him all the kingdoms of the world in a moment of time; and the devil told him, "I will give you all these splendid kingdoms and

their glory—for they are mine to give to anyone I wish—if you will only get down on your knees and worship me." Jesus replied, "We must worship God, and him alone. So it is written in the Scriptures."

Then Satan took him to Jerusalem to a high roof of the Temple and said, "If you are the Son of God, jump off! For the Scriptures say that God will send his angels to guard you and to keep you from crashing to the pavement below!" Jesus replied, "The Scriptures also say, 'Don't experiment with God's patience.' "   Luke 4:1-12

The first temptation, we might say, was to accept the life principle of *pleasure*. Jesus had fasted, a total fast from all food, and was very hungry. The promise of the devil was the satisfaction of his physical hunger. The reply of Jesus was: "Other things in life are much more important than bread!"

So the devil takes Jesus up to a high place and shows him all the glittering kingdoms of the world and promises him *power* over all these places and peoples. Jesus firmly rejects this life principle: "We must worship God, and him alone." Jesus will give his heart neither to the pursuit of pleasure nor the flattery of power.

So Satan takes Jesus up to the pinnacle of the Temple and urges him to throw himself off. "Let your Father catch you in the arms of his angels!" the devil taunts, but Jesus is resolute. He will not abdicate his personal responsibility for his life. I see this third temptation precisely in this way. It implies that we are not really free anyway. It asks us to accept a kind of determinism that rationalizes an *avoidance of responsibility.* Jesus is firm: "Don't experiment with God's patience."

In this clarification of his own life principle, Jesus is stating firmly: "I will not live for pleasure! I will not live for power! I will not surrender responsibility for my life and my actions!"

Life Principles:
Freud, Adler, Skinner

These same three principles, rejected by Jesus, have been proposed by three of the great names in the history of psychology as *the* life principles of all human beings.

Everyone has one dominant life principle.
It may be difficult to lure it out
of the dark . . . but it is there.

Sigmund Freud (1856–1939) has been tradition-
ally associated with the *pleasure drive* or *pleasure
principle*. In the first part of his career he thought
that all neuroses were due to sexual repression. Later
he realized that there are other personal factors
involved, but he continued to use the word *libido* (the
Latin word for "desire" or "lust") to describe the
instinctual energies and desires that are derived from
the so-called *id*. In the Freudian construct, the *id*
represents our (animal) drives: vanity, gluttony, lust.
It is the source of energy which manifests itself in
emotional drives. These impulses are unrefined and
primitive, bent only upon immediate gratification.
Of course, Freud taught that this basic desire for
pleasure had to be moderated. This moderation is
done by the *superego* (censor), which means that there
is a constant tension in every person between wish
and morality. This tension is to be resolved by the
ego (the self or the "I"). The ego is a kind of executive
part of our psychological makeup, which tries to
regulate our desires by adjusting them to reality.
The point is that human drives are strongly
animalistic—drives for pleasure, for personal gratification. Whether frustrated or moderated, the pleasure principle is the fundamental drive in all humans,
according to Freud.

Alfred Adler (1870–1937) was Freud's pupil and
disciple until 1911, when he left the "Master" to start
his own school of "Individual Psychology," so called

because he thought that every human being repre-
sented a unique psychological problem. He accused
Freud of applying a general formula indiscriminately
to all. More specifically, Adler believed Freud's basic
error was his universal application of the assumption that frustration of *libido* (the pleasure principle)
was always at the heart of every human problem.
However, as Adler progressed with his own thought,
he fell into the same fallacy of universal application
in his formula of compensation-for-inferiority. Adler
saw sex and *libido* only as a setting for the *struggle
to gain power.* He interpreted all relationships as
struggles for power: the child trying to throw off
parental authority, a husband and wife each striving
for dominance, and so forth. It all begins, according
to Adler, with an inferiority complex. This complex
is universal, and there is in everyone a desire to
compensate for a sense of inferiority. Of course, Adler
proposed that the basic desire and struggle for power,
as a compensation for inferiority feelings, should be
channeled into positive and useful accomplishments.
But this was his assumption and interpretation: The
basic drive in people is for power and accomplish-
ment.

B. F. Skinner is a contemporary psychologist who
proposes that it is neither pleasure nor the pursuit
of power that writes the script for human life. He
contends that we are the irreversible result of our
conditioning or programming. This logically invites

us to *avoidance of responsibility* for our lives. "Operant conditioning" is based on the assumption that if we find a certain type of behavior rewarding, we tend to repeat it. If it produces negative results, we avoid it and try something else. In his book *Beyond Human Freedom and Dignity,* Skinner attempts to refute the theory that we can choose our own life principle. According to him, it is not our lot to choose anything. His is a theory of behaviorism that amounts to determinism. If one were to accept this, it would mean abdication of all personal responsibility for one's life and actions. The attitude of such a person would be to wait and see what life holds in store, to see how things turn out. One would regard his or her life story as a phonograph record, already imprinted, complete in all details, as the result of programming in infancy. During one's lifetime the phonograph record is in the process of spinning out. The process is automatic. The story cannot be changed. We are predetermined. No adult really exercises either freedom or responsibility. Or so says Skinner.

What you and I will become in the end will be just more and more of what we are deciding and trying to be right now.

Inroads into My Own Life

Of course, there is *some* truth in what each of these three men has written. (It is hard to be totally wrong.) We have only to consult our own personal experience to know that there is in us a drive toward pleasure and toward power. We are likewise aware that certain reactions, prejudices, phobias, and so forth have been programmed into us. We have to acknowledge that our freedom has been limited to some extent by the early experiences of our lives.

Still each of us has a leverage of freedom, an ability to choose, to clarify our own values, and to act on chosen motives. It is good for us to look back over the choices of the past: Which of the proposed life principles has tended to dominate my life? Has the story of my life been a pursuit of *pleasure?* Or have I been competitive, ambitious, intoxicated by the raw liquor of *power?* Perhaps neither has been the driving force in my life. It may be that there has been no driving force in my life. Perhaps I have let life roll over me. I have decided by not deciding. It may be that I have accepted the *avoidance-of-responsibility* life principle, which has led me to abdicate responsibility for the direction and outcome of my life. (There is a consensus, by the way, that most people today have given up all serious hope that they can determine or even change their lives.)

Gospel Characters:
Life Principles Illustrated

In the Gospels we find individuals who seem to be personifications of these three life principles. Herod seems to be dominated by the pleasure principle. I think that Herod was drunk when Jesus was brought before him for judgment.

> Now when Herod saw Jesus, he was very happy. He had wanted for a long time to see Jesus since he had heard so much about him. He was hoping to see some exhibition of his magical powers. He asked Jesus a string of questions, but Jesus didn't answer any of them. Now the chief priests and the Scribes were standing around and were angrily accusing him. Finally, Herod, joined by his soldiers, began to treat Jesus with a mocking contempt. They finally clothed him with a bright robe and sent him back to Pilate.
>
> **Luke 23:8–11**

"I will not live for pleasure!
I will not live for power!
I will not surrender responsibility
for my life and my actions!"

My suspicion that Herod was drunk comes not only from secular history's portrayal of him as a weak, pleasure-bent man, but is also based on the fact that Jesus would not speak to him. He would not speak to him because it would have done no good. This man, who had been educated at the imperial court of Rome, was surrounded by his own "nobility," called the Herodians. They supported him in all his whims, including his divorce from his wife in order to take his half-brother's wife, who was his own niece, Herodias. When John the Baptist fearlessly denounced this marriage as sinful, Herod imprisoned him. He seems to have been completely controlled by Herodias, who persuaded her daughter, Salome, to ask for the head of John the Baptist. I think that Herod was drunk on this occasion, too, when he expressed such great pleasure with Salome's dancing that he promised her anything . . . up to half of his kingdom.

When Jesus came before Herod, I think that Herod regarded him only as some kind of magician, who would do a few sleight of hand tricks for the entertainment of his court. When Jesus met his intoxicated demands with silence, Herod in effect pronounced this sentence: "I am ready to pronounce judgment. This man is crazy! Here I have the power over his life and he just stands there, a silent fool. He is crazy, insane. Take him back to Pilate, clothed in the robe of a fool."

Poor Herod had a ring in his nose. It was the ring of pleasure. It was his life principle, the underlying motive that ruled all his choices and shaped his entire life. He was owned by the pursuit of pleasure.

On the other hand, I see Pontius Pilate as a man whose life was ruled by the desire for power. About five to ten years before he sentenced Jesus to die, he was appointed by Rome to rule Judea, Samaria, and Idumea. Like many power-thirsty people, Pilate was a cruel man. He flaunted the religious sensibilities of the Jews, whom he was sent to rule, by erecting graven images of the emperor. He confiscated money from their Temple treasury to finance an aqueduct. He ruthlessly slaughtered a group of worshiping Galileans. He minted coins bearing the image of offensive pagan religious symbols. At one time Pilate was ordered back to Rome to stand trial for cruelty and oppression. A letter from Herod Agrippa I to Caligula describes him as "inflexible, merciless, and corrupt." He was often accused of holding executions without trial. An uncertain tradition, reported by the historian Eusebius, has it that he killed himself on orders from Caligula, shortly after he sentenced Jesus to die.

Pilate's life clearly reveals that his life principle was power. It is easy to imagine him as he uses his barbarian soldiers to inflict terrible cruelties in order to establish his privilege of power. He knows that if he succeeds in his present commission, he will get a higher, more prestigious post. It is all he really cares about.

So when Jesus is brought before him, the charge for which Jesus was convicted in the Sanhedrin—that he claimed to be the Messiah and the Son of God—is not even mentioned. It would have meant nothing to Pilate, who was a polytheist. He could have shrugged that off. With all the gods that Rome worshiped, divinity was not a serious concern for him. And so the charge before Pilate was tailored for one whose only concern was power: "He claims to be a king!" Ah! This would indeed impress poor Pontius Pilate. If word got back to Rome that some simple Jew claimed to be a king and Pilate did not crush him, his political career would be over. He would lose his power. So Pilate offers to interview Jesus.

In effect he says to him: "You're not really a king, are you? Is that what they said out there? You don't look like a king to me." Jesus responds: "I am truly a king, but my kingdom is not of this world. I am not

It may be that there has been no driving force in my life.

competing with you. But I am a king. This is why I was born and why I have come into this world. This is the truth, and those who really want the truth will hear my voice." (*See* John 18:33–37.)

Then Pilate asks his famous question: "What is truth?" What does it matter if you have truth on your side? It is power that counts. Pilate can think only in terms of power: he cannot recognize any other value.

But something happens to Pilate in that interview with Jesus. He does everything he can to avoid pronouncing the sentence of crucifixion. He returns to the porch of his palace and raises his hands for silence: "I find him not guilty!" he bellows. When the demand is chanted again and again, "Crucify that Galilean!" Pilate becomes aware that Jesus is a Galilean. He recalls that Herod has power to preside over cases involving Galileans. So he tries the escape of sending Jesus off to Herod. When Jesus is returned to him, Pilate tries a second subterfuge. In one of history's classic *non sequiturs,* he says: "I find him not guilty. Therefore, I will chastise him and release him." It proves futile.

Another avenue of escape occurs to Pilate: the custom of the Procurator of Rome to release a prisoner at festival time. He gives the crowd a choice between a notorious criminal, Barabbas, or Jesus. They choose Barabbas. When Pilate's wife, Claudia, sends a message to him at this point, saying that she has had a bad dream and warning him not to yield to the demands of the mob, Pilate is irritated. He is trying with all his strength to get out of this predicament. He offers again to have Jesus chastised before release, but the mob's clamoring for his death is unyielding.

Pilate makes a last attempt to escape the inevitable. "Do you want to see blood? I will show you blood!" He orders Jesus to be scourged. When Jesus is brought before the crowd, a red mask of agony, Pilate moans: "Do you see this? What you see here is a man. Look at the man." Once more he pronounces: "Take him yourselves and crucify him. I find him not guilty."

But the mob cries: "If you release this man, you are no friend of Caesar; for everyone who makes himself a king sets himself against Caesar!" (John 19:12).

"Shall I crucify your king?"

"We have no king but Caesar."

So Pilate breaks a small, dry twig in the face of Jesus and pronounces the sentence: *"Ibis ad crucem!"* ("You will go to the cross!") The mob senses his weakness. They have Pilate where he hurts. His power is at stake. Power, power, power.

In a last ironic gesture, he calls for a boy with a bowl of water: "I wash my hands of the blood of this man." But Pilate's lust for power had owned him and had led him into places he did not want to go. He had built a life on the pursuit of power, and in the end it destroyed him.

The Gospel personality who seems to suggest, if not personify, the avoidance-of-responsibility life principle is the invalid at the Bethesda pool.

Inside the city, near the Sheep Gate, was Bethesda Pool, with five covered platforms or porches surrounding it. Crowds of sick folks—lame, blind, or with paralyzed limbs—lay on the platforms (waiting for a certain movement of the water, for an angel of the Lord came from time to time and disturbed the water, and the first person to step down into it afterwards was healed). One of the men lying there had been sick for thirty-eight years. When Jesus saw him and knew how long he had been ill, he asked him, "Would you like to get well?"

"I can't," the sick man said, "for I have no one to help me into the pool at the movement of the water. . . ." Jesus told him, "Stand up, roll up your sleeping mat and go on home!" Instantly, the man was healed!

John 5:2–9

Actually we know very little about this poor man, and perhaps our use of him as an example is unfair. However, he seems to have been assigning his plight to the unwillingness of others to help him. He also seems to have lost hope. Like many people who do not want to assume responsibility for their lives, he talks only about what others are not doing for him. Apparently he has not given much thought to how he might help himself. He is so absorbed in the limitations of his condition that he does not explore the creative possibilities of the situation.

And so Jesus asks the man a question that moves him to probe his own inner attitudes: "Would you really like to get well?" Some people, as we know, make a vocation of being sick, either physically or emotionally. It is the easiest, if not the only, way for them to relate to others: by being needy. Sometimes sickness provides an excuse for not trying. The American Academy of Psychosomatic Medicine has theorized that 92 percent of all physical illness is psychologically induced. It would seem that many people, at least subconsciously, prefer to be sick— even to the point of resisting obvious means to health—simply because they have given up on their capacity to cope with life. They cannot accept the challenges of life so they retreat into some physically or emotionally disabling condition. Illness is passive. Involvement is active. They choose passivity rather than activity in life.

There are many other rationalizations, besides the excuse of sickness, which are used to justify the avoidance-of-responsibility life principle. Sometimes we let our fears or our self-inflicted judgments of inferiority shield us from taking the risks and facing the challenges of a full life. We substitute "I can't" for "I won't even try." I remember a former student of mine explaining to me why he was withdrawing from all his classes just before final exams. "It is easier not to have tried than to have tried and failed. If you don't try, you can always console yourself by saying: 'I probably could have done it.' If you try and fail, you don't even have that dubious consolation."

When one sets out to look for avenues of escape, the possibilities are infinite. "This is the way I am!" Some people blame their life condition on their genes. Others claim that their level of education is responsible for their life's outcome. Still others assign their fixed state to ethnic background or lack of connections. A large group of people "blame it on the stars." This tendency to use astrology as a way out of personal responsibility is an old one: a tried and true rationalization.

> "Men at some time are masters of their fate.
> The fault, Dear Brutus, is not in our stars,
> But in ourselves. . . ."
>
> ***Julius Caesar*** (I, ii, 134)

Not to Judge
But to Understand

The point is not to set oneself on the throne of judgment, or to pity from a privileged position those who have been duped by the fountains of pleasure or lured into the palaces of power. Nor can we diagnose with disdain those who seem to have given up and accepted life as a passive spectator sport. The point is, rather, that to some extent all three of these life principles have made inroads and left an imprint on our own life-styles.

So you and I must look into ourselves at the deepest level, the point at which few people, if any, are ever permitted to know us. What do we *really* want from life? What do we *really* think would make us happy? You and I are now practicing a life principle, which may not be obvious from a surface view. Someday it will amount to a life wager. In the end everyone gambles his or her life on something, or someone, as the way to happiness.

The Christian
Life Principle

In the Gospel narrative of the final Passover Feast (the Last Supper), Jesus dramatizes his own life principle and lays before the Apostles and all of us the condition of our own Christian discipleship. Almost immediately after Jesus gives his disciples the bread of his Body and the cup of his Blood, a dispute arises over "which one in their group should be considered the greatest" (Luke 22:24). After three years of tutelage under the greatest of all spiritual directors, the disciples still labor under their old delusions. They are petty, competitive, self-centered.

So in the last hours of his life, Jesus tries to remind them of his central message. He washes their feet. According to Jewish custom, if the host of a dinner was honored by the presence of his guests, he would wash their feet. If, on the contrary, the guests considered themselves honored by the invitation, the host did not wash their feet, presumably indicating his higher social status. You will recall that when Jesus ate with Simon the Pharisee (Luke 7:36–50), Simon did not extend this courtesy.

During the Last Supper or Passover Meal, Jesus

> . . . got up from the supper table, took off his robe, wrapped a towel around his loins (as a servant would do). He poured water into a basin and began to wash the feet of his disciples and to dry them with the towel he had around him.
>
> When he came to Simon Peter, Peter said to him: "Lord, are you really going to wash

my feet?" Jesus explained, "You may not understand this now, but someday you will understand."

"No!" Peter protested, "you will never wash my feet."

Jesus replied: "If you don't let me wash your feet, you cannot be my partner!"

Simon Peter then exclaimed: "If that is the case, then wash my hands and head, too, not just my feet."

John 13:4-9

During his three years with the Twelve—spending most of the time alone with them, teaching and preparing them for their mission—the central message of Jesus was the kingdom of God. Much of the Gospel narrative concerns the preaching and parables of the kingdom. If this kingdom could be briefly defined, it would certainly imply two things.

First, the kingdom is an invitation from God. It is an invitation to all humankind to come to God in an intimate relationship of love. More vividly, we might imagine God, smiling at us with a warm look of love, stretching forth his arms to embrace us: "Come to me. I will be your God. You will be my People, the children of my heart!" It should be noted that this call or invitation is not extended to us merely as individuals. In the kingdom of God we are never less than individuals, but we are never merely individuals. We are the Body of Christ. We are called to come to God's embrace of love as brothers and sisters in the Lord. The French poet Charles Peguy wrote: "Do not try to go to God alone. If you do, he will certainly ask you the embarrassing question: 'Where are your brothers and sisters?' " In other words, the invitation to the kingdom is extended to us together. I can say "yes" to God only if I say "yes" to you, my brothers and my sisters. It is one and the same "yes" which embraces my God and my human family, all in the same act of love.

Second, on our part, the kingdom of God implies a free response of love. "In the head of the book it is written of me that to do your will is all my delight. Behold I come . . . running!" When we pray in the Lord's Prayer "Thy kingdom come!" we are praying that all of us will say the big "yes" (and all the little "yeses" which will be inside it) to one another and to our Father.

I can say "yes" to God only if I say "yes" to you, my brothers and sisters.

It was this, I feel sure, that Jesus wanted so much to make clear to Peter and the disciples. In all his days with them, but especially at the Last Supper, in his last moments with them, he wanted to underline the truth: My kingdom is a kingdom of love! It is not a place where power rules or people compete. It is not a playground of pleasure or a haven for those who have no heart to try. The solemn and solitary requirement for entrance into the kingdom of God is the choice of love as a life principle. There is only one badge of identification: "By this shall all men know that you are my disciples, that you love one another as I have loved you" (John 13:35).

"If you cannot accept this," Jesus was saying to Peter, "you cannot be my partner. The only power in my kingdom is the power of love!" In the wake of their silly squabbling over who was the most important, Jesus washed their feet and left them with a rather solemn reminder:

> "In this world, kings lord it over their subjects, and those in authority insist that they be called their country's 'benefactor.' Don't let it ever be this way with you. On the contrary, the highest among you must bear himself as though he were the youngest, and the chief among you must act like a servant. Who is greater: the one who sits at table or the servants who wait on him? Surely the one

who sits at table. Yet here I am—I am your
servant!"   Luke 22:25-27

Jesus wants to know if the lesson has come
through. He apparently found in the Apostles the
same lack of understanding that I so often find in
myself. In Mark's Gospel, Jesus asks the Apostles
seventeen times (I once counted them!): "Are you still
without understanding?" John writes:

After washing their feet he put on his robe
again and sat down with them. Then he
asked: "Do you know what I was just doing?
You call me 'Master' and 'Lord' and you do
well to say this because it is true. And since
I, the Lord and Teacher, have washed your
feet, you ought to do the same for one another.
I have given you an example to follow: do as
I have done to you. . . . If you keep this in
mind and put it into practice you will be very
happy."   John 13:12-17

I must ask myself the same question again and
again: Do I really understand? Do I really believe
that Jesus calls me to accept as my own the life
principle of love? Do I really understand that such a
commitment is the only way to true and abiding
happiness? These are the questions whose answers
lie deep inside me. I must at least attempt a search
of those deepest parts. My whole life is at stake.

C H A P T E R   T W O

The contemporary crisis of love

The crisis of our time
As we are beginning
Slowly and painfully to perceive
Is a crisis not of the hands
But of the hearts.
ARCHIBALD MACLEISH

The English author Gilbert Keith Chesterton once said that there is a double problem with proclaiming the Gospel as the "Good News." First, he suggested, it is not really "news" to many people who have heard it repeated and repeated. Second, it does not sound like "good" news to most people.

Something in me eagerly agrees. To my ears a lot of religious exhortation seems to be aimed about two or three miles above where most people really live. The level of the ideal offered is so clearly beyond reach that all we are left with is inevitable failure and the consequent guilt feelings. Of course, I am not suggesting a massive compromise of our ascetical and moral principles. Such a "cave-in" would be even worse.

The question at hand is this: Is loving really the way to human fulfillment? If I choose love as my personal life principle, will I find satisfaction and true gratification? Are all the Gospel paradoxes about love really valid in the laboratory of life? If I seek myself and my own happiness, is it certain that I will lose both? Does the seed really have to fall into the ground and die before there can be a full and happy life? Is the Gospel beatitude of unselfish and unconditional love really the path to true human joy? These are indeed hard and practical questions— questions which are today the subject of considerable debate.

In fact, I would say that this is the major crisis facing contemporary society. Is a life of love, which involves a permanent and unconditional commitment to the happiness of another, really the way to personal satisfaction and human fulfillment? Or must one rather stay free and unencumbered from all such relationships in order to experience the pleasure, the power, and the variety of sensations which life can offer? Is personal satisfaction and gratification the most fulfilling life goal, or is the deepest meaning in life to be found only in a committed and permanent relationship of love? Should we lay our lives and our persons on the line, or is it better never to say "forever"?

The Denial of Love

Love as the life principle of a meaningful existence has not been accorded the status of a beatitude by contemporary society. In fact, there is a library of recent literature challenging the life principle of love. In the life-styles chosen by many people today, and in the motives they offer for their life-styles, there is a persistent and ruthless questioning of the reality— the very *possibility*—of true, permanent human love. Books pour off the presses—many of them high on best-seller charts—proposing trendy techniques to get the most pleasure and personal satisfaction out of life. The suggested basic mind-set and only pertinent question is: *What's in it for me?*

As a result of this philosophy, many people have taken to reevaluating the investment of their lives. They have measured their life experience according to the recommended criterion: What have I gotten out of life for myself? An alarming number of these people have fallen into a regret-filled despondency as they look at their lives, their jobs, their marriages, and their families. They feel that they have been somehow defrauded, cheated of an exhilarating happiness that could have been theirs. "You only go around once. You have to grab all you can . . . for yourself." They look at what they have grabbed and it is not enough. They are haunted by the fear that they have missed all the tingling satisfactions that could have been theirs. They are sad and wonder where they went wrong. The depressing words repeat themselves slowly and sadly: Is this all there is?

Opportunistic authors have come running with reams of advice and pages of instructions · on self-satisfaction and self-fulfillment. "I will turn these stones to bread. . . . I will give you these cities to rule. . . . I will free you from the struggles of

To my ears a lot of religious exhortation seems to be aimed about two or three miles above where most people really live.

personal responsibility and commitments!" These authors have given detailed instructions on taking care of Number One (me, me, me!), on getting power and keeping it, on winning by the intimidation of others. They have extolled the virtues of selfishness. They have portrayed life as a cutthroat competition and warned that "nice guys finish last!" They have deluged an already sex-drenched generation with the "how to" books, guaranteed to produce increased erotic pleasure. Sexploitation.

These authors have relegated love, marriage, and family to the oblivion of "old-fashioned" ideas. The "in thing" now is creative divorce: how to make the death of a deep relationship the birth of something bright and beautiful. One group actually wrote a ritual to "celebrate" divorce among its members. The authors have encouraged us to shift gears, to pull up all the old roots in order to develop exciting new selves! They have urged us to focus all our attention on ourselves, to be our own best friends now and forever.

Underlying all these suggestions is the belief that human fulfillment is found by the direct pursuit of one's own happiness. To do this, one must be free—free from once-made promises, free from responsibilities and love commitments, free from all the claims others make upon one's life and one's love. This has led many to see their spouses and families as obstacles to their personal fulfillment.

At best these books are dehumanizing; at worst they are positively cruel. In either case they are part of a vast societal rationalization of the self-centered existence. They lie at the farthest point on the spectrum from the commitment of unconditional love. The assumption of this self-fulfillment cult seems to be that to give your word of commitment and your promise of faithfulness to another is really to surrender your own individuality and personal identity.

To me it is obvious that this is simply not true—that the very opposite is true. Unless you give your word and your promise of fidelity to another, there can be no real trust and consequently no authentic relationship or secure framework in which two people can grow.

The Cult of Experience
vs.
Unconditional Commitment

Of course, all of us should at times take inventory of our personal growth and sense of fulfillment. The question "Am I really enjoying my life?" can and very likely will reveal valuable information and put me in touch with unrealized parts of myself. If we find inside us some painful voids, we should reassess our attitudes and perhaps redirect some of our energies. But this is not the issue of contention.

The heart of the matter and the crux of the problem is this: Do we get fulfilled by trying to have all the experiences we can? Is it true that the more experiences a person has, the more developed and fulfilled he or she will be as a person? Or is the contrary true, that a person is fulfilled by making a commitment and then choosing experiences according to whether they honor, promote, and reaffirm the commitment?

Trying to choose all available experiences is like trying to mix oil and water: they just don't blend. The result is confusing, fragmenting, and disintegrating to the human person. For a fulfilling life, we must conceive reality as somehow ordered and meaningful. This implies a value structure, priorities. It is in the light of these values and priorities that we must evaluate experiences. I would like to quote from my own book on religious faith, *A Reason to Live, A Reason to Die:*

> *The depressing words repeat themselves slowly and sadly: Is this all there is?*

To try to open himself to all possible experiences can only result in an interior chaos; it would break him apart. If a man decides to be a true husband and father, to be loyal and faithful to his marriage commitment, the experience of having a mistress or visiting prostitutes will make his heart and soul a divided city. If a person is determined to grow through contact with reality, which is the only way to grow, the experience of drunkenness or hallucinogenic narcotics will be very crippling to his personal growth.

Becoming a person, therefore, involves the sacrifice of some experiences in order to experience more deeply the values which are connected with and which promote one's own destiny. Having decided what we want to be and want to do, we must exercise some selection in the experiences we seek, choosing those which are conducive to our goals and refusing those which could only detour us.

Making a commitment to permanent, unconditional love will mean for me that certain experiences, which might otherwise have been mine, are now impossible for me. The man who chooses one woman for his wife and life partner by his very choice has eliminated all other women as possible wives and life partners. It is this very elimination that frightens us on the brink of commitment. Every commitment is like every moment in life: there is a birth and a death in every moment. Something is and something else can never be again. There is a choice and a surrender, a "yes" and a "no." To love is indeed costly. To love unconditionally is a life wager. In love we put ourselves on the line and there is no going back. It is at this brink that so many seem to collapse. Within arms' reach of greatness, they faint at the thought of never returning. It is the less traveled road.

The Road Not Taken

Two roads diverged in a yellow wood,
And sorry I could not travel both
And be one traveler, long I stood
And looked down one as far as I could
To where it bent in the undergrowth;

Then took the other, as just as fair,
And having perhaps the better claim,
Because it was grassy and wanted wear;
Though as for that, the passing there
Had worn them really about the same,

And both that morning equally lay
In leaves no step had trodden black.
Oh, I kept the first for another day!
Yet knowing how way leads on to way,
I doubted if I should ever come back.

> I shall be telling this with a sigh
> Somewhere ages and ages hence:
> Two roads diverged in a wood, and I—
> I took the one less traveled by,
> And that has made all the difference.
>
> **ROBERT FROST**

The cult of experience urges us to grab all we can while passing through this world. Besides being internally confusing, such a program is a practical impossibility. It can leave us so fragmented that we might never be able to put our pieces back together again. It will certainly leave us with broken dreams and shattered hopes. If we listen to the preachers and propagandists of this cult, we will resemble the person who wants it all so badly that, in the end, everything is lost. I am reminded of the graphic description of such a person, given in *The Bell Jar* by Sylvia Plath:

> I felt like a racehorse in a world without racetracks or a champion college footballer

Without fidelity there cannot be an authentic relationship.

suddenly confronted by Wall Street and a business suit, his days of glory shrunk to a little gold cup on his mantel with a date engraved on it like the date on a tombstone.

I saw my life branching out before me like the green fig tree in the story.

From the tip of every branch, like a fat purple fig, a wonderful future beckoned and winked. One fig was a husband and a happy home and children, and another fig was a famous poet, and another fig was a brilliant professor, and another fig was Ee Gee, the amazing editor, and another fig was Europe and Africa and South America, and another fig was Constantine and Socrates and Attila and a pack of other lovers with queer names and offbeat professions, and another fig was an Olympic lady crew champion, and beyond and above these figs were many more figs I couldn't quite make out.

I saw myself sitting in the crotch of this fig tree, starving to death, just because I couldn't make up my mind which of the figs I would choose. I wanted each and every one of them, but choosing one meant losing all the rest, and, as I sat there, unable to decide, the figs began to wrinkle and go black, and, one by one, they plopped to the ground at my feet.

The ultimate delusion and cruelty of the cult of experience lie in this, that in the end we are always left with the same painful emptiness which we were led to believe we could fill. Human nature abhors a vacuum; but when empty people reach out to eat, drink, and be merry as a program of fulfillment, the hangover is worse than the hunger. The hangover is not confined to the next morning. The original emptiness becomes a deeply painful bankruptcy. Like a gull that circles over shining waters, we swoop down to be filled with the cool, refreshing waters of pleasure. But the waters of pleasure, sought for all they can give, are always bright on the surface but, sadly, only one inch deep. We always come up with sand in our mouths.

Good Times
vs. a Good Life

Human fulfillment and true satisfaction cannot be measured by the yardstick of "fun." This would be sadly superficial. Fulfillment and satisfaction likewise cannot be measured by counting the moments of exhilaration that can be crammed into each day. And finally, true happiness cannot be the result of a tensionless existence. Fun, exhilaration, and the absence of tension—which are all good in themselves and have a place in every life—can never add up to human fulfillment or a meaningful life.

A meaningful life can result only from the experience of love, and this implies a commitment and dedication to another. Love rejects the question "What am I getting out of this?" as the only criterion of fulfillment. Love understands by direct experience those often-quoted words of Francis of Assisi: "It is in giving that we receive." Egoistic concern and concentration on self can lead only to the loss of self. It is a strange and painful paradox that we must all learn. The most perceptive insight of contemporary personalism is that I become a person only if I receive my personhood from someone else through the gift of affirmation. If I never see myself valued by others, I will never value myself. To this the psychiatrist Viktor Frankl enjoins this absolutely necessary advice: True self-esteem and a true sense of identity can be found only in the reflected appraisal of those whom we have loved.

Giving the gift of myself in love leaves me with a deep and lasting satisfaction of having done

In the end we are always left with the same painful emptiness which we were led to believe we could fill.

something good with my life. I live with the sweet memory of having contributed a gift of love to the lives of others. Likewise I am left with a sense of having used well the gifts which God has invested in me. Love takes time, demands a history of giving and receiving, laughing and crying, living and dying. It never promises instant gratification, only ultimate fulfillment. Love means believing in someone, in something. It supposes a willingness to struggle, to work, to suffer, and to join in the rejoicing. I doubt that there has ever been one recorded case of deep and lasting fulfillment reported by a person whose basic mind-set and only question was: What am I getting out of this?

It is, of course, the paradox of the Gospels: satisfaction and fulfillment are the by-products of dedicated love. They belong only to those who can reach beyond themselves, to whom giving is more important than receiving.

Sometimes we are tempted to confuse "good times" with "a good life." The successful pursuit of endless "good times" is a Camelot that never existed and can never exist. It can only result in the inevitable sadness and disappointment of unfulfilled expectations. G. Marian Kinget writes:

Many a life may be regarded—and experienced by the subject—as good, yet may comprise a relatively scant measure of what is commonly called fun and enjoyment. Among those who hold an examined view of the subject, few would deny that a fair share of the goodness of life befell to such persons as Abraham Lincoln, Ghandi, Louis Pasteur, Albert Schweitzer, Dorothea Dix, Dietrich Bonhoeffer, Pope John XXIII, Martin Buber, and Martin Luther King. Hardly anyone, however, would say that these persons' lives were marked by lots of fun. Such contamination of the notion of the good life with that of a good time obscures and distorts the issue.

On Being Human

"Doing My Thing" vs. I-Thou

The tension between self-fulfillment directly sought and self-fulfillment as a by-product of loving is, in my judgment, the greatest crisis facing our society today.

There are two poetic expressions which do not precisely define these opposing positions, but seem to reflect something of their diverse spirits. The first is the familiar "Gestalt Prayer" of Fritz Perls.

I do my thing, and you do your thing.
I am not in this world to live up to your
    expectations,
And you are not in this world to live up
    to mine.
You are you and I am I;
If by chance we find each other,
    it's beautiful.
If not, it can't be helped.

FRITZ PERLS

These lines express very forcibly the human need for independence and self-expression. I must have my own thoughts and feelings and I must assert my right to express them freely. I must make my own choices and be able to live by them. No doubt these were the practical good purposes in the mind of Fritz Perls. I feel sure that he wanted his lines to expose the clinging dependency and jealous possessiveness which are, in fact, counterfeits of true love.

But the waters of pleasure . . .
are always bright on the surface but,
sadly, only one inch deep. We always
come up with sand in our mouths.

At the same time his verse opens itself to serious criticism. In itself and without qualification it sounds like a creed of "subjectivism" which waves the banner-slogan: "Do your own thing!" This kind of subjectivism ignores the fact that we are interrelated and interdependent social beings. I cannot do my thing without somehow affecting you. I cannot light up my big, fat cigar if it will make you sick.

But more profoundly, this subjectivism ignores one of the deepest truths of human existence: For a person to be is to-be-with-others. Human life and human fulfillment are essentially relational. In other words, the Perls credo reflects the human need for independence, but ignores the need for true and deep relationships. Perls prescinds from the warmth, the caring, the empathy and commitment which are so essential to loving, which is in turn so essential to the process of becoming a person.

The supplement, offered by psychologist Walter Tubbs, speaks for itself. It redresses the imbalance in the thought of Perls, giving a fuller view of the human condition. True human fulfillment is found only in relationships of love: "The truth begins with two."

Beyond Perls

If I just do my thing and you do yours,
We stand in danger of losing each other
And ourselves.

I am not in this world to live up to your
    expectations;
But I am in this world to confirm you
As a unique human being.
And to be confirmed by you.

We are fully ourselves only in relation
    to each other;
The I detached from a Thou
Disintegrates.

I do not find you by chance;
I find you by an active life
Of reaching out.

Rather than passively letting things
    happen to me,
I can act intentionally to make them
    happen.

I must begin with myself, true;
But I must not end with myself:
The truth begins with two.

WALTER TUBBS

CHAPTER THREE

The meaning of love

"It is only with the heart
that one can see rightly;
what is essential
is invisible to the eye."
ANTOINE DE SAINT-EXUPÉRY,
The Little Prince

I would like to review briefly at this point some things that I have treated in greater detail in another book, *The Secret of Staying in Love.* Love should be generally supported by favorable feelings, but it is not itself a feeling. If it were a feeling, love would be a very fickle reality and those who construed it to be a feeling would be very fickle people. Rather love is a *decision* and *commitment.* My Christian vocation is to love all people. This means that I must try to do for each person with whom I interact whatever I can to promote that person's true growth and happiness. However, I cannot enter into an actual and ongoing love relationship with everyone. I must therefore decide—and it should be a careful choice— to whom and at what level of commitment I wish to offer my love.

Having made such a decision, on the presumption that my offer of love has been accepted and reciprocated, I am now by my own free choice committed to the happiness, security, and well-being of the person I love. I will do everything I can to help that person build whatever dreams he or she has. It is this commitment which I make when I offer my love. When I question myself about the place love has in my life, I must therefore ask if there is any person in my life whose growth and happiness is as real or more real to me than my own. If so, love has truly entered my life.

I might even ask if there is any person or cause for which I would give my very life. Jesus has told us that this is the greatest love. "No one can give a greater proof of love than by laying down his life for his friends" (John 15:13).

Obviously the commitment to love will involve me in much careful and active listening. I truly want to be whatever you need me to be, to do whatever you need done, and I want to say whatever will promote your happiness, security, and well-being. To discover your needs, I must be attentive, caring, and open both to what you say and to what you cannot say. However, the final decision about the "loving thing" must be mine.

This means that my love may be "tough" love, not at all sweet and coddling. You may ask me for another drink when you are already inebriated, or you may ask me to join you in some deception. Of course, if I truly love you, I must say an emphatic "No!" to these requests. If you are on a self-destructive course, like alcoholism, you will meet in me a firm and confronting love. But, when needed, my love will also be "tender." If you have tried and failed, and you just need a hand in yours in the darkness of disappointment, you can count on mine.

I may read you wrongly on occasion and misjudge your needs. I have done this so often to so many in the past. But know this, that my decision is to love you and my commitment is to your true and lasting happiness. I am dedicated to your growth and fulfillment as a person. If I should fail you, for lack of wisdom or because of the abundance of weakness in me, please forgive me, try to recognize my intention, and know that I will try to do better.

True Love
Is Unconditional

There is no third possibility: love is either conditional or unconditional. Either I attach conditions to my love for you or I do not. To the extent that I do attach such conditions, I do not really love you. I am only offering an exchange, not a gift. And true love is and must always be a free gift.

The gift of my love means this: I want to share with you whatever I have that is good. You did not win a contest or prove yourself worthy of this gift. It is not a question of deserving my love. I have no delusions that either of us is the best person in the world. I do not even suppose that, of all the available persons, we are the most compatible. I am sure that somewhere there is someone who would be "better" for you or for me. All that is really not to the point. The point is that I have *chosen* to give you my gift of love and you have *chosen* to love me. This is the only soil in which love can possibly grow. "We're gonna make it together!"

Erich Fromm writes of the so-called conditional love:

> Unconditional love corresponds to one of the deepest longings, not only of the child, but of every human being; on the other hand, to be loved because of one's merit, because one deserves it, always leaves doubt; maybe I did not please the person whom I want to love me, maybe this, or that—there is always a fear that love could disappear. Furthermore, "deserved" love easily leaves a bitter feeling that one is not loved for oneself, that one is loved *only* because one pleases, that one is, in the last analysis, not loved at all but used.
>
> *The Art of Loving*

The Message of Unconditional Love

The essential message of unconditional love is one of liberation: You can be whoever you are, express all your thoughts and feelings with absolute confidence. You do not have to be fearful that love will be taken away. You will not be punished for your openness or honesty. There is no admission price to

my love, no rental fees or installment payments to be made. There may be days when disagreements and disturbing emotions may come between us. There may be times when psychological or physical miles may lie between us. But I have given you the word of my commitment. I have set my life on a course. I will not go back on my word to you. So feel free to be yourself, to tell me of your negative and positive reactions, of your warm and cold feelings. I cannot always predict my reactions or guarantee my strength, but one thing I do know and I do want you to know: I will not reject you! I am committed to your growth and happiness. I will always love you.

Unconditional Love and Personal Growth

There is nothing else that can expand the human soul, actualize the human potential for growth, or bring a person into the full possession of life more than a love which is unconditional. We have labored for so long under the delusion that corrections, criticism, and punishments stimulate a person to

"We're gonna make it together!"

grow. We have rationalized the taking out of our own unhappiness and incompleteness in many destructive ways. For example, recent surveys revealed that 80 percent of the inmates in this country's prisons were brutalized as children. Only recently have the behavioral sciences reached the point of enlightenment to show us that unconditional love is the only soil in which the seed of a human person can grow.

Of course, free will is a factor in every human life. Everyone must say his or her "yes" to growth and integrity. But there are prerequisites. And one of these is that someone must empower me to believe in myself and to be myself. Only someone who loves me unconditionally can do this.

When we think of conditional love, we immediately think of manipulative parents. We think of parents giving their children affection and affirmation only when the conditions are met: when the children get good grades, obey the rules, make their parents proud, and so forth. We think of husbands and wives who do the same things to each other. The games people play. The hugs and kisses when the house is clean, in return for punctuality or a special dinner. The pan-scales always show through conditional love: it is an exchange, a reciprocal bargain, not a free gift. We often overlook a more subtle form of conditional love: the "operant conditioning" of which B. F. Skinner writes. We give to those whom we wish to manipulate appropriate rewards for being what we want them to be. We assign to them an identity of our choosing. We paint them into a small corner of life, allowing them to be only what we have decided they should be. Unconditional love is liberating. It frees the loved one to be authentic and real. Operant conditioning leaves the loved one only the course of conformity.

The Story of Katie

A few years ago a woman named Margaret Stern Mattisson shared with us a shattering episode from her own life. She called her story, published in *Reader's Digest*, "Love Is Not Enough." The summary line beneath the title read: "Our daughter was bright, loving, popular, successful—'perfect,' we felt, in every way. And then one awful night she tried to end her life."

Margaret Mattisson very courageously told the story of her child, Katie, the ideal daughter. She told of the unexpected phone call which came to the church hall during the production of a musical in which Margaret Mattisson was playing a part. It was Katie gasping, struggling: "Mother, come home. . . . I've taken sleeping . . . sleeping . . . sleep . . ." Then the crash of the phone and Katie to the floor, the frantic phone calls to neighbors, the ambulance siren, the white hospital sheets, and the still unconscious form of Katie, the perfect daughter, who tried to end her life. The unspoken question that ached in her mother and father at her bedside was: Why? Fortunately Katie did revive. But when she sat up in the first glimmerings of consciousness, it was anger, not pathos, that spewed from her: an astonishing array of angry, vulgar epithets. Katie had never, never sworn before. These words it was supposed she did not know. Katie was snapping like an animal. She bit the nurse on the wrist and sent an angry fist flush into the face of an intern, bloodying his nose. New curses, kicks, and angry screams.   .

Hours later, after waking from a sedated sleep, Katie whispered: "I sort of remember . . . I hated everything, everything."

"Us, Katie? Mostly us?" Katie's father asked.

"No. Mostly me," she said, closing her eyes.

Later the staff psychiatrist visited Katie and reported to the bewildered parents: "Katie is a very upset young woman. She doesn't think much of herself. That's why she took the sleeping pills."

"But she's wonderful—always has been," the distraught Margaret Mattisson blurted out. "She must know it!"

The doctor remained calm. "She knew you thought so, and she tried to be, felt she *had* to be, what you thought she was. That's what she was telling us last night."

"Why didn't she tell it to us before? We always talked," the puzzled mother asked.

"She didn't want to disappoint you—didn't want anyone to think she wasn't as nice as they all thought she was. We all want to be loved, you know. She thought acting nice is what made people love her—even her parents. She doesn't think she is a person, so dying doesn't matter."

Katie's parents responded that they had loved her, and asked how it was possible that Katie could hate herself.

The doctor replied: "Love is not enough. You can't exist as the reflection of someone's love. You have to be your own person."

All the time that Katie presented herself as the ideal daughter and young lady there was inside her a seething resentment and self-contempt. Her parents had built a pedestal for her and she climbed up on it. For years she played the role because she thought it was the admission price for being loved.

At last—thanks perhaps to Katie's shattering and almost disastrous attempt to die—the parents understood and Katie recovered. The essential and most valuable thing she recovered, of course, was her self, her own individual, unique, and unrepeatable person.

Thank you, Margaret Mattisson, and thank you, Katie, for sharing your story. The lesson is so easy to lose, to forget. We must all be sure that those to whom we are committed in love know that there is no price tag, no admission price on our love. I have given you my love freely. It is my gift to you. There is no fine print in the contract, no hidden agenda. Love is the purest and simplest of gifts. Most people want to be very sure that their love is not taken for granted. Unconditional love says the very opposite: "Take me, and take my love for granted." In the words of the contemporary hymn: "All I ask of you is forever to remember me as loving you."

Giving and Receiving Love

When we talk about the kind of love with which we want to be loved, most of us would clearly and emphatically specify that it be unconditional. I don't want you to love me for what I can do for you or because I please your expectations. I want you to love me for better or worse, in sickness and in health, in good times and in bad, for richer or for poorer, with no strings attached. I can't sell out my person to buy your love.

However, when we are discussing the kind of love which we are willing to give, it is not so clear. Most of us want to be more tentative in case things don't work out. To give my word and to promise unconditional faithfulness to that word is more than a little frightening. We want to leave a back door open, an escape hatch. It is so much easier to be an unencumbered butterfly, flitting from flower to flower. It is so much harder to take the plunge into an unconditional commitment. It seems much less frightening to travel with a tent than to build a permanent home.

In Fear and Trembling: Commitment

What do we fear in the promise of unconditional love? For sure there are many uncertainties. I almost always think at weddings what a marvelous act of trust two people make in themselves and in each other when they promise that nothing will ever come between them with a power to separate them. As they make their vows, they certainly know something at least of what this will involve. There will be days when the well of warm feelings will run dry, when the decision of fidelity will be tested. There will be long and gray days when the rewards of loving will seem like distant memories or faint hopes. And still they will have the courage to say before all the

world: "As long as I shall live, I will be your man
... your woman." It is a real profession of belonging,
a life wager, a choice that will change two lives and
unite two persons forever in love.

When a couple exchanges rings on their wedding
day, I think of the symbolism. The circle of the ring
is symbolic of the endlessness of love. There are, of
course, other young people who express cynicism
about marriage, saying that it is "only a piece of
paper." I feel very sympathetic when I hear this,
because I presume that such people have never
experienced a committed and unconditional love. But
I also feel very sad because I see marriage as the only
public profession of unconditional love which we
have left in our society.

I do have a very real sympathy for the doubters.
As in so many other similar matters, experience
seems to lie at the heart of the matter. We tend to
generalize from our own experience. If I have never
had the experience of unconditional love—either as
a giver or receiver—I tend to doubt its existence. I
tend to disbelieve those who claim the experience.

*"Love is not enough. You can't exist
as the reflection of someone's love."*

On the other hand, if I have ever, even once, known the security of a love without conditions, I need no further explanations or proof.

The Haunting Fear

Perhaps the most disturbing of all fears is that my commitment of unconditional love will somehow be a denial or surrender of my self, a sad farewell to a sense of separate identity. I fear that I will have to give up my individual interests and personal tastes. In fact, if these fears were realized, there could be no relationship of love because relationship means two. Kahlil Gibran in his book *The Prophet* says that unconditional love should not be conceived as making two islands into one solid landmass. A love relationship, he suggests, should rather be like two islands that remain separate and distinct, but whose shores are washed by the shared waters of love. Rainer Maria Rilke says: "Love consists in this: that two solitudes protect and touch and greet each other." A person might possibly surrender his or her own identity to another out of lack of respect for self or out of the need for approval, but one can never do this in the name of true love.

More specifically, loving you does not mean that I cease to love myself. On the contrary, the idea that I cannot love you unless I love myself is universally accepted by psychologists. Those who do not love themselves are sad, plagued by a constant sense of emptiness which they are always trying to fill. Like a person with a toothache, they can think only of themselves and they are constantly in search of a dentist, someone to make them feel better. If I do not love myself, I can only *use* others; I cannot *love* them.

My loving you can never be an abdication of my own self. I could possibly give my life for you out of love, but I could never deny my identity as a person. I will try to be what you need me to be, to do what you need done, to say whatever you need to hear. At the same time I am committed to an honest and open relationship. As a part of my gift of love, I will always offer my thoughts, preferences, and all my feelings, even when I think they may be unpleasant or even hurtful to your feelings. If we are committed to total honesty and total openness, our relationship will never be a sticky one, marked by hidden agenda, repressed resentments, displaced emotions, acting out in adolescent ways what we do not have the courage to speak out. Unless we agree to honor honesty and openness, we will never be sure of each other. Our relationship will seem more like a charade than a real life drama.

I Promise You a Person

Finally, in my commitment of unconditional love I promise you a person, not a piece of putty. A "person" means that I have rights, as well as responsibilities. I have a right, for example, to express my own thoughts and feelings, to have my own preferences and the liberty to follow them. I also have an area of personal choice which is mine, and I must insist on keeping this area for myself. Making my own decisions and taking responsibility for them is an essential part of the human maturation process. Of course, I will never make decisions which involve both of us, but there are decisions that I must make for myself. These are some of the rights implied in being a person, and I intend to assert these rights and to insist that you respect them. Be ready to find in me a person you can bump into. Of course, you have a corresponding set of rights, and I will try to be very careful in respecting them. I will not only respect your rights, but I will expect you to exercise your own personhood in asserting these rights and in insisting on my respect for them.

And please have the courage to tell me at all times what you are thinking and feeling. I have no X-ray eyes to know your hidden thoughts or feelings. I cannot guess your preferences. You must tell me. Making assumptions is a dangerous game. Do not think you are loving me by playing chameleon or by twisting yourself into a pretzel shape trying to please me. If you do, I will probably tire of you or become bored with you. I will certainly feel unchallenged by you and by our relationship.

Lastly, I cannot ever let you use or manipulate me. We must love persons and use things. I am a person, not a thing. To let you use me would be no act of love, either for you or for myself. Please understand that I will never set myself up as your judge. I cannot now nor will I ever be able to read your intentions. I can know your intentions only by asking you. But I will never allow your temper tantrums or your tears to compromise my communication. If I feel suspicious of you, I will confront you with my feelings. If I feel hurt by something you have said or done, I will say "Ouch!" When you affirm or console or congratulate me, I will forever be visibly grateful to you. The me that shall be yours will be the unabridged and unedited version. In the words of the poet Richard Lovelace: "I could not love thee, dear, so much/Lov'd I not honor more."

I am an actor, not a reactor. This means that I must always decide how I am going to act. I cannot put this responsibility in your hands. I will try to combine as much tact and kindness as I can with my honesty and openness, but I can never allow myself to be manipulated into a compromise, either in conduct or in communication. My thoughts and my feelings are not for hire. I will not be used.

Whatever else love may ask of us, it does not ask us to be doormats or peace-at-any-price persons. The primary gift of love is the offering of one's most honest self through one's most honest self-disclosure.

The dynamics of love

When I want to be free at all costs
I am already beginning to bind myself
When I pursue my own wishes
I throw myself in chains
I do what I don't want to do
I am at my own mercy

And when I finally consider myself free
Freedom becomes a burden
Because I must make decisions
Which I am unable to make
And my freedom turns into a new prison

I can only find freedom
In the ropes that bind me
To you

ULRICH SCHAFFER

The Three Stages of Love

In the process of loving there are three important stages or moments:

1. **Kindness:**
   a warm assurance that "I am on your side. I care about you."

2. **Encouragement:**
   a strong reassurance of your own strength and self-sufficiency.

3. **Challenge:**
   a loving but firm exhortation to action.

It has been said that loving is an art and this means that there are no scientific-type formulae that can be applied to guarantee successful results. One must take constant readings of the relational situation and try to judge what is needed, when to apply it, and how much of it to apply. Just as an artist-painter uses canvas and oils to achieve certain desired effects, so the artist-lover must try to sense when the need is for more kindness, more encouragement, or more challenge. It is never easy.

Kindness.   Someone has wisely said that "people do not care how much you know until they know how much you care." I am sure that this is the foundation of love: a communicated caring about the happiness of the one loved and an affirmation or reassurance of that loved one's worth. To build a relationship on any other foundation is to build on sand. I have to know that you really want my happiness and my growth, that you really are "for me," or I won't open at all to your influence.

I must understand that I am a person to you, not just a thing. I must know that I am not simply a "case" to be treated, or a "problem" to be solved. And so, the first thing that love must do is communicate these three things: I truly care about you. I really want your happiness and I will do all I can to assure it. You are a uniquely valuable person.

Encouragement. For a long time in my own life, I would like to admit to you, I thought of love as doing acts of kindness for others. I even fell victim to the delusion that doing things for others which they could have and should have done for themselves was really love. If a person were painfully shy, I would leap into action, saving them from the distress involved in self-assertion. For the indecisive, I was a repository of answers. Every person who ever submitted a problem to me was immediately blessed with an instant solution. I never let others struggle long enough to win a victory for or over themselves.

Gradually the truth settled in on me. The settling in started when someone suggested to me: "Give a man a fish and he can eat for a day. Teach him to fish and he can eat for a lifetime." The application was obvious. Shy, indecisive, and struggling people may welcome or even invite us to provide for them. They may even say "I can't" when they really mean "I don't want to put out whatever is needed." They may try various forms of manipulation to hitchhike on the stability, decisiveness, or assertiveness of others. And we average persons are tempted. We are very vulnerable, in fact, to such manipulation. It is more immediately gratifying to say, "Of course, I will do it for you," or to offer the advice, "What you really need to do is this. . . ." The right response in such cases usually provides much less immediate gratification. "Oh, come on, you can do it. . . . I don't know what you should do. You have a good mind and you are capable of making decisions. What do you think you should do?"

When we cave in and allow others to be only persons-by-proxy, we train them to need us. They have to come back to us to get their deeds done and their problems solved. We develop clienteles of progressively weaker people in need of a "fix." We train them to be addicts in need of us. It is not at all loving.

One of the hardest-to-accept facts about true love is that it is liberating. Love offers a person *roots* (a sense of belonging) and *wings* (a sense of independence and freedom). What people really need is belief in themselves, confidence in their own ability to take on the problems and opportunities of life. This is what is meant by the second stage of love: encourage-ment. To en-courage means to put courage in. It instills into the recipient a new and fuller awareness of his or her own powers, strength, and self-sufficiency. Encouragement says: You can do it!

Challenge. The final stage of love is challenge. After conveying kindness ("I am for you!") and implanting courage ("You can do it!"), true love should then invite the beloved to "stretch," to grow beyond the old limitations, to attempt what was always considered too difficult, to break a self-destructive habit that has always been too overpow-ering, to rise above a fear, to give up a grudge, to open a repressed feeling, to confront a difficult situation, to offer a painful apology.

If encouragement makes the one loved aware of his or her strength, challenge is the loving push to actually use this strength: "Try. Stretch. Do it. If you succeed, I will be in the front row clapping my hands off. If you fail, I will be sitting right at your side. You won't be alone. Go ahead now. Give it your best shot. You can do it!"

Loving and "Growing Up"

Many nice, bland things can be said of love. For example, "Love divides one's burdens in half." An old monastic saying has it that "where there is love there is no labor." We sometimes roast the people we love, but we always have a toast for love: "If we only have love . . ." Love should indeed be toasted as the secret of a full and meaningful life, but it is no favor to love to romanticize it. T. S. Eliot once remarked that sometimes we "cannot stand too much reality." And Ionesco has made the observation that we are "forever trying to turn real life into literature."

The truth about love, I think, is that it is indeed a profound comfort, but it is also a monumental challenge. Love immediately challenges me to break the fixation I have with myself. It will drag me all the way from my infantile *id* to a complete self-donation to a cause or to a person in freely given love. Love demands that I learn how to focus my attention on the needs of those I love. It will ask me to become a sensitive listener. At times love will insist that I postpone my own gratifications to meet the needs of those I love. The kind of communication which is the lifeblood of love will require me to get in touch with my most sensitive feelings and my most buried thoughts, and to share these in the frightening act of self-disclosure. Love will make me vulnerable. It

It is no favor to love to romanticize it.

will open me to the honest reactions of others whom I have allowed to penetrate my defenses. If I have built protective walls around my vulnerable places, love will tear them down.

Love will teach me to give and to receive without pan-scales. Love transcends pan-scale justice. If love divides the burdens of life in half by sharing, it also doubles one's responsibilities. Two do not eat as cheaply as one, unless one of the two does not eat. It is also true that two cannot make decisions as quickly as one. Two are not as mobile as one, and so forth.

In other words, if you don't want to—

- break the fixation with self and give up your self-centeredness,
- learn how to care about and be sincerely dedicated to the satisfaction of another,
- become a sensitive listener, who hears what is said and some things that are not able to be said,
- postpone personal gratification to meet the needs of another,
- get in touch with your deepest feelings and most hidden thoughts,
- share your most vulnerable self as an act of love,
- get honest feedback from someone who really knows you through your own self-disclosure,

- give up your pan-scales and be prepared to give 100 percent,
- take on the added responsibilities for a "we,"
- work at the delicate art of dialogue and shared decision making,

... if you don't want these things, then obviously you don't want love. If you prefer to be an island, a recluse, a narcissist, preferring to live in a world that has a population of one, love would rip out of your hands everything that you hold dear and clutch tightly.

And yet, it seems obvious to me, as I feel sure it will seem to you, that these very challenges of a true love relationship, which assault our self-centeredness, are in fact the bridge to human maturity and ultimate human fulfillment. Viktor Frankl writes:

A thought transfixed me: for the first time in my life I saw the truth as it is set into song by so many poets, proclaimed as the final wisdom by so many thinkers. The truth— that love is the ultimate and the highest goal to which man can aspire. Then I grasped the meaning of the greatest secret that human poetry and human thought and belief have to impart: *the salvation of man is through love and in love.*

Man's Search for Meaning

Another great psychiatrist, Dr. Karl Menninger, liked to repeat: "Love cures. It cures those who give it and it cures those who receive it." Even the great doctors, with whom we had previous occasion to disagree, are unanimous in the praise of love and love relationships as the chief source of human maturation. When Sigmund Freud was asked for a definition of mental and emotional health, he said: "It is the capacity to work and to love." Likewise, Alfred Adler said that "all human failures are the result of a lack of love." More and more psychologists are coming to esteem the capacity for intimacy. People with low capacities for love relationships are ten times more likely to be labeled psychiatrically ill. The command of Jesus that we love one another seems to be a human imperative rather than an option. The experimental evidence for the crippling effects of a loveless life is found in the office of every psychiatrist, filled with children and adults who have no awareness of their own worth, no sense of identity, who are filled with hatred and fear and tortured by anxieties. Love is costly, but the alternatives are deadly.

Love demands that I learn how to focus my attention on the needs of those I love.

The Challenges
and the Comforts

Michael Novak has written of marriage and family
in words I would like to share with you. What he
says in the following lengthy excerpt, originally
published in *Harper's Magazine,* is applicable, I think,
to any true commitment of love:

> In our society, of course, there is no need to
> become an adult. One may remain—one is
> daily exhorted to remain—a child forever. In
> such a life, the central aim is self-fulfillment.
> Marriage is merely an alliance, entailing as
> minimal an abridgment of inner privacy as
> one partner may allow. Children are not a
> welcome responsibility, for to have children
> is, plainly, to cease being a child oneself.
> One tries instead to live as the angels were
> once believed to live—soaring, free, unen-
> cumbered.
>
> People say of marriage that it is boring,
> when what they mean is that it terrifies them:
> too many and too deep are its searing
> revelations, its angers, its rages, its hates, and
> its loves. They say of marriage that it is
> deadening, when what they mean is that it
> drives us beyond adolescent fantasies and
> romantic dreams. They say of children that

they are piranhas, brats, snots, when what they mean is that the importance of parents with respect to the future of their children is now known with greater clarity and exactitude than ever before.

Being married and having children has impressed on my mind certain lessons, and most of what I am forced to learn about myself is not pleasant. The quantity of sheer impenetrable selfishness in the human breast (in *my* breast) is a never-failing source of wonderment. I do not want to be disturbed, challenged, troubled. Huge regions of myself belong only to me. Seeing myself through the unblinking eyes of an intelligent, honest spouse is humiliating. Trying to act fairly to children, each of whom is temperamentally different from myself and from each other, is. baffling. My family bonds hold me back from many opportunities. And yet these bonds are, I know, my liberation. They force me to be a different sort of human being in a way I want and need.

MICHAEL NOVAK,
"The Family Out of Favor"

Novak goes on to say that it would be a lie to write only of the difficulties and not of the beauty of love. In fact, I think, weathering the storms of the love process is the only way to find the rainbows of life.

The comforts that one finds on the "less-traveled road" of love are found nowhere else. Life has a much deeper meaning when I truly love another. The loneliness of a world that has a population of one is filled by a new and warm presence when love enters a life. The self-alienation of the old person who could not interact intimately is replaced in the person renewed by love by a sense of self and of self-worth. It is what we call today a sense of "identity." It has become a truism that we can know and love only as much of ourselves as we are willing to share with another in love. The aimless wandering of the loveless person finds in love a sense of belonging and a place called home.

Going out to another in love means risk—the risks of self-disclosure, rejection, misunderstanding. It means grief, too, from the temporary separations, psychological or physical, to the final separation of death. Whoever insists on personal security and

*The crippling effects of a loveless life
are found in the office of every psychiatrist,
filled with children and adults
who have no awareness of their own worth,
no sense of identity.*

safety as the nonnegotiable conditions of life will not be willing to pay love's price or find love's enrichments. Whoever shuts himself or herself up in the cocoon of self-protective defenses, keeping others always at a safe distance and holding on tightly to personal possessions and privacy, will find the price of love far too high and will remain forever a prisoner of fear. Erich Fromm writes:

> To be loved, and to love, need courage, the courage to judge certain values as of ultimate concern—and to take the jump and stake everything on these values.
>
> *The Art of Loving*

CHAPTER FIVE

The God of love

Some day,
after we have mastered the winds,
the waves, the tides and gravity,
we will harness for God
the energies of love
and then for the second time
in the history of the world
man will have discovered fire.
PIERRE TEILHARD DE CHARDIN, S.J.

In the Old Testament God reveals himself to the People of Israel as a God of unconditional love. His gift of himself in the choice and creation of "my People" is totally unsolicited, undeserved, and unmerited. In the seventh chapter of Deuteronomy it is very clear that God's love for his People was not based on anything they were or had. The Hebrew word used to describe this kind of covenanted and unconditional love is *hesed*. It can be translated as "loving kindness," but *hesed* clearly implies that this love is an unmerited gift and an irrevocable commitment. God decides, God chooses, God offers his gift of love. He is by his own free act forever committed to his People. The prophet Hosea uses the image of God taking a bride: "And I will betroth you to me forever" (2:19–20). Through the prophet Isaiah, God says: "Even if a mother should forget the child of her womb, I will never forget you" (49:15).

The unconditionality of God's love for his People is a constant refrain in the Old Testament. God has promised and God will always be faithful to his promise. Jeremiah writes of God's constant willingness to forgive: "With an eternal love I have loved you. Therefore, in loving-kindness I draw you to myself" (31:3). It is a striking anticipation of Jesus' parable of the prodigal son: "And while he was still a long distance away, his father saw him coming, and was filled with loving pity and ran and embraced him and kissed him" (Luke 15:20).

Jesus: God's Word of Love

Saint Paul calls Jesus the "visible image of our invisible God" (Colossians 1:15). To his contemporaries Jesus was a rabbi, and by the tradition of the times should have spent his time deciding cases of the law. But Jesus kept talking about love, and his contemporaries found this very irritating. They encouraged him to be a legal interpreter; they kept presenting to him cases to be adjudged. "Good Master [Rabbi], this man's oxen have fallen into a ditch on the Sabbath, and we want to know if he can pull them out. . . . Good Master, are we obliged to pay taxes to Rome? . . . Good Master, we have caught this woman in the sin of adultery. Now we have a law that says she should be stoned to death. . . . Good Master, what do you say? . . . Good Master. . . ?"

And Jesus kept telling them that this kind of microscopic attention to the letter of the law kills the spirit of love. "Oh, don't worry," he assured them, "I have not come to destroy the law but to fulfill it, to subsume, to elevate the whole law into one great commandment: love! You can self-righteously keep the law in every detail without loving, but you can't truly love without keeping the law. If you really love, you will keep the law: you won't steal or lie or kill, not if you really love." This was the summary response of Jesus, if not his exact words.

He was telling them something like this: "Don't deal with God legalistically. That's the way you deal with someone you fear. You worry about the punishments of an authority whom you fear, so you do everything he demands and then you feel safe. Then you can say, 'I have done everything you demanded. You cannot punish me now!' This is not really a 'Yes!' of love to either God or neighbor. It is really a small and frightened person saying an emphatic 'No!' to personal insecurity. God is not calling you to this fearful submission, but rather to love him with your whole mind and heart and soul and your neighbor as yourself!"

But they didn't understand. And it really wouldn't have been so bad, they whispered to each other, if only he weren't so soft on sinners. He kept associating with tax collectors and prostitutes. He kept eating and drinking with socially, if not totally, disreputable people.

He thought of himself as some kind of "Good Shepherd in love with and in search of straying sheep." He said he was the "Divine Physician" who did not come for the healthy and wealthy but for the poor, the sick, and the needy. He once scandalized the whole self-righteous set when he allowed a prostitute to cry all over his feet and then to dry them with her bleached hair at the house of Simon the Pharisee. The worst part was that he praised her for her . . . get this, love! He said that wherever the story of his life was told, down through the centuries and out to the ends of the earth, the story of that woman and what she did for him would also be told. It was just too much!

The Confrontation and the Parable

So the doubters confronted Jesus one day, and pressed the question they knew he couldn't safely answer. They stood around him like an iron horseshoe of hostility. It was his last chance. If he didn't conform or at least compromise now, then it would be better that one man should die than that the whole nation (and all its laws) should perish. They knew it. He knew it.

They asked: "What does God think of a sinner?"

So he told the story of unconditional love. We call it the parable of the prodigal son. It is the story of a kind and loving father and his two sons. The younger son feels that he has outgrown his father, and wants no part of his father's life-style or home. He lays claim to his inheritance and leaves his father without even looking back over his shoulder. The father allows his son this liberty of choice, but he waits on the front porch of the little farmhouse every night, hoping and watching the road from the city. Others coming back from the city deliver shattering reports.

"Hey Mister, you ought to be declared 'Father of the Year' for siring that fuzzbrain son of yours. You should see your little blue-eyed boy—seducing every available and vulnerable woman, when he isn't too drunk or involved in some other stupidity."

But the father continues to wait there every night until darkness settles over the land. When it is dark, he goes inside and goes to bed, saying a tearful prayer for his boy, his lost but always dear son.

Then one night, there on the front porch, his heart nearly explodes with excitement. He sees a figure coming down the road. He can tell . . . it is his son! His son is coming home. The father runs down the road, his heart pounding and his eyes filling with tears, the tears of relief. All Scripture scholars say that no father in that time and culture would have run to his son. It would have seemed totally strange and out of place. It could have happened only to someone whose explosion of joy overcame all sense of time and place and social custom.

The father hugs his boy tightly, huge racking sobs of joy shaking his body. Warm tears roll down his cheeks. The boy is saying something about not being worthy to come home as a son, and asking only to hire on as a field worker. The father hears nothing of this. His heart is saying: "I don't care where you've been or what you've done. All I really care about is that you are home . . . you're home!" The father

swallows hard, swallows the warm tears gathered
in his throat, and calls for rings and robes and music
makers. He orders the fatted calf killed and roasted
over an open fire. This is to be a party to end all
parties. "My boy is home!" When the older son comes
in from the fields to discover the party in full swing,
he does not understand. He is angry: "You never
gave a party for me and my friends."

"Oh Son," the father says, "I do understand. I
love you so much. And I am very grateful for your
faithfulness. You have stayed here with me. Everything I have is yours. Anytime you want a party for
yourself and your friends, everything I have will be
at your disposal. But there is something I must ask
you to understand. Would you please try to understand what goes on in the heart of a father when his
lost child comes home?"

The question hung there in the emotionally
charged atmosphere: "Would you please try to
understand what goes on in the heart of a father
when his lost child comes home?" Jesus looked
squarely around the horseshoe of hostile faces and
said: "This is what God thinks of a sinner!"

The question was answered. He would offer his
life in the end for that answer. But he would die as
he had lived, unconditionally loving.

He would say "Shalom! Be at peace. I understand" to the frightened Apostles who had left him

to die alone. He would die praying for the very people who had crucified him: "Father, forgive them, for they do not know what they are doing." In the end he would die between two thieves. It was somehow fitting that he who spent his life caring for and searching out the rejected should die between two thieves. One of the thieves looked at the plaque over the head of Jesus, indicating the crime for which he was dying. It read: "This is Jesus of Nazareth, the King of the Jews." The thief looked with plaintive eyes into the eyes of Jesus: "I know nothing about your kingdom, but when you come into your kingdom, would you remember me?"

These were the last words that Jesus would speak to any person before his death. He said: "This day you will be with me in paradise."

Under every crucifix, depicting the Lord with his heart opened and his hands stretched out as if to embrace all the weak and the wounded of this world, there should be a caption reading:

"This is what I mean when I say I love you!"

But he would die as he had lived,
unconditionally loving.

If the parable of the prodigal son is the story of unconditional love, Jesus on his cross is the portrait of such love. Like love itself the person of Jesus is both a comfort and a challenge. The comfort is more profound than anything we have ever experienced. The "Shalom! Be at peace. I understand" is always held out to us, and especially at those times when we feel like old Peter the rock and sometimes sandpile: "Depart from me, Lord," Peter moaned, "for I am a sinful man!" But, of course, unconditional love doesn't ever depart. Jesus asked Peter, as he asks us, only this: "Do you love me?" He does not ask about our weakness but only about our love.

The challenge is: "Love one another as I have loved you!"

Love: God's Port of Entry

God's love for each of us is just as unsolicited, unmerited, and unconditional as was his love for the People of Israel. Jesus is the Word of this love, uttered into the world. God comes to us in him, wanting to share, to communicate his goodness, joy, and love. He wants to love us into the fullness of life.

On the human level all of us have at some time experienced this kind of inner urge and insistence to share something good: good news, a good joke, a good tip. At an even deeper level it is the inner urge of artists to share with others a vision of beauty, the music that they have heard inside themselves. At the deepest human level it is the desire of procreation: when two people love each other very much, they want to share their love and their lives with a new life, fashioned by God from their own flesh and blood. It is something like this with God. The impetus of God's love comes from within himself, to share with us his life and love. It is a free gift, freely given, not earned or deserved or claimed by any right of ours. It is a beautiful, eternal gift, held out to us in the hands of love. It is an unconditional covenant.

All we have to do is say "Yes!" All we have to do is open ourselves to receive this pearl of great price, this love that will transform us and every moment of our lives. The key word is openness.

The little child who is inside me wishes that openness were simple. The fact is that the big "Yes!" of openness has many other little "yeses" inside it. Some of them will be very costly. Some will call for great courage. Some will be uttered in darkness.

Saying "Yes!" to God's gift of love and life primarily and above all means *choosing love as a life principle*. The Apostle John, for whom Jesus seemed to have a special love, says in his First Epistle:

> We know how much God loves us because we have felt his love and because we believe him when he tells us that he loves us dearly.

God is love, and anyone who lives in love is living with God and God is living in him.

1 John 4:16

Saying "Yes!" to God is not a simple matter because making our lives into lives of love is not a simple or easy thing. To choose love as a life principle means that my basic mind-set or question must be: What is the loving thing to be, to do, to say? My consistent response to each of life's events, to each person who enters and touches my life, to each demand on my time and nerves and heart, must somehow be transformed into an act of love. However, in the last analysis, it is this "Yes!" that opens me to God. Choosing love as a life principle widens the chalice of my soul, so that God can pour into me his gifts and graces and powers.

Tommy

About fifteen years ago, I stood watching my university students file into the classroom for our first session in the Theology of Faith. That was the day I first saw Tommy. My eyes and my mind both blinked. He was combing his long flaxen hair, which hung six inches below his shoulders. It was the first time I had ever seen a boy with hair that long. I guess it was just coming into fashion then. I know in my mind that it isn't what's on your head but in it that counts, but on that day I was unprepared and my emotions flipped. I immediately filed Tommy under "S" for strange . . . very strange.

Tommy turned out to be the "atheist in residence" in my Theology of Faith course. He constantly objected to, smirked at, or whined about the possibility of an unconditionally loving Father-God. We lived with each other in relative peace for one semester, although I admit he was for me at times a serious pain in the back pew. When he came up at the end of the course to turn in his final exam, he asked in a slightly cynical tone: "Do you think I'll ever find God?" I decided instantly on a little shock therapy. "No!" I said very emphatically. "Oh," he responded, "I thought that was the product you were pushing." I let him get five steps from the classroom door and then called out: "Tommy! I don't think you'll ever find him, but I am absolutely certain that he will find you!" He shrugged a little and left my class and my life (temporarily). I felt slightly disappointed at the thought that he had missed my clever line: "He will find you!" At least I thought it was clever.

Later I heard that Tom was graduated and I was duly grateful. Then a sad report. I heard that Tommy had terminal cancer. Before I could search him out, he came to see me. His body was badly wasted, and the long hair had all fallen out as a result of chemotherapy. But his eyes were bright and his voice was firm, for the first time, I think. "Tommy, I've thought about you so often. I hear you are sick!" I blurted out.

"Oh, yes, very sick. I have cancer in both lungs. It's a matter of weeks."

"Can you talk about it, Tom?"

"Sure, what would you like to know?"

"What's it like to be only twenty-four and dying?"

"Well, it could be worse."

"Like what?"

"Well, like being fifty and having no values or ideals, like being fifty and thinking that booze, seducing women, and making money are the real 'biggies' in life."

I began to look through my mental file cabinet under "S" where I had filed Tom as strange. (I swear that everybody I try to reject by classification God sends back into my life to educate me.)

"But what I really came to see you about," Tom said, "is something you said to me on the last day of class." (He remembered!)

He continued, "I asked you if you thought I would ever find God and you said, 'No!' which surprised me. Then you said, 'But he will find you.' I thought about that a lot, even though my search for God was hardly intense at that time. (My "clever" line. He thought about that a lot!)

"But when the doctors removed a lump from my groin and told me that it was malignant, then I got serious about locating God. And when the malignancy spread into my vital organs, I really began banging bloody fists against the bronze doors of heaven. But God did not come out. In fact, nothing happened. Did you ever try anything for a long time with great effort and with no success? You get psychologically glutted, fed up with trying. And then you quit. Well, one day I woke up, and instead of throwing a few more futile appeals over that high brick wall to a God who may be or may not be there, I just quit. I decided that I didn't really care . . . about God, about an afterlife, or anything like that.

"I decided to spend what time I had left doing something more profitable. I thought about you and your class and I remembered something else you had said: 'The essential sadness is to go through life without loving. But it would be almost equally sad to go through life and leave this world without ever telling those you loved that you had loved them.'

"So I began with the hardest one: my dad. He was reading a newspaper when I approached him."

"Dad . . ."

"Yes, what?" he asked without lowering the newspaper.

"Dad, I would like to talk with you."

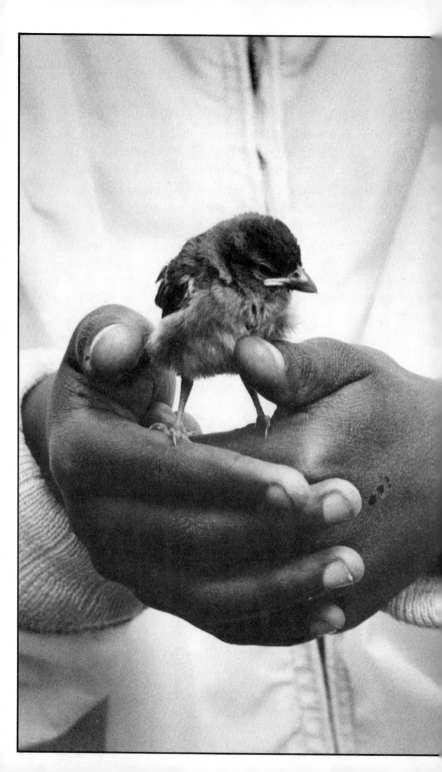

"Well, talk."

"I mean . . . It's really important."

The newspaper came down three slow inches. "What is it?"

"Dad, I love you. I just wanted you to know that."

Tom smiled at me and said with obvious satisfaction, as though he felt a warm and secret joy flowing inside of him: "The newspaper fluttered to the floor. Then my father did two things I could never remember him ever doing before. He cried and he hugged me. And we talked all night, even though he had to go to work the next morning. It felt so good to be close to my father, to see his tears, to feel his hug, to hear him say that he loved me.

"It was easier with my mother and little brother. They cried with me, too, and we hugged each other, and started saying real nice things to each other. We shared the things we had been keeping secret for so many years. I was only sorry about one thing: that I had waited so long. Here I was, in the shadow

The big "Yes!" of openness has many other little "yeses" inside it.

of death, and I was just beginning to open up to all the people I had actually been close to.

"Then, one day I turned around and God was there. He didn't come to me when I pleaded with him. I guess I was like an animal trainer holding out a hoop, 'C'mon, jump through. C'mon, I'll give you three days . . . three weeks.' Apparently God does things in his own way and at his own hour.

"But the important thing is that he was there. He found me. You were right. He found me even after I stopped looking for him."

"Tommy," I practically gasped, "I think you are saying something very important and much more universal than you realize. To me, at least, you are saying that the surest way to find God is not to make him a private possession, a problem solver, or an instant consolation in time of need, but rather by opening to love. You know, Saint John said that. He said 'God is love, and anyone who lives in love is living with God and God is living in him.'

"Tom, could I ask you a favor? You know, when I had you in class you were a real pain. But (laughingly) you can make it all up to me now. Would you come into my present Theology of Faith course and tell them what you have just told me? If I told them the same thing, it wouldn't be half as effective as if you were to tell them."

"Oooh . . . I was ready for you, but I don't know if I'm ready for your class."

"Tom, think about it. If and when you are ready, give me a call."

In a few days Tommy called, said he was ready for the class, that he wanted to do that for God and for me. So we scheduled a date. However, he never made it. He had another appointment, far more important than the one with me and my class. Of course, his life was not really ended by his death, only changed. He made the great step from faith into vision. He found a life far more beautiful than the human eye has ever seen or the human ear has ever heard or the human mind has ever imagined.

Before he died, we talked one last time. "I'm not going to make it to your class," he said.

"I know, Tom."

"Will you tell them for me? Will you . . . tell the whole world for me?"

"I will, Tom. I'll tell them. I'll do my best."

So, to all of you who have been kind enough to hear this simple statement about love, thank you for listening. And to you, Tom, somewhere in the sunlit, verdant hills of heaven:

"I told them, Tommy . . . as best I could."

Acknowledgments *Continued from page ii*

Richard and Clara Winston. Copyright © 1963. Reprinted by permission of Pantheon Books, a Division of Random House, Inc.

Excerpt from G. Marian Kinget, *On Being Human.* Copyright © 1975. Reprinted by permission of Harcourt Brace Jovanovich, Inc.

The text of Colossians 3:14, John 5:2-9, I John 4:16, Luke 4:1-12, and Luke 15:20 are taken from *The Living Bible,* copyright © 1971 by Tyndale House Publishers, Wheaton, Ill. Used by permission.

Poem by Archibald MacLeish. Reprinted by permission of Houghton Mifflin Company. All rights reserved.

Excerpts from Margaret Mattison, "Love Is Not Enough." Adapted with permission from the February 1976 *Reader's Digest.* Copyright © 1976 by The Reader's Digest Association, Inc.

Excerpt from Michael Novak, "The Family Out of Favor." Copyright © 1976 by *Harper's Magazine.* All rights reserved. Excerpted from the April 1976 issue by special permission.

Frederick S. Perls, "Gestalt Prayer" on page 63. © Real People Press 1969. All rights reserved.

Specified excerpt from pages 84-85 from *The Bell Jar* by Sylvia Plath. Copyright © 1971 by Harper & Row, Publishers, Inc. Reprinted by permission of Harper & Row, Publishers, Inc., and Faber and Faber Ltd.

Poem on page 21 of *Searching for You* by Ulrich Schaffer. Copyright © 1978 by Ulrich Schaffer. Reprinted by permission of Harper & Row, Publishers, Inc.

Excerpt from Antoine de Saint-Exupéry, *The Little Prince,* translated by Katherine Woods. Copyright 1943. Reprinted by permission of Harcourt Brace Jovanovich, Inc., and William Heinemann, London.

Adapted excerpt from Pierre Teilhard de Chardin, S.J., "The Future of Chastity." Reprinted by permission of Georges Borchardt, Inc.

Walter Tubbs, "Beyond Perls," from *Journal of Humanistic Psychology,* 12 (Fall 1972), p. 5. Reprinted by permission of *Journal of Humanistic Psychology.*